Ultimate
AUTO
Detailing

Your hands-on guide to the professionals' and concours winners' secrets

David H. Jacobs, Jr.

Motorbooks International
Publishers & Wholesalers Inc.
Osceola, Wisconsin 54020, USA

First published in 1988 by Motorbooks International Publishers & Wholesalers Inc, PO Box 2, 729 Prospect Avenue, Osceola, WI 54020 USA

Printed and bound in the United States of America

The information in this book is true and complete to the best of our knowledge. All recommendations are made without any guarantee on the part of the author or publisher, who also disclaim any liability incurred in connection with the use of this data or specific details

We recognize that some words, model names and designations, for example, mentioned herein are the property of various manufacturers. We use them for identification purposes only. This is not an official publication

Library of Congress Cataloging-in-Publication Data
Jacobs, David H.
    Ultimate auto detailing.

    1. Automobile detailing.   I. Title.
TL152.J295 1988   629.2′6   88-9470
ISBN 0-87938-310-0 (soft)

On the front cover: The ultimate detailing for an ultimate automobile, a Ferrari 308GTS, courtesy of Bloomington Acura. *Michael Dregni*
On the back cover: Detailing the details on an Alfa Romeo, Cadillac and BMW, courtesy of Bloomington Acura. *Tim Parker*

Motorbooks International books are also available at discounts in bulk quantity for industrial or sales-promotional use. For details write to Special Sales Manager at the Publisher's address

Contents

Acknowledgments

I would like to thank a number of people for helping me to write this book. Art Wentworth was invaluable. He spent a considerable amount of time detailing and posing for pictures. He was also instrumental in locating and securing cars used to demonstrate various detailing techniques in the pictures. His knowledge of automobiles and years of detailing experience proved to be a great asset.

George and Kathy Ridderbusch provided much information pertaining to Concours d'Elegance events. I appreciate the time and friendliness they afforded me. One must recognize the countless hours they have spent researching and detailing to become consistent concours winners. I would also like to thank Mike Wiley for his input as a concours judge.

Dan Mycon, owner of New Look Autobody in Kirkland, Washington, offered his shop as a photo studio and provided information about auto detailing from a body and paint shop's perspective. Squire Tomasie and Randy Cavanaugh of Squire's Autowerke in Bellevue, Washington, offered detailing tips from their experience as auto racers and mechanics.

Barney Li, owner of Eagle 1, was very gracious in providing information and car care products.

Thanks also go to Mel Miller of Meguiar's, Peter Huber of Turtle Wax, Al's Auto Supply of Bothell, Washington, and Wesco Autobody Supply of Everett, Washington.

The following folks were very kind for allowing the use of their cars in the photographs: Clint Worthington, owner of the 1985 Porsche 944; Diana Coffin, owner of the 1987 Toyota MR2; Jerry McKee, owner of the 1972 E-type V-12 roadster; Mary Jo Wertheimer, owner of the 1985 BMW 635 CSi; Terry Skiple, owner of the 1974 Corvette roadster and 1974 De Tomaso Pantera; Marsha Templeton, owner of the 1977 Porsche 911 Targa; Art Wentworth, owner of the 1970 Buick GS 455 convertible; and George and Kathy Ridderbusch, owners of the 1979 Porsche 928.

I also appreciate the efforts of Van Nordquist and John Blackburn of Gallery & Sons, Ltd. Photographic Studios, who developed the film and processed the prints for the book, taking extra time to make sure each photograph turned out just right.

Finally, I want to thank Tim Parker, Michael Dregni and Barbara Harold of Motorbooks International. Their continued support and editorial assistance have made this a very enjoyable project.

Introduction

For years, farmers washed their tractors with kerosene. This petroleum product removed grease and dried with a thin, protective film that prevented rust. I think it is safe to say that we all want our vehicles to be clean and rust-free, but there are now better answers than washing with kerosene.

Professional detailers and show car people have been cleaning automobiles for a long time. Over the years, many have developed "secret" methods that help them to clean and polish faster and more effectively. Try as one may, it is difficult to get them to reveal these personal treasures. Fortunately, I was able to talk to a number of auto enthusiasts who shared their tried-and-true methods for making cars sparkle. Included in this book are tips for cleaning, polishing, waxing, shampooing and detailing which have worked for them and will help you to make your car look great.

Auto detailing is the process of making an automobile look its best with the least amount of dismantling. Beyond auto detailing is total restoration. The difference between the two is hundreds of hours of work and hundreds of dollars for new parts and paint work.

Consider taking pictures of your car before getting started. This will be a big help in remembering how jacking equipment and the spare tire go back in the trunk, how engine compartment parts are reassembled and just what the car looked like before you detailed it. You may want to use a video camera to include voice instructions that describe how you dismantled particular items and where you may want to place special emphasis in cleaning and polishing.

Although this book shows you how to detail cars as the professionals do, it is not intended to be a complete manual for preparing show cars and concours winners. If you plan to restore a car to show quality, the information in this book will help you get started and reach the baseline. You must realize that it takes much more than cleaning and waxing to build such unique vehicles, and the chapter "Is concours any different?" will explain why. Most of all, this book is designed to help the conscientious owner keep his or her car looking its best and maintain its highest value, using proven methods, products and techniques.

Chapter 1

What does detailing mean?

The reflections on the hood of this neglected 1985 Nissan 300ZX show the paint to be in good shape. Tree sap and bird droppings that are allowed to accumulate detract from the beauty of the automobile and will eventually ruin the paint.

Two automobiles parked side by side. They can be the same color, year, make and model and have identical options but appear different. Why?

The reasons vary. An obvious difference may be that one car is covered with stickers, has broken glass and scratched paint and appears to have never been washed. If both have been cared for, however, the differences may be subtle.

Subtle differences don't reach out and grab you. They are, however, noticed, and under close scrutiny you can detect them. They are things like bent license plates, broken license plate frames, wax residue in emblems, smeared windows, dirt lodged in the back side of bumper guards, dirty tires. They don't catch your eye right off the bat but neverthe-

Mary Jo Wertheimer's 1985 BMW CSi is clean and crisp. It would look even better with the dealer's license plate frame removed; note how the frame tends to draw your eye toward it.

less give you an uneasy feeling about a car—especially when it is parked next to an identical car that has been detailed.

Detailing defined

You'll find that every owner has a different definition of car cleaning. One will say his or her car is clean if washed once a month, another will insist it be washed weekly and some will clean their cars only after the windows are so dirty that they can't see out of them!

Auto detailing is the process of making an automobile look its best without major dismantling or repainting. Much more than a quick wash and vacuuming, detailing requires careful planning and methods. Detailing is a systematic cleaning, polishing and waxing from front to back, top to bottom. Interior detailing is also a systematic, labor-intensive cleanup that could take you right down to the floorboards. A simple vacuuming may do well for a car that is frequently cleaned. It, however, will not rid an interior of dirt, grime, debris and odor if only done once a year. It is not unusual for a conscientious detailer to spend days detailing a "clean" car. He or she expects to spend a day on the interior, a day or two on the engine and two to three days on the exterior and extras.

Detailing can be described as cosmetic car care that falls somewhere between a run through the automatic car wash and total restoration. You can give your car a minimal detail on a Saturday afternoon with an exterior wash and wax, interior vacuuming and wipe. A moderate detail will generally take an entire day and consist of a thorough exterior wash, polish and wax as well as a conscientious cleaning and dressing effort for the interior. A first-time or once-a-year total detail will require a

Dirty exhaust tips and fenderwells are subtle items that detract from the overall appearance of Terry Skiple's 1974 DeTomaso Pantera. Cleaning, polishing and some painting will bring life back to these parts to help them blend with the rest of the car.

Weekly washing and frequent waxing is what keeps this Mazda RX-7 looking good. Because black paint so readily shows swirls, use a soft cotton wash mitt and a mild car wash soap. Dry with thick fluffy towels and wax with a liquid or cream.

Diana Coffin's 1987 Toyota MR2 is standing tall. The fenderwells and side underbody have been maintained clean and black, accenting the white body and black trim.

Stickers do not mar the glass, and the wheels and tires look new.

number of days to clean, polish, wax and dress every part of the car to near perfection. The final and highest degree of detailing is preparation for a Concours d'Elegance event.

Detail shops

Nearly 8,000 detail shops are in operation throughout the country. For $125 to $150, most of them can make used cars look new in about four hours, using special equipment, cleansers, polishes

Inexperienced car people sometimes opt for harsh chemicals to make cleaning jobs go faster. You must consider what long-term effects these products may have on your car and you should realize that old-fashioned soap, water and elbow grease are generally the easiest on paint, chrome, vinyl and other surfaces.

and waxes. They use these various chemicals to help speed the detailing process. You can use the same materials and equipment but must realize the potential risks involved.

Harsh chemicals clean quickly and are safe when used properly. Misuse can result in paint blemishes, fabric stains and other damage. Some car enthusiasts are afraid of chemicals and prefer old-fashioned soap, water and lots of elbow grease. Most professionals cannot afford the time it takes to detail a car without the use of chemicals, although there are a small number of specialty shops that detail by hand, using very mild methods and taking days to gently bring an automobile to its fullest potential. For the pampering, these detailers charge $350 and up.

Most used cars on a dealer's lot have been detailed. They exhibit shiny black tires, velvety paint, clean windows, fresh upholstery and a glossy engine compartment; there is no question that the car has been professionally prepared.

One must realize that most dealers' used cars are detailed generically in just a few hours. In many instances, professionals must take short cuts to get the car looking its best in the least amount of time. Dealers want the car on the lot as soon as possible and detailers must work within strict budgets.

Due to these constraints, many generic detailers rely on clear lacquer paint to make engine compartments, trunks, doorjambs and vents look new and shiny. They use ample amounts of dressing on the interior to quickly achieve the best cosmetic appearance in the shortest time. Paint is buffed and then hand waxed with a liquid for speed and high gloss.

Don't get me wrong, the cars look good, but they look "detailed." They look like something that just came out of a gloss factory. Everything is too glossy, too shiny, the car doesn't look real, especially when compared to an identical vehicle that has been meticulously detailed by hand and maintained that way.

The best way to see the difference first hand is to look at used cars on a dealer's lot and then compare with a Concours d'Elegance winner. Gloss on the concours car will be minimal but perfect. The entire car will be cleaner than new and look like it has been lovingly cared for.

These same professionals know how to meticulously detail and without all the high gloss expected on dealers' used cars. They cannot justify the extra time and labor on most dealer cars, however, because of the minimal fee dealers pay. When they get $150 to $350 to detail a privately owned vehicle, they can afford to spend a few days detailing by hand and not have to count on dressings and clear lacquer for a quick fix. You can do the same thing for your car and save hundreds of dollars.

If you should opt to have a professional detail your car, ask to see a sample of his or her work. Check to see if the interior is clean or just bathed in dressing. Look for swirls and spider webbing on the paint and wax build-up in emblems. Inspect the engine compartment for paint overspray and the use of clear lacquer paint, a no-no for nice cars. Inquire as to the methods used for preparing a car, be it with buffers and chemicals or by hand.

Personal viewpoints

Auto detailing, real detailing, is much more than surface cosmetics. For some, it is knowing that every part of the car has been cleaned, polished, waxed or dressed. It is the feeling and fresh aroma cleanliness brings with it.

Have you ever noticed that most winning race cars are also the best looking? Besides the enjoyment of driving a machine that looks good, racers acknowledge the psychological edge an outstanding car presents. As a former racer, Squire Tomasie says, "You know the guy with the clean stuff is serious." Sponsors prefer to have their advertisements displayed on clean cars. Mechanics detect problems more quickly and easily on clean engines,

Wax residue around the Countach emblem on this Lamborghini is disgraceful. A small paintbrush with the bristles cut to about a half inch, or a soft toothbrush, will remove the residue. Future wax applications should be carefully applied around the emblem.

and to spot problems even more easily, some mechanics paint the entire underbody white, making for better light distribution and visibility. For the driver, a meticulously maintained and detailed race car instills a continuing vote of confidence.

Art Wentworth is a true car enthusiast. He has owned more cars than I care to count, including a Rolls-Royce, a Jaguar, Cadillacs and twenty-six brand new Corvettes. Wentworth speaks for many car people when he says, "I prefer a car that has not been generically detailed. Rather, I like the ones that have been well cared for, like somebody's baby —not all that gloss."

Wentworth does his own detailing. Convinced that buffers and chemicals do more harm than good, he will spend days hand polishing and waxing the paint and weeks preparing the rest of the car, using mild soaps, toothbrushes and cotton swabs.

Clean race cars give mechanics and drivers a continuing vote of confidence. An engine like this is easy to work on and allows mechanics to quickly notice obvious problems.

Quality detailing will increase the value of almost any automobile. Special cars, like this Pantera, are no exception.

Terry Skiple is sales manager for a large Seattle dealership. He started in the car business at the age of fourteen, buying, fixing and selling cars. He bought and sold cars on his own until age thirty when he was reprimanded for selling too many units without a dealer's license. He has a favorite three-step method for paint restoration: two hand applications of polish, two hand applications of cleaner wax and three applications of carnauba wax. Now that's dedication.

As an auto sales manager, Skiple believes that many times the difference between a $2,000 car and a $3,000 car is a $100 detail. In most cases, trade-ins can bring an additional $300 if they are detailed. Skiple advises cleaning the car in such a way that it doesn't look detailed, just taken care of. "At the least," he says, "a five-dollar car wash can increase trade-in value by fifty dollars."

George Ridderbusch is a consistent Concours d'Elegance winner with his 1979 Porsche 928. When

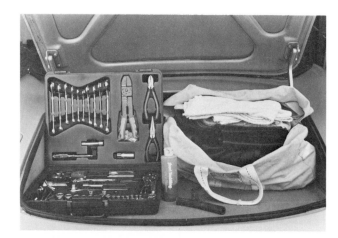

This is just a part of the immaculate underbody of George and Kathy Ridderbusch's concours-winning 1979 Porsche 928. Thousands of hours have been spent cleaning and polishing this car to perfection. Hard to believe this underbody has undergone 30,000 miles of road travel.

Jerry McKee bought this tool kit and carries it in the trunk of his 1972 Jaguar E-type V-12 roadster. In the bag are a car cover, road cleaning kit and some miscellaneous parts which come in handy on trips.

The rear underbody of McKee's Jaguar roadster looks good. This part of the car is mostly noticed by other drivers, as opposed to those who may be admiring the car from a standing position. During the detail, be sure to spend an adequate amount of time cleaning these lower body areas.

I first looked at his winning car, with 30,000 miles on the odometer, I was impressed. It was clean, tidy and standing tall. Despite the car's fine condition, Ridderbusch said it would take three weeks to prepare it for a concours event. It was hard for me to see what had to be done.

Most true car enthusiasts will not drive a dirty car. For trips they carry a road kit in the trunk, including a bucket, cotton wash mitt, car wash soap and towels. The owner will get up early in the morning and wash the car before hitting the road. Wentworth used to have white towels in his road kit until he got tired of funny looks from motel people; it seemed the motel folks thought he was using their towels to clean his car. Now, he carries a set of special black towels in the kit.

More than cleaning

Detailing consists of much more than a wash and wax. Sure, you can spend an entire day washing and waxing, but have you addressed the details? Do the fenderwells look dirty? How about the bottom rear? When stopped at a red light, does the driver behind you see rust-colored axles, gas tank or spare

Smeared wax on the taillight cover of Clint Worthington's 1985 Porsche 944 is almost impossible to remove completely. It will take lots of toothbrush scrubbing with soap and water to get the residue out of the textured surface. A light coat of dressing applied with a cotton swab can be added for a finishing touch. Controlled wax application is a must around these areas.

11

Like the rear underbody of this Jag roadster, the front underbody should be cleaned and polished. If the front license plate is not required in your state, you may consider running without it. This car looks much better from the front without the plate jutting out from one side of the grille.

Undercarriages on 4x4s are almost always plainly visible, like this one on a four-wheel-drive muscle truck. In order to keep the vehicle looking its best, you must take time to clean these areas thoroughly and repaint as necessary.

tire well? Does the visible frame, below the doors, stick out like a sore thumb? Is there wax in the lettering on the taillight lens?

Dan Mycon is the owner of New Look Autobody. He is well known for his excellent auto body and paint work. Says Mycon, "If you want your car to be different, clean and wax it. Clean everything." This is especially true underneath the rear end of 4x4s and Corvettes. The axle, gas tanks and shocks are plainly visible on 4x4s; exhaust and fuel tank on Corvettes. Be sure to clean these areas and paint accordingly. You can clean with a power washer at the automatic self-serve car wash or use a bucket, brush and wash mitt. Black paint usually looks best. Clean the shocks on 4x4s and repaint with the original color.

Tires and wheels are of great concern to car people. As a dealer, Skiple prefers trade-ins to have bald tires or brand new ones. He feels tires and wheels are the first thing to catch a customer's eye. Thoroughly cleaned and smartly dressed, tires and wheels stand out and accent the beauty of any car.

For Mycon, dirty fenderwells are an immediate eyesore, and he can't understand how anyone can spend hours and hours washing and waxing the body and completely ignore the fenderwells. "Body rust starts from the inside and eats through to the outside," he says.

Inexperienced car people make a very common mistake when waxing. They feel if a little is a little good, then a lot will do a lot of good. Not true with car wax. Every can of wax carries instructions that advise the reader to apply sparingly. In other words, two light coats are much better than a single heavy one.

Keep wax away from emblems, seams, black anodized trim, bumper guards, door guards and the like. Wax build-up in these areas is unnecessary, unsightly and a pain in the neck to remove. Use the applicator in a systematic manner and take care to apply the wax where you want it. The chapter about tools and chemicals will give you more information about wax, applicators and application.

Trailer hitches can be another eyesore. Refrain from painting hitches and brackets a color that

While the tire and wheel are off the car for cleaning, Wentworth will spend time cleaning and undercoating the fenderwell on his GS 455. Along with an improved appearance, the removal of dirt and residue build-up in fenderwells helps to reduce the potential of rust corrosion.

Wheel and tire on Art Wentworth's 1970 Buick GS 455 convertible which has been at the body shop for over a month. Both need to be cleaned and polished on the front side, as well as the back.

Stock chrome spoked wheel and Goodyear Wingfoot tire have been on McKee's Jag since 1972. Gentle and consistent upkeep have kept this combination in excellent condition, adding to the overall attraction of the car.

Wax build-up around the base of this Corvette radio antenna is unsightly. Gentle scrubbing with a soft toothbrush, soap and water will clean and should not scratch the paint. The use of a small rectangular sponge for wax application will allow greater control and help prevent this kind of overwaxing in the future.

stands out in contrast to the car. Black supporting brackets blend with the bottom of the car, while bright silver paint allows tongues and balls to blend well with chrome bumpers. Chrome hitches are nice, if affordable.

Getting things right

Some "car nuts" regard detailing as a two-step process. First is cleaning, polishing and waxing. Second is *getting things right*. Things like license

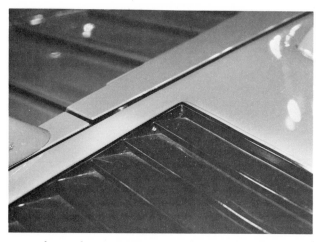

Dust, dirt and wax residue can be easily removed from the louvers on this Lamborghini Countach by using a soft paintbrush with car wash soap. More than one application may be necessary, but using the soft brush is much safer than the high water pressure from a pressure washer.

plate frames, floor mats and jacking equipment. Does the license plate frame blend with the back of the car? Or pull your eye directly to it? Specialized frames are OK if in good taste. Dealers like you to advertise for them, but does their frame make your car look better? Does the painted frame match the color scheme of your car?

Wentworth likes simple chrome frames on cars with chrome bumpers. For him, stock Corvette frames are perfect. They are thin, have no projections for screws and are made of stainless steel. They cost around twenty dollars. Black frames look best on cars with black bumpers and those with black paint around the license area.

When you put new tabs on the license plate, take pains to place them on square. Car people have used hair dryers to loosen crooked tabs and adjust them square with the plate. This is a minor consideration, one that catches your eye. You can also line up the screws holding the license plate in place. Wentworth likes all the screw slots running vertical. He tells people this helps the slots to drain water, reducing rust potential. In reality, he is just finicky and prefers things in order.

Some foreign cars come equipped with tool kits. When you go to use this kit, you will probably *really* need it. Don't hesitate to take a look at it once in a while to make sure all tools are in working order. Take a few minutes to lubricate the pliers and rust-proof the rest of the tools with a light coat of WD-40. The jacking equipment is equally important. Clean and remove unnecessary grease. If the tool kit is

A stock Corvette frame dresses the license plate on a Jag roadster. The stainless steel frame blends well with surrounding chrome. Note the even position of the month and year tabs. Mounting screws should be the same color and their slots should all be in line with each other, running vertically.

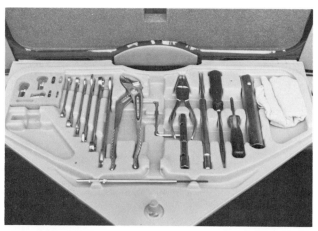

You generally need to use a tool kit when something goes wrong. Therefore, it is a good idea to keep tools clean and in working condition, like these in a factory, trunk-lid-mounted BMW tool kit. Check tools once a month. Operate pliers and apply a light coat of WD-40 to keep them from freezing in the closed position.

plainly visible in the trunk, wax or paint a compatible color.

Decals and stickers are more popular now than ever before. Hardly a car rolls by without one. They represent parking permits, fraternal organizations, unions, places visited and messages of various intent. Some decals and stickers are necessary, such as parking permits. Instead of placing them just anywhere, take a minute to find an appropriate spot. If a window seems most logical, place the sticker in the corner and be sure the bottom edge is square with the window trim. Don't put it on cock-eyed. If the bumper is more suitable, keep the sticker square with the bumper's bottom edge. Never, I mean never, put a sticker on the painted surface of the trunk. If you ever attempt to remove it, you

Although Worthington keeps his 1985 Porsche 944 in perfect condition, he neglected to check the tool kit. Here, we found the pliers rusty and frozen in the closed position. They were cleaned with an SOS pad and freed with WD-40 and twenty minutes of gradually increased opening and closing.

Jacking equipment needs to be serviced once or twice a year in order to maintain proper lubrication and keep tools clean. The knock-offs on this Jaguar roadster cannot be properly removed without its special equipment, generating a valid need to keep this equipment in top condition.

McKee took time to place this service sticker in a neat position on his 1972 Jag driver's door. Most car people would appreciate the careful application but much prefer to keep such reminders out of sight in the glovebox. These stickers are not factory items and tend to make the car look cheap.

15

After sitting in the body shop for extensive body and paint work, the engine compartment of Wentworth's Buick convertible needs a complete detail.

stand a good chance of taking paint with it. Once the sticker is removed, you'll notice the paint underneath is darker than the paint on the rest of the car.

The bottom line

The ultimate secret to detailing is time, patience and elbow grease. The more quality time you spend, the better results you will achieve. If your time is limited, spend it on one area, as opposed to a little time on a lot of areas. Take one day to clean nothing but the wheels. Use another day on the interior. Plan a weekend for the exterior and another for the engine.

You should also realize that a complete and thorough detail is only necessary once, providing you have a consistent system for regular maintenance. Car enthusiasts routinely go through a rig

Wentworth's 1970 Buick GS 455 convertible's engine compartment after detailing. Garden hose water pressure, Simple Green soap, paintbrushes, toothbrushes, a wash mitt and plenty of rags were used to clean it. The black inner fenderwells and firewall were repainted with spray cans and the hoses and wires were treated with a cloth sprayed with Armor All. The black air cleaner housing was waxed with Meguiar's Car Cleaner Wax.

once or twice a year. Then, they wash the car weekly, waxing one section each time. They concentrate on the hood, top and trunk in the summer, sides in the winter. It doesn't take too much time and assures adequate wax protection.

Keep detailing as simple as possible. During the one-time, major detail, dismantle as necessary to reach dirt around parts such as the grille, moldings, emblems, seats and knobs. After that, stay on top of those areas by cleaning frequently, not giving dirt a chance to build up. If you question the use of certain chemicals, always remember that you won't go wrong using mild soap, water and a soft touch.

A perfect detail followed by regular weekly and monthly maintenance is the best way to keep an automobile looking good, standing tall and remaining valuable.

Once or twice a year, or as often as necessary, pull the spare tire out of the trunk and clean. This Porsche spare was cleaned front and back. Afterward, wax was applied to both sides of the wheel for protection against dirt and rust.

Checklist for major detailing and upkeep
Engine compartment
Clean, paint, wax or dress as needed:
1. Carburetor and air cleaner
2. Intake manifold
3. Heads and exhaust manifold
4. Front of block
5. Rear of block
6. Alternator; front, sides and back
7. Air-conditioning unit; front, sides and back
8. Power steering unit; front, sides and back
9. Wires and hoses; top and bottom
10. Inner fenderwells and firewall
11. Frame and steering members
12. Radiator; top, sides, front and back
13. Space between grille and radiator

Interior
Vacuum, clean and dress as needed:
1. Dashboard; vents, slots, knobs, steering wheel, mirror, glovebox
2. Headliner; sun visors, seatbelts
3. Seats; along beads, seams and the space between the cushion and seatback
4. Carpet; under and along the sides of seats
5. Console
6. Side panels; door panels, cranks, handles, pouches
7. Seatbelts
8. Foot pedals
9. Floor mats
10. Rear deck
11. Speakers
12. Trunk; jacking equipment, tool kits

Exterior
Wash, clean, wax, dress, paint as needed:
1. Tires and wheels
2. Fenderwells; fenderwell lips, mudflaps
3. Underbody; front, rear and sides, including steering and suspension members, fuel tanks and shock absorbers
4. Spoilers
5. Bumpers and bumper guards
6. Exhaust tips
7. Trim; emblems, lettering, door handles, key holes, antennas, around windows
8. Grille; pop-up headlights
9. Light lenses
10. Doorjambs; hood and deck lid edges
11. Vinyl or convertible top
12. Glass; wiper blades front, back and headlights
13. Side mirrors

Chapter 2

Work area and materials

All the tools and chemicals discussed in this chapter have been used successfully by many detailers and car enthusiasts. It is imperative that you follow the instructions on the label of each product you use. If you question directed usage, seek advice

Before you start detailing, always remove rings, watches and other jewelry. If Wentworth's hand were to slip off the towel, his ring or watch would surely scratch the paint on this beautiful Guard's Red Porsche. Be alert to belt buckles and rivets on jeans as well. You will be leaning over the car a number of times during cleaning and these objects present a real scratch hazard.

from an auto body paint and supply store or your local detailer.

Appropriate attire

During the course of detailing, your hands, arms and body will come in contact with the car. If you wear rings, imagine what will happen if your hand slides off a towel and onto the painted surface. Watches and bracelets can also scratch paint. Remove all jewelry before detailing.

Clothes are important. You want to be comfortable while bending and twisting to reach all parts of the car. Be wary of jeans that have rivets at the pockets. You will be leaning over the fenders to reach parts in the engine compartment. A cotton warm-up suit is great. It allows you easy and comfortable movement and has no protruding rivets or zippers that can cause scratches.

Tennis shoes are fine as long as they don't have treaded soles that trap dirt and debris. When you sit in the interior to clean, you won't want all that stuff coming off your shoes and onto the carpet. If you must wear shoes with such soles, lay a towel on the floor for your feet.

Some detailers wear a long apron while waxing or buffing. The apron serves two purposes. First, it keeps the detailer's clothes clean. Second, it protects the body of the car while the detailer has to lean against it.

Work area

The area in which you choose to work should be appropriate for the type of job that you are planning. For a preliminary cleaning, including the engine compartment, you must realize the amount of dirt, grease and grime that will fall off onto the ground. Is your driveway suitable for this mess, or should you find somewhere else?

A good place to wash engines and fenderwells is a self-serve car wash. It offers high-pressure

Skiple prefers to wash his Pantera in the driveway. Since the car is frequently cleaned, he doesn't worry about excessive dirt and grease staining the concrete.

Self-serve car washes offer an ideal place to clean engines and underbodies. Wentworth uses this facility to occasionally rinse the fenderwells on his Buick when they need the added strength of a pressure washer to remove heavy accumulations of dirt and debris. Note that some self-serve car wash proprietors prefer you not clean engines at their facilities. In those cases, you will have to find an alternative location.

The added strength of a power washer cleans this Pantera engine compartment quicker than garden hose pressure. When using high-pressure water, you must remember that the force can easily remove stickers and peel paint.

Hold the wand away from the surface, going in closer only to remove extra dirty spots on surfaces that can withstand the force.

water and soap mixed through a high-pressure wand. Each bay is equipped with drains in the floor, allowing for heavy residue runoff. Self-serve car washes are inexpensive and useful places to remove

High-pressure water is not designed for normal body washing. Used incorrectly, the water force from a pressure washer can dislodge license plate tabs and decals, such as the Toyota MR2 insignia on the right side of this trunk lid.

heavy accumulations of dirt and grease. Afterward, relocate to your driveway for detailed cleaning.

Use caution with the high-pressure wash. Aiming the tip of the wand too close to stickers in the engine compartment will remove them. Some paint will come off the engine, which is to be expected. You can repaint later. Watch out for water ricochet. Pointing the wand at the top of the intake manifold, with your head directly behind the wand, may splatter water and grease in your face and possibly your eyes. Stand to the side and plan for splatter to go away from you; consider wearing goggles.

I don't recommend using high-pressure water on the body, except for rinsing during engine cleaning. The force of the water could damage paint and emblems. Save the body wash for your driveway.

You can do all the preliminary washing in your own driveway or yard if the car is reasonably clean. Just remember that car washing should be done in the shade although you can do it in the sun as long as you rinse frequently. The object is not to allow soap to dry on the car. Wash the shady side first, sunny side last. Dry the entire car immediately after washing.

Almost all work can be done on the driveway. You can clean the trunk, paint the engine and detail the interior. The sole exception is waxing, which must be done in the shade. A garage or carport is perfect. The sun dries wax too fast which makes it hard to remove and leaves streaks. If one of your favorite hobbies is car waxing at the beach or park, find a shady spot. If nothing else, wax the shady side first; then, reposition the car so the opposite side is in the shade.

Washing equipment
Water applicators

Portable power washers offer the same high water pressure as self-serve car washes for cleaning engines and underbody. They can be rented at any local rental yard. Your need for them is disputable; other than for washing the engine and underbody, you shouldn't need one, and it is far cheaper to use the self-serve car wash. Don't get me wrong, the use for which they are intended is good. High-pressure water sprays help to clean wheels, grilles and vinyl tops. You must consider the damage that can

Light engine compartment cleaning can be done on the driveway without much worry of staining the surface. Here, an old wash mitt is used to remove dust and light dirt from a Pantera engine compartment.

A small, portable pressure washer works well for cleaning heavily soiled wheels, fenderwells and engine compartments. This unit was used to clean the neglected wheels on a Nissan 300ZX.

be done, however, if not used properly. Decals and stickers can be blown off, paint peeled and vinyl torn. I feel it is much safer, in the long run, to use the gentlest techniques available.

Ordinary household water pressure is sufficient for most purposes. If higher pressure is needed, use a high-pressure nozzle. (Be careful not to drop the nozzle in such a way that it careens off the ground and hits the car.)

An open-ended garden hose is best for car washing. Softly flowing water will remove soap and leave the waxed paint almost dry because water will fall off the car in sheets. Applying water through a nozzle will result in thousands of water spots, an added drying chore.

Most auto parts stores carry multiuse wash wands. They are long metal tubes with a hose connection at one end and a brush at the other. Soap is mixed with water and comes out through the brush.

Advertised as work-savers, I wonder what effect they have on car paint?

These wands may be well suited for washing windows, vinyl house siding and garden furniture, but not quality cars. The brush will leave fine scratches. Scrubbing a particularly tough spot will result in deeper scratches. It may be all right for the person who has a regular driver that gets washed once every six months, but not the person who cares enough about his car to wash it every week.

Car wash soaps

Almost every car enthusiast I talked to has a different preference for car wash soap. Some feel mild dish soaps are best; others prefer name brand products designed specifically for washing automobiles.

All agreed, however, that powdered soaps are out of the question. They feel that a single grain of powder, not dissolved completely, can scratch paint.

A small assortment of car wash soaps as displayed at a local auto parts store. Although many car people successfully use dish soaps for car washing, you minimize damage risk by using products designed for use on auto paints. The cleaning mitt at the right is a cotton type recommended by many car enthusiasts.

Also stay away from household cleaners such as 409 and Mr. Clean; for car washing, they are too alkaline or abrasive. These cleaners can be used later for other detailing chores.

The biggest question seemed to focus around the soap's ability to remove wax. Most dish soaps contain degreasers. While the degreasing feature is good for removing road grime, it could remove wax. This poses no problem if you always wax a small portion of the car after each wash. On the plus side, some dish soaps help to reduce water spotting.

Eagle 1, Turtle Wax, Meguiar's and many other manufacturers of car care products make car wash soaps that have been tested on cars, not dishes. You can't go wrong using any of these products. Try each at different times until you find one that works best for you.

Mitts

Washing a car is easiest with a wash mitt. It holds plenty of soap and water, covers a good-sized area and protects your hand. There are a few different types on the market. Some are synthetics that look like lamb's wool. Car enthusiasts feel the synthetics are too rough. The myriad minute scratches left on paint after washing with a nylon mitt look like webbing left by a thousand spiders. The thin lines are accented by sunlight and are exceptionally visible. To remove spider webbing, polish with a sealer and glaze like Meguiar's #7.

Car enthusiasts prefer cotton wash mitts, which are often made of chenille, a type of cord. The fibers are soft and do not promote swirls. I recommend the use of two mitts: one for the body and one for underbody, fenderwells and engine compartment.

A wash mitt will collect grit. It is very important to rinse it frequently. You should also rinse the wash bucket occasionally and refill with clean, soapy water, remembering that anything collected in the mitt or the wash bucket is a potential scratch hazard.

You can also use towels for car washing. They are cumbersome if too big, so cut them in half. Baby diapers are soft and a good size. The disadvantage of using cloths and towels is that your hand can slip off of them, resulting in cuts from sharp edges on emblems or other projections. Cloths and towels don't seem to hold as much soap as a mitt, either.

Brushes

To detail an automobile thoroughly, you need a small assortment of brushes. A three-inch, soft natural-bristled paintbrush works wonders around headlights, mirrors, window trim, emblems and wheels. The soft bristles will not scratch paint and will reach areas your mitt or cloth cannot. Since the brush is soft, you may have to use more than one

A soft-bristled paintbrush works very well to clean inside grooves and seams along the door trim of this 944. Carry it in the wash bucket and use it right after sudsing up with the wash mitt.

Cotton wash mitts often come made of chenille. This new cotton mitt features a long fluffy nap with a wristband designed to help keep the mitt on your hand. I recommend you place your hand inside the mitt to prevent scratching it while washing next to metal bumpers and sharp edges.

23

application on tough spots. Be patient. The value of using a nonscratching brush is well worth the effort. As a precaution, place a strip of duct tape around the metal frame of the brush. This will prevent paint damage while brushing in tight areas.

A smaller paintbrush, about one inch in width, works very well in close quarters. The small size allows easy access to spots around the grille,

A paintbrush is also handy during engine cleaning. On this Buick 455 V-8, the brush was used with solvent to quickly clean around bolts, wires and hoses.

between lug nuts on wheels and in tight pockets near taillights and bumpers.

A plastic-bristled brush can be used on tires, fenderwells and underbody areas. The stout bristles knock off dirt and debris and scrub rubber clean. This brush can also be used to shampoo carpets and upholstery, vinyl tops and convertibles. If necessary, it can be used under the hood to remove extra-heavy accumulations of dirt.

Whitewall brushes are small, short-bristled wire brushes. They are not nearly as strong as the larger painter's wire brush. The bristles are closely cropped together and make short work of removing dirt and stains.

Toothbrushes are used in every detail shop. Old toothbrushes with soft bristles work best. These handy tools can be used to remove dirt and wax build-up around light lenses and in emblems, dirt in upholstery seams, stubborn spots on carpet and almost anything else you deem necessary. Have more than one on hand since you may find yourself using one in the engine compartment and won't want to use it later on the interior.

Cotton swabs are very useful. Their size, texture and absorbing qualities are perfect for removing dust around radio buttons, cracks in dash panels and slots around heater controls. They can also be used to apply and remove wax inside painted vent openings and around emblems.

Finally, a small, one-inch paintbrush, with the bristles cut to about three-quarters of an inch, works exceptionally well to remove wax from em-

This all-purpose plastic brush can be used to scrub dirty convertible tops. The stout bristles help to dislodge dirt embedded in the grain. Note the plastic sheet protecting the body on this 1974 Corvette roadster from soap stains.

During detailing, a toothbrush is a must. Older toothbrushes are best because the bristles are soft. Here, one is used to remove wax build-up from the lettering on a Porsche 944 sidelight lens.

blems, cracks and trim. The bristles will not scratch, so the brush can be used as a final detailing tool. The short length of the bristles gives them the strength to remove wax build-up.

Steel wool soap pads

SOS pads are a familiar item at most supermarkets. They are pads of steel wool impregnated with soap. Designed for scrubbing pots and pans, they also work well on chrome, whitewalls, vinyl tops, convertible tops, some wheels and engines.

The texture of the pad is soft and should not scratch real chrome. The soap adds cleaning and degreasing power. Since they fall apart rather

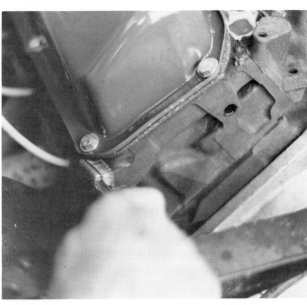

Have more than one toothbrush on hand. You wouldn't want to use this one on the interior after using it to clean the V-8 in your Pantera.

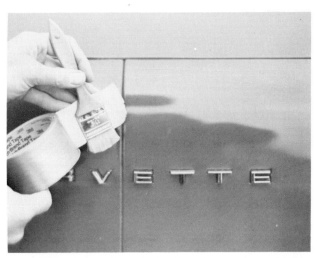

A small paintbrush with the bristles cut to a half or three-quarters of an inch works very well to remove wax build-up around emblems and lettering. A piece of thick tape around the metal band of the brush helps to prevent the bare metal from scratching paint.

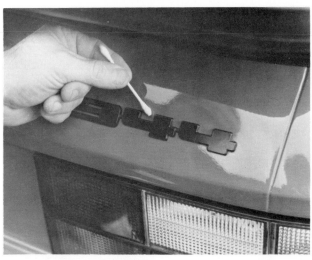

Cotton swabs are useful on the exterior as well as the interior. Inside, they are used to remove dust from vents, slots and grooves. Outside, you can use them to remove wax from emblems and to apply wax and dressing in tight spaces.

SOS pads have a number of uses during an auto detail. Used mostly on chrome and unpainted engine parts, you can gently scrub some painted parts to remove heavy accumulations of dirt and grease. In this case, an SOS pad is carefully applied along the bottom edge of a Jaguar engine compartment to remove dirt build-up.

Simple Green is a degreasing soap designed for auto and household use. Wentworth has found this product to *work very well on most auto cleaning chores, from engine compartments to wheels, and vinyl tops to tires.*

Some concours winners don't like to bring moisture into the interior of their winning car. For them, a foam cleaner like Tuff Stuff is a good compromise. This product cleans well without the excessive moisture content of liquid cleaners like Simple Green.

quickly, you will need more than one during the course of a complete detail.

Steel wool can be used for some cleaning jobs. Used with a window cleaner, it can remove stubborn bug residue from windshields. Used with wax, it can polish, clean and protect real chrome in one application. Always use soft steel wool. I have found #00 and softer works best.

All-purpose cleaners

Detail shops use heavy-duty cleaners supplied by wholesale outlets. Some similar products are available retail. Simple Green is a heavy-duty cleaner available at most auto parts stores. Wentworth has had good luck using it for many cleaning jobs, including engines, tires, trunks and wheels. It is a mild cleaner that penetrates dirt—just what you want. Other household cleaners may work just as well.

Use all-purpose cleaner to clean the engine compartment, jacking equipment, underbody and vinyl. Such cleaning agents are too harsh for washing the car body but work well for cleaning other parts. I have had good luck buying all-purpose cleaner in gallon size, diluting it to recommended standards and applying through squirt bottles. Simple Green and other cleaners also come in spray bottles that you can refill from the larger container.

Use this type of cleaner on vinyl interior parts. Spray it on one side of a folded towel to clean the headliner, use the other side of the towel to wipe dry. Do the same for dashboards, seats and seatbelts. Clean ashtrays with this product and a toothbrush.

The brand you purchase is up to you. As in choosing car wash soaps, you have to find the cleaner that works best for you and your needs. Under no circumstances mix cleaners. They may react chemically and damage the material you are cleaning.

Toothpaste is a mild abrasive that can be used to clean stained metal parts. Some detailers have used it to scrub metal emblems. Since it has not been designed for use on cars, you may have better luck using chrome polish first, saving toothpaste for a last resort.

Upholstery and carpet cleaning equipment
Shampoos

To clean carpet and cloth upholstery completely, you need to use shampoo. Most supermarkets carry an assortment of such products. I won't recommend one over the other. Used with a stiff plastic-bristled brush, shampoo makes most upholstery turn out beautiful. Use it as you would for household furniture. It is best to have a wet-and-dry vacuum cleaner available to remove excess water and soap. If not, use lots of dry towels to soak up moisture.

Shampooing the carpets can be done just like the upholstery. I like to fill a small bucket and spray bottle with shampoo mixed with water according to the label instructions. I use the plastic-bristled brush to work up a good lather. The spray bottle comes in handy for stubborn stains.

If carpeting is merely spotted, you should not have to shampoo the entire area. Supermarkets also carry many carpet cleaners designed for spot removal. These products do not require the use of water or a wet-and-dry vacuum cleaner. They are easy to use and work well.

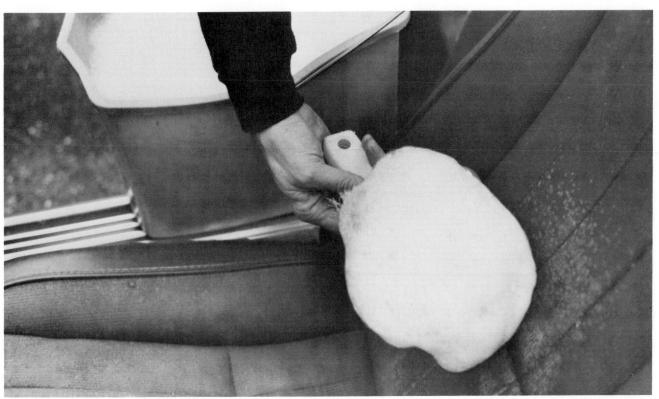

This Corvette was stored in a garage with sheepskin covers over the seats. The white spots on the seatback are mildew, caused by moisture trapped between the sheep-skin cover and the vinyl seat. Plenty of upholstery shampoo suds on the plastic-bristled brush made short work of cleaning and left the seats in excellent condition.

27

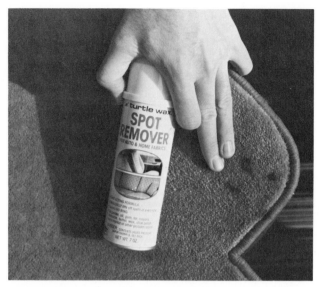

Most spot removers like this Turtle Wax product do not require the use of a wet-and-dry vacuum. The remover dries to a white powder and is brushed off or removed with a dry vacuum.

Vacuum cleaners

A wet-and-dry vacuum cleaner is most versatile. Generally stronger than household units, it picks up larger items, as well as water. Unless you plan to shampoo the carpet and upholstery, there is no need to purchase or rent one. Dry carpet cleaners work well and the powdery residue can be removed with a dry vacuum cleaner.

If the interior of your car warrants the power of a wet-and-dry vacuum cleaner and you don't have one, drive to a local self-serve car wash. Most of these facilities have three or four vacuum units on site. They have wet-and-dry capabilities and can also be used to remove shampoo.

The small 12 volt vacuum cleaners powered by cigarette lighters are fine. Since they lack power, you can sweep debris into a pile using a plastic-bristled brush. Then vacuum away. These units do not have enough power to loosen stubborn grit, hence the need for a brush. The same holds true for battery-powered vacuum cleaners.

The powerful suction of a wet-and-dry vacuum works best for cleaning auto interiors. A small unit like this can be used to remove heavy concentrations of dirt and grit from upholstery and carpet. It can also be used to remove water and suds after shampooing.

If you need the power of a wet-and-dry vacuum and don't have access to a personal unit, try a self-serve car wash.

Most of these facilities are equipped with four to eight units.

Drying cloths

You will need towels to dry the car and clean areas other than the body. Bath towels are great, except for their size. Cut them in half and fold into quarters. Medium-sized fluffy hand towels with long naps are perfect. Nap refers to the surface tex-

ture of cloth, towel or carpet. As opposed to flannel, which is smooth, towels and carpet are made with thick woven fibers (pile) that stick up out of the base material and form a soft cushiony texture.

Drying the car requires at least two towels. If you used free-flowing water, as opposed to a nozzle,

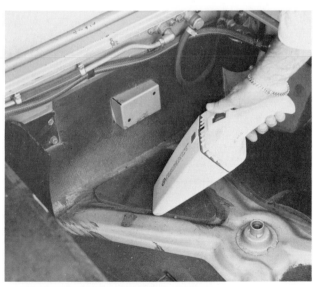

For light work during weekly cleaning, a small battery-powered vacuum is fine. This type of unit lacks real suction power, however, and you may have to sweep dirt and grit into a pile with a brush to remove with this vacuum.

Anything that touches the paint on your car should be soft. Like soft cotton wash mitts, cotton towels are a favorite with most car people. Thick fluffy naps are gentle on paint and tend to keep small particles of grit tucked deep inside the material, away from paint.

This round sponge-like wax applicator came with the can of Simoniz Paste Wax. As long as it is kept clean, it will work just fine.

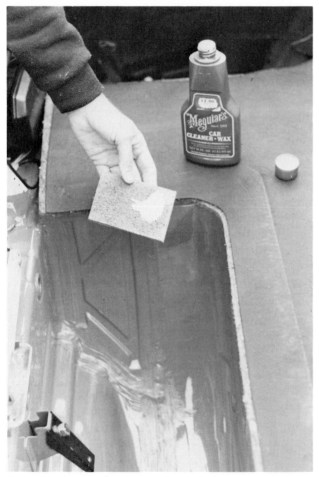

A small rectangular sponge is perfect for wax application. The square edges allow good control around emblems, letters and other obstacles. It is also good for waxing unusually shaped areas like this trunk space in a Porsche 944. After each use, rinse the sponge in clean water.

there won't be much water on the car. Use the first towel to absorb the majority of water and the second to dry the car completely. Later, use the dampest towel to wipe doorjambs, trunk lid and hood edges.

You will need towels or cloths for other cleaning chores such as doing the interior. The coarse nap on hand towels helps remove dirt and imbedded grime. Folding them in quarters allows you to refold and use clean sections as needed.

Paper towels can be used to wipe greasy parts and plug wires. Inexpensive and plentiful, they are useful for the dirtiest and greasiest jobs. Paper towels can also be used to keep ignition parts dry while cleaning the engine. Their absorbing qualities help keep the distributor and carburetor dry during engine cleaning.

Wax application and removal require a different set of cloths. Some waxes come with a round, spongelike applicator. These are OK. I have had better luck using a rectangular sponge. The straight edges on the sponge allow greater control while waxing along seams and sunroof edges. The sponge may be cleaned and reused. Since they are quite inexpensive, having an ample supply on hand is easy.

Removing wax raises another point of disagreement among car enthusiasts. What cloth works

Soft cotton cloths are best for removing wax. Wentworth has had good luck buying soft white flannel at the yardage store and using it for wax removal. A yard of flannel is inexpensive and works best when it is cut into small sections about two feet square. After each use, clean the cloths in the washing machine and clothes dryer.

best for rubbing and polishing? The only criterion is that the material be very soft, inexpensive and easy to use. Again, fold the cloth into quarters; refold as a side becomes dirty.

Baby diapers are a favorite. They have never been exposed to harsh materials that may scratch, such as metal chips or grit. The only problem may be availability. You can buy new ones but must consider the cost. Skiple likes cheesecloth. It is inexpensive, soft and works very well to remove wax. The only drawback is that it can only be used once. Old cotton shirts are fine, but how many do you have hanging around? Which brings us to the fabric store. Wentworth uses plain, white flannel. It is soft, removes wax adequately and can be used over and over again. After each use, he puts the cloth into the washing machine and dryer. When done, it looks clean and soft as new. When it wears out, he buys another yard for under two dollars. All of these types of cloth work well.

Dressings

Of all the dressings on the market, Armor All is probably the name most frequently heard. It may be because it was one of the first or because it is the most widely used. Other manufacturers of car care products make similar polypenetrants. The differences can be argued by the manufacturers; you will have to choose which works best for you.

Jerry McKee has used Armor All on the tires of his 1972 Jaguar V-12 roadster for over twelve years. The tires look like new. Others, however, have complained that weekly use of tire dressing causes the rubber to crack.

I have heard similar complaints about dashboards. It seems that once a dressing has been applied, you need frequent reapplication to keep the vinyl looking good. One explanation may be that the dressing makes the vinyl look so good, that after the vinyl dries to its normal appearance, it looks terrible in comparison. Again, you have to be the judge. As with anything, too much is not too good. Used sparingly, dressings—such as Armor All, Turtle Wax Clear Guard, Meguiar's #40 Vinyl/Leather/Rubber/Cleaner/Conditioner and Eagle 1 Concours Tire Dressing & Protectant—work well to rejuvenate dry vinyl and bring back the rich texture it had when new.

Paints

During the course of the detail, you will need paint. Many paints are available at auto parts stores. You can select the color you want and the type needed for each special application. You can also buy touch-up paint for newer model cars. If yours is a vintage model, you may have to have a special mix of paint made at an auto paint supply store. If you need a stock color, the manufacturer's plate on the doorjamb or dashboard will give the color code.

Auto parts stores carry a number of vinyl and rubber dressings. Auto enthusiasts have different preferences for a variety of personal reasons. Wentworth prefers Armor All, Ridderbusch uses Meguiar's and others have had good results with Eagle 1 and Turtle Wax. You will have to try each one until finding the brand that best suits your taste.

Too much is seldom too good. Worthington has sparingly applied Armor All to the Pirelli tires on his Porsche since 1985. The rubber looks good and has not been damaged in any way. Excessive amounts of dressing do not look good cosmetically, and the added moisture content could possibly cause problems in the long run.

Semigloss black looks good on black engine compartments, fenderwells and underbody areas. The engine block will need special heat-resistant paint, the same color as the stock engine—for example, Chevy orange or Ford blue. The trunk can be painted with special trunk paint. It is a spatter paint that coats the trunk with a combination of gray, black and white. Different colors are available.

Bright silver is the best color to use on dock bumpers and metal ashtrays. The newly painted part will look new if it is properly prepared. Dock bumpers should be free of peeling. Use wet-and-dry sandpaper for smoothing. Cover decals, manufacturer labels and license plate lights with masking tape. One heavy coat is not as good as two light coats. The same holds true for painting metal ashtrays.

If the fenderwells have been completely cleaned, you may consider painting them with undercoating. Not a rustproof formula, undercoating helps to reduce road noise. For true rustproofing, you need

This is a typical assortment of spray paint available at most auto parts stores. The various brands range from body touch-up to heat-resistant engine paints. For special color mixes, you will have to go to an auto body paint and supply store.

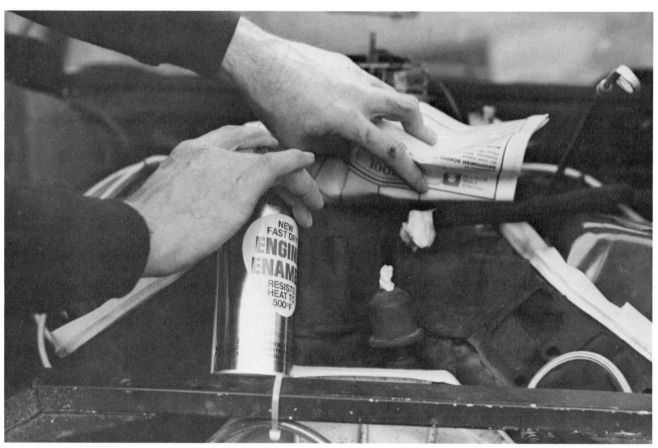

Because of high operating temperatures, engines require special heat-resistant paint. Ford Blue is being applied to this Pantera engine, matching the original color. Some metal parts and the valve cover gaskets are masked because they came stock from the factory unpainted.

In lieu of painting fenderwells and underbody with black paint, you can apply undercoating. Rustproofing products are not the same as undercoats. Read the labels on the different products to see which one will do the job you are planning.

to buy a can of rustproofing material or visit your local rustproofing specialist.

Some detailers like to spray crystal clear lacquer over a detailed engine compartment. Just about every car on a used car lot has had the engine shot

Rocker panel sprays protect lower body parts against rock chips and other road hazards. Auto body paint and supply stores carry the widest assortment of these types of products.

Black lacquer works well for fenderwells, visible frame members and black engine compartments. Crystal Clear makes plastic ashtrays look new and Bright Silver is the right tint for wing nuts, metal ashtrays and other silver or metal parts.

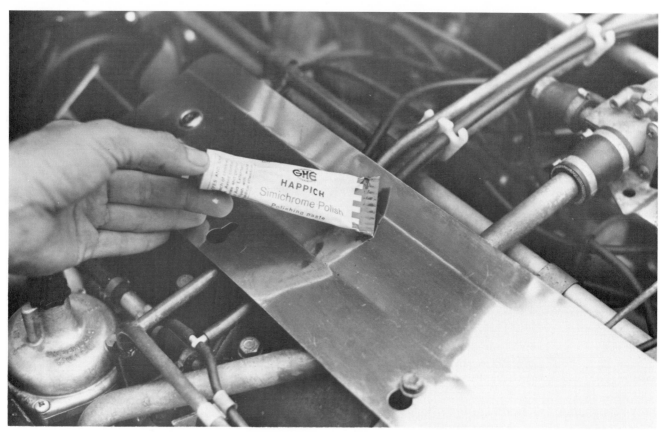

Happich Simichrome Polish is excellent for chrome and polished metal. It was used to polish this flat deflector which sits under the louvers on the hood of McKee's Jaguar, protecting electrical engine parts from water.

Eagle 1 Mag & Chrome Polish made short work of removing rust and dirt from this Corvette side mirror.

with clear. It looks great at first. It covers small imperfections and some dirt.

You will not want to use clear lacquer in the engine compartment of a really nice automobile, however. The paint will yellow in time and look bad. It is best to avoid using clear lacquer unless it is absolutely necessary to make the car you are selling look better. One application is worthy of note: Clear lacquer makes clean plastic ashtrays look new.

Polishes

There are two types of polish: one for metal and one for paint. Metal and chrome polish removes rust, pits and blemishes. It contains a fine grit. Happich Simichrome and Eagle 1 Mag & Chrome Polish work well. It is important to remember that a polish is not a wax. It is not designed to protect; rather, it is intended to clean and shine. After each use, you should apply a coat of wax for lasting protection.

Paint polish also contains grit, but it is different from chrome polish. This type of polish comes in a variety of textures. Rubbing compound is by far the harshest; you should never have to apply rubbing compound. Polishing compound is similar but softer. It is needed on paint that is heavily oxidized, stained and just about dead. Almost as a last resort, a detailer will use polishing compound before recommending a new paint job. Be careful using heavy polish because you don't know how much paint is left on the car.

Meguiar's offers a large assortment of polishes and waxes. Although many are available at most auto supply stores, the greatest variety can be found at auto body and paint stores. Determining the right product depends on the condition of the paint on your car and whether you plan to use a buffer or hand application. The safest way to choose the right product is to ask the store clerk or a detailer. If you want to choose the product yourself, read the label and use the one that contains the least grit. It is better to apply a mild polish two or three times than to use a polish that is too harsh a single time.

Waxes

Choosing the right wax can be quite a dilemma. By far the most common question I have been asked

Not all glazes and sealer waxes are designed for machine use. Products like Meguiar's Professional Machine Glaze #3 will specifically state they are for use by buffers. Polishes designed for hand application contain more grit than those made for machine use. Buffing with the wrong polish can result in the removal of too much paint and will present a greater paint burning hazard.

Meguiar's has the widest selection of automotive waxes and polishes. These are just a few found at a local auto parts store. Each product has a specific use. Read the labels to see which one is best suited for the degree of oxidation you need to remove from your car. Hi-Tech cleaners and waxes are recommended for the new types of high-tech paints, such as urethane and clear coats.

Meguiar's Car Cleaner Wax is an excellent one-step polish/wax. Wentworth uses it to polish chrome, remove sticker glue, get rid of road tar and wax paint. He has even used it under the hood to shine various metal parts.

Carnauba-based waxes last longer than most other wax products. This kind of wax is for paint protection only. They do not contain grit and will not remove oxidation or other paint blemishes. Application is made after paint is polished and all oxidation is removed.

is, "What is the best wax to use on my car?" The answer is not simple, nor is there common agreement among car enthusiasts.

Art Wentworth loves cars. I describe him as the Felix Unger of cars. He will not use anything but Meguiar's Car Cleaner Wax. He swears by its ability to polish and wax at the same time. It even removes residue left by stickers. While he says this, we must recognize that Art waxes a portion of his car every time he washes it. In the summertime, he will wax the roof one week and the hood and trunk the next. During winter months, he'll wax one side the first week and the other side the next.

Dan Mycon likes carnauba waxes. He feels the lasting quality is well worth the effort of application. Once the paint is in good condition, all it needs is protection. Once a year he will use a cleaner wax to remove old carnauba and oxidation that may have slipped in. Then, wax again with carnauba.

Terry Skiple applies polish, one-step cleaner wax and then carnauba. His method is labor-intensive. He only does this once to get the paint right. Later, he waxes with a cleaner wax when the paint needs it and keeps a coat of carnauba on for protection.

Auto parts stores and discount stores are filled with racks of auto wax. Choosing the right one is difficult. You can try each until you find the one best suited for your needs. Talk to other car enthusiasts to see what they use. There is no clear-cut definition of a perfect car wax. The car enthusiasts I have talked to have found their "perfect" wax by trial and error and word-of-mouth endorsement. I feel that Meguiar's offers the biggest variety of polishes, cleaner waxes, glazes and sealers. Auto body paint and supply stores carry all of them.

Buffers

Using a buffer to polish the paint on your car can be a real time-saver, providing you know how to use one. Most detailers use buffers to remove heavy concentrations of oxidation. Afterward, they hand

Auto body paint and supply stores generally carry most of Meguiar's large assortment of waxes and polishes. If the labels fail to provide you with the product usage information you need, ask the store clerk for help. These folks are well versed in auto body and paint needs and can be of valuable assistance.

This is a typical buffer used to polish paint. The pad attached to the machine is a cutting pad used to remove oxidation and scratches. The pad next to the buffer is a very soft finishing pad used with soft creamy wax to remove swirls and exceptionally light scratches.

This is a paint burn caused by the application of too much pressure on the buffer next to the ridge, or by holding the buffer in one position as opposed to keeping it moving. Carefully buff up to ridges, never directly on top of them.

It is also a good idea to start out using a mild polish with little grit and graduate to one with more grit as the need arises.

wax. The buffer has its place, and it is up to you to determine if your car's paint needs buffing.

Buffers are available at rental yards for about $10 a day, or can be purchased for around $175. The rpm range is from 1750 to 3000. Only the most experienced detailers use the high-speed 3000 rpm model. If you decide to use one, use the slower 1750 rpm buffer; it will save the paint on your car.

Buffers are used in conjunction with liquid wax. Depending on the oxidation of paint, a low-grit wax is generally preferred. The high-speed buffer helps to remove oxidation, allowing good paint underneath to shine. Using a wax with too much grit will result in paint burning (the wearing away of paint to the primer or metal).

Most paint jobs can be saved by hand. Although exceptionally difficult and labor-intensive, hand polishing does not present the hazards a buffer does. You don't have to worry abut peeling off emblems, whipping radio antennas into your face, ripping off windshield wipers, pulling off bodyside moldings or burning paint.

If the paint job on your car is so badly oxidized that you feel you need to use a buffer, so be it. Rent one with low rpm and practice on an inconspicuous place. Use extreme caution around moldings, wiper blades, antennas and ridges.

The pad you use is of equal importance. There are two types of pads: a cutting pad and a finishing pad. The cutting pad should be used to remove oxidation. Polishing a small part of the car at a time, you must clean the pad frequently as it will be removing wax and old paint.

If you are buffing a car with dark-colored paint, you must buff a second time with a finishing pad and a nongrit wax. The second buff with the finishing pad will remove swirls and spider webbing. You won't notice the imperfections in the shade, but once in the sunlight, they will stick out like a sore thumb.

Wheel cleaners

With the availability of so many different types of wheels, a number of easy-to-use wheel cleaners have also become available. As much as wax is a controversy among car enthusiasts, so are wheel cleaners. Eagle 1 has the largest assortment of wheel cleaners on the market. Barney Li, owner of Eagle 1, has a high interest in wheels. He feels that almost every wheel needs a separate cleaner and no single wheel cleaner is right for every wheel.

Wire wheels, mags, anodized aluminum and painted wheels need special treatment. I highly recommend, as does Mr. Li, that you read the label

Buffing pads are readily available at auto body paint and supply stores. Cutting pads are on top and finishing pads on the bottom.

Many detailers wear aprons while working on cars to protect paint against scratches. Consider wearing coveralls or an apron to protect fenders while working on the engine and the side of the car while polishing the hood, top and deck lid.

39

This is a small assortment of chemical wheel cleaners available at the auto parts store. It is extremely important to match the correct wheel cleaner with the wheel. Using the wrong product may result in permanent wheel damage. Eagle 1 has a large assortment of cleaners designed for special wheels. Carefully read the product label to make sure it is safe for your wheel and follow the application instructions exactly.

Using the wrong chemical cleaner could ruin this beautiful Jaguar chrome-spoked knock-off wheel. Improper application of chrome spoke wheel cleaner could also result in damage to the spokes and nipples. Some auto enthusiasts fear extended use of harsh chemical cleaners and prefer to clean such wheels with soap, water and toothbrushes.

of each wheel-cleaning product before you decide to buy. Mr. Li is proud of the assortment of products his company provides. He realizes the special applications needed for each wheel and has tried to provide the right product for each.

Some wheel cleaners claim to be good for all-purpose use. This is true because of the weak nature of the product. Basically, an acid mixture is used to rid the wheel of stains and dirt. Too strong a mixture will ruin certain wheels. Hence an all-purpose product must be weak.

To save damage and heartbreak, some car enthusiasts prefer to use old-fashioned methods like time and elbow grease. It is perfectly all right to use an acid-based wheel cleaner one time. Then, stay on top of the cleaning problem by washing frequently. Use a toothbrush and soap. Use your fingers if necessary. Realize that constant exposure to harsh chemicals will take its toll in time. Be sure

After the upholstery is clean and dry, consider applying a fabric protector like Scotchgard. This type of product will help to prevent deep upholstery and carpet stains.

Whitewall cleaners work well to clean whitewalls and raised white letters. SOS pads and whitewall brushes with soap also work well to brighten whitewalls. Auto parts stores carry a number of such products as well as tire cleaners like Eagle 1.

Auto parts stores carry a variety of upholstery cleaners, spot removers and protectors. Some products combine cleaning power with protecting agents. Read the different labels to determine which brand will do the best job for you.

Deodorants come in liquids and solids. The best interior scent is the smell of "clean." Detail the interior to get rid of odor-causing problems. If you still wish to incorporate a different scent into the interior, read the directions on the product you choose before applying full strength.

to read the label of any wheel cleaner you decide to use.

Cloth protectorants

These products are designed to protect cloth upholstery against stains. Scotchgard is a familiar name. It works. Similar products are available, made by various companies. They work equally well and can be used on carpet, too.

Most new car dealerships offer this type of protection at a nominal fee. I contend that you can do the same job for much less. I recommend the use of cloth protectorants only when the upholstery material is clean and dry. Spray the fabric in an orderly fashion and allow it to dry. Be sure to spread the pleats and maintain complete coverage. Always read the directions and follow the instructions.

Deodorizers

Deodorizers come in solid and liquid form. The solid types come shaped like trees, rainbows and such. Hang them from a knob, a lever under the dash or hide them under the seat. The deodorizing power is supposed to be unleashed a small amount at a time, determined by the degree to which the package is opened.

For severe odor problems, I suggest you use a solid full force. Open the package, toss the element under the front seat and lock the car for three to four days. This will work, provided you removed the cause of the odor before you tossed in the deodorant.

Liquid deodorizers can be sprayed directly on the carpet. I recommend you spray them under the front seats, just in case they contain a product that may stain.

"New car smell" products are available. You will have to try them yourself to see if they meet your needs.

By far, the best way to make your car smell good is to keep it clean. There is nothing better than the smell of clean. It is impossible to describe, but easy to detect. Keep the interior vacuumed, wipe it down frequently and remove the cause of bad odors immediately.

Chapter 3

Under the hood

A clean engine compartment serves more than cosmetic purposes. Repairs and maintenance are easier, problems are more readily detected, exposed linkages move more freely and the engine usually operates a bit cooler.

Tomasie's repair shop serves Porsches exclusively. Prior to any repairs or maintenance, he cleans the engine. This way, he doesn't get dirty and doesn't have to worry about grit or grease falling into an open carburetor or other part. Before return-

Besides eye appeal, clean engines are easier to maintain and repair.

ing the car, he washes the body, vacuums the interior and cleans the windows inside and out. Tomasie feels this service helps the driver better recognize the service performed. After all, does anyone expect a dirty car to run better?

For detail jobs on neglected cars, start with engine compartment cleaning before any other phase. Cleaning a dirty engine is messy work, and chances are you will inadvertently splatter grease and grime on fenders, cowling and windshield.

Complete detailing of the engine compartment that takes place once a year or one time may require the use of high-pressure water spray and solvent-based cleaners. With this, you must be concerned about water and caustic cleaners being forced into electrical connections and ignition parts by the pressure washer. Controlled spraying and a planned approach will minimize problems.

Work area

Engines suffering years of grease and grime build-up should be cleaned in a place where residue will not be a problem. A self-serve car wash with large drains is ideal. Your driveway is not. Consider removing the big stuff at a self-serve car wash and

With the air cleaner off, you can see that this Buick 455 V-8 needs detailing. Garden hose water pressure, all-purpose soap, a wash mitt, toothbrush and paintbrush should be all the equipment needed to completely clean this engine compartment. The firewall, inner fenderwells and engine can be repainted with spray cans without removing the engine.

High water pressure may be needed to help remove heavy accumulations of grease and build-up on neglected engines. By holding the nozzle away from the engine, less force is applied which reduces damage to stickers and *peeling paint. The white towels over the fenders were sprayed with water to keep them in place while protecting the paint from grease and solvent splatter.*

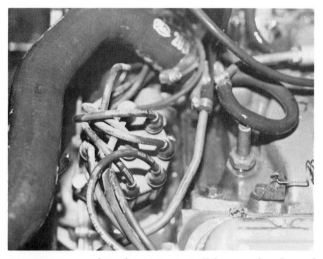

In some cases, distributor caps will have to be cleaned with soap and water. A paintbrush helps to remove dirt and dust. Be sure to dry the distributor cap when engine compartment cleaning is complete.

performing the detailed cleaning at home. Detailed cleaning will not cause residue problems because most grease and grime will be gone. You will be concentrating on wires, hoses, polishing and towel cleaning.

The work site for detailed cleaning should provide a water source and plenty of light. Good water drainage will help keep your feet dry, and a source of electricity will allow use of a droplight for better visibility. For maximum brightness, line the inside of your droplight with aluminum foil. Place the shiny side out, and keep it away from the socket of the droplight to prevent a short.

Preparation

Consider initial cleaning as the first step in detailing a neglected, grease-covered engine compartment. For this you will need a degreaser, brush, soap, old wash mitt, water source and towels to

A hair dryer is used to dry the distributor cap on a Buick GS 455 V-8. Use a clean towel to remove excessive moisture and then apply hot air from the blow dryer to evapo-rate any residual. Hold the dryer about four to six inches away from the cap as high temperatures could possibly damage plastic.

cover and dry the distributor and carburetor. If you choose to work at a self-serve car wash, plan a time when you won't be hurried by a long line of other people waiting to use the stall.

Although covering the distributor is recommended, there are times when it needs a bath in degreaser and water. In those cases, plan to dry it before attempting to restart the engine. A hair blow dryer works well, as do a clean dry towel and air pressure. To keep excess water from entering the distributor, remove the cap and place a piece of plastic over the entire exposed surface. Then snap the cap back in place. Water condensation may appear on the inside of the cap; dry it with a clean towel. After detailed cleaning, again remove all moisture in and on the distributor by drying with a towel, blow dryer or air pressure.

Wentworth likes to cover the entire distributor with paper towels, folding and wadding them between ignition wires. Then he covers it with aluminum foil, using tape as needed. Paper towels quickly absorb moisture that seeps around the aluminum foil. You can also cover the distributor with a thick Ziploc freezer bag. There must be enough slack in the wires to allow the bag to fit over the entire distributor.

No water should be allowed to enter the carburetor either. With the air cleaner off, gently fill the throat with rags and cover with a plastic bag taped

A thin towel was gently placed in the throat of the carburetor with the excess wrapped over the top to prevent water from entering the fuel system. Duct tape was used to keep the towel in place. When the bulk of the cleaning has been done, the towel will be removed and a toothbrush used to clean those areas covered by the towel. The foil under the radiator hose at the right of the picture covers paper towels formed over the top of the distributor, helping to keep it dry.

Before washing an engine with soap, solvent and water, remove the distributor cap and put a piece of plastic over the rotor and inner workings. Replace the cap over the plastic to form a nice seal which will protect the points and other electrical parts from moisture.

Another way to keep water out of the carburetor is to tape a thick plastic bag over the top of it. This method is suitable for light cleaning with low water pressure, as tape doesn't adhere strongly enough to withstand the force of high water pressure.

Duct tape works well to seal the hole in this Pantera valve cover left open with the removal of the air cleaner and attached breather hose and fitting. Note: This valve cover was previously repainted and a new valve cover gasket installed before the engine was detailed.

to the top outer ring. If tape won't stick to the greasy surface, tie with a string. Aluminum foil can be used in lieu of plastic with good results. Any method is good as long as it keeps out water.

Use a strip of duct tape to cover holes in the tops of battery caps. Duct tape also works well to cover holes in valve covers left open by the removal of air cleaner hoses. Other electronic parts may be protected as you see fit; use plastic wrap, paper towels, rags, tape, foil or anything else you feel will keep the part dry.

Initial cleaning

Auto parts stores carry a variety of engine degreasers. Gunk in the spray can is easy to apply and removes grease handily; it is also available in quart and gallon containers. Solvent and kerosene work equally well. Many enthusiasts have had the best luck buying solvent in the gallon can and applying it with a spray bottle. The nozzle on the

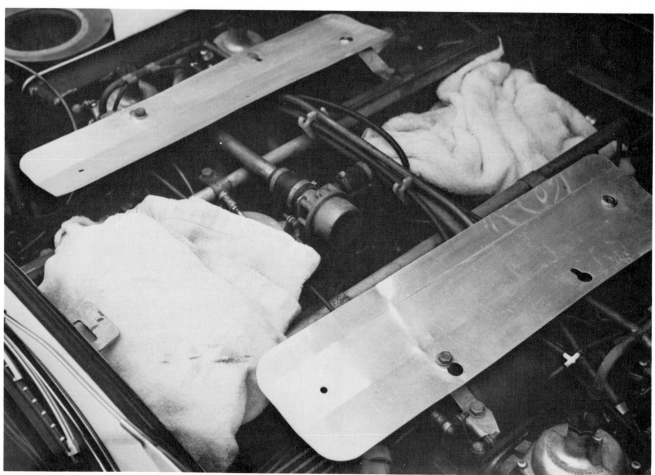

The valley on this Jaguar V-12 engine is loaded with electrical equipment. The first of three steps to protecting this area from water during engine cleaning was to carefully mold towels into place.

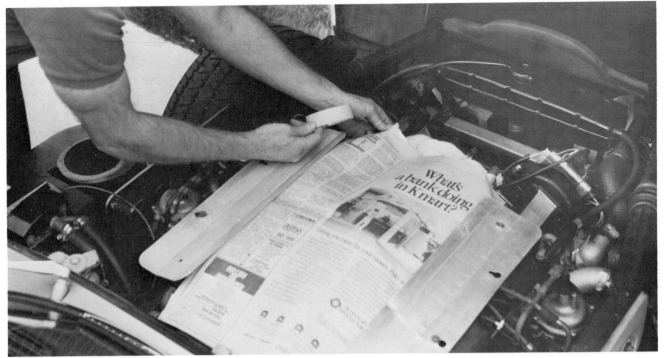

The second step on the V-12 was to cover the towels with about six to ten pages of newspaper to form a flat surface free of deep pockets. The ends of the paper were taped down to help water run off the edges and not puddle in the center.

Finally, clear plastic wrap was placed over the top of the newspaper to prevent water penetration into the valley of the V-12. Aluminum foil can be used in lieu of plastic and you can take advantage of the foil's ability to mold around objects and stay in place.

Good results were found using Gunk to clean off grease on this Pantera V-8. The spray can features a solid spray pattern with a good reach and enough pressure to break loose light grease accumulations. For neglected engines, plan to use at least two cans.

bottle adjusts from a spray to straight stream, and a clear bottle shows when solvent is running low.

Let the engine warm up to operating temperature before starting. Grease is easier to remove from a hot engine. With the air cleaner in place, spray the engine and all greasy spots with solvent. Let it soak into hot grease for a couple of minutes. Then, use water pressure to rinse clean. Aim the nozzle in such a way that water and grease don't splatter you. Because of the powerful cleaning ability of degreasers, consider wearing goggles or glasses to protect your eyes and rubber gloves to prevent your hands from drying out. Remember that the engine and radiator will be hot, so watch where you rest your arms and hands.

After rinsing, look closely at the engine. Note remaining spots of grease and spray again. Use a paintbrush on stubborn spots to work in the degreaser and help loosen build-up. Spray under the air cleaner and behind the power-steering unit and alternator. Rinse with water. Next, spray the entire engine compartment with a cleaner like Simple Green. Use an old wash mitt on the air cleaner,

Grease build-up is easiest to remove when hot. Allow the engine to warm up to operating temperature before tackling this cleaning job. Along with solvent and high water pressure, a small wire brush may be needed to remove the encrusted grease on this V-8 head.

This Pantera V-8 engine was first sprayed with a pressure washer to remove the big stuff. Gunk was then sprayed on greasy spots and allowed to soak for three to four minutes. Rinsing was done with the pressure washer and resulted in the removal of most of the grease and grime build-up.

A paintbrush works well to agitate solvent and help dislodge grease in the tight corners of engine accessory parts. For added scrubbing power, cut the bristles to about an inch in length.

After the Pantera V-8 was degreased, Simple Green is liberally applied to the entire engine compartment. A wash mitt and paintbrush will be used to remove dirt and light amounts of grease on the inner fenderwells, firewall and engine.

Use high water pressure judiciously to prevent damage to paper stickers, electrical parts and paint. Hold the wand at least two feet away from any part you feel may be damaged by high pressure.

The towel is being removed from the carburetor after the heavy engine cleaning was accomplished on the Pantera. Gunk will be sprayed onto a toothbrush and then applied to the top of the carb for cleaning. A towel will be used to absorb runoff and remove residue. Puddled water on the intake manifold at the bottom of the picture can be removed with a wet-and-dry vacuum or absorbed with towels.

fenderwells, firewall and radiator. Rinse with water.

Two initial applications of degreaser and one of soap should have removed heavy accumulations of grease and grime. At this time, dry the top of the air cleaner and remove it from the engine. Have you covered the carburetor as described? Concentrate on one side of the engine, spraying degreaser on all remaining rough spots. Use the paintbrush freely. Look at areas around spark plugs, bell housing and air-conditioning units. Stick your head inside the engine compartment, and look for grease. Spray, brush and rinse with water until all grease is gone. Do this around the entire engine, including intake manifold and carburetor.

Assured of a grease-free engine, spray everything with Simple Green, or cleaner of choice. Use the paintbrush and wash mitt to remove dirt around the battery, windshield washer bucket, compartment edges and fan. Rinse with water. Continue until you are satisfied that the engine compartment is as clean as it is going to get.

Cautions

While cleaning engines warmed to operating temperature is recommended for easiest grease removal, it is not suited for all engines. Turbochargers and headers get extremely hot, even at normal engine operating temperatures. Spraying cold water on them while they are still hot may cause cracks, warping and other damage. Clean turbocharged engines and those with headers while they are cold. If you had to drive to a self-serve car wash, let the car sit and don't start cleaning until the turbocharger or headers have cooled to the point that you can touch them with your hand.

Strong degreasers and powerful water spray can easily remove stickers and decals. To keep an engine looking original, factory-installed stickers should be kept in place. Gently use a paintbrush to

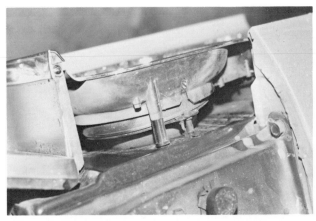

The back of this GS 455 headlight must be cleaned, as well as the rest of the space between the grille and the radiator. Reaching into these tight spots is difficult. Spray the area with liquid cleaner and allow to soak for two to three minutes before rinsing. Use a toothbrush to clean areas of build-up. A baby bottle brush can be covered with a thin cloth and inserted in narrow spaces to clean around headlights and the sides of support brackets.

A paintbrush with shortened bristles is cleaning the carburetor on a Pantera V-8. Use the paintbrush along with a spray bottle filled with solvent to remove caked-on grease in corners and around bolts and linkages. Foil to the left of the carburetor is covering and protecting the distributor.

Batteries this dirty must be removed for complete cleaning. Use soap, water and a brush. High-pressure water is not necessary, as a toothbrush can easily clean the lettering on the caps. Besides, high-pressure water will surely remove the paper warranty sticker.

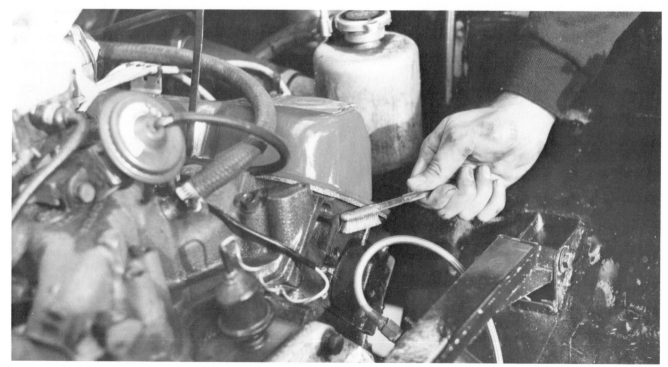

Instead of reapplying more and more solvents, cleaners and high-pressure water, use a toothbrush to clean along valve cover edges, around bolts and in corners.

clean them, and rinse with the nozzle at a distance to reduce the water's force.

High-pressure water can cause other problems, too. Water, cleaner and degreaser can be forced into electrical connections, creating a potential corrosion hazard. Improperly applied, it can peel paint and cause other damage.

Engines can be cleaned using low-pressure water; high pressure just makes the job go faster. For engines in high-performance cars, classics and those where high pressure may present special problems, use a garden hose. Lower the pressure by closing the spigot. As you rinse, agitate dirty areas with a paintbrush to help float away grease and grime.

Fenders and cowlings can be protected with towels. Before you start cleaning, drape towels over parts you want covered. A light water spray on the towels will help keep them in place.

Towels are draped over the Pantera fenders to protect them against grease splatter and from scratches while the detailer leans over to clean the engine compartment. Lightly spray towels with water to give them weight and help them stay in place.

Engine compartments on special cars can be cleaned with mild methods to aid in the longevity of paint, wiring and electrical components. Most car enthusiasts use solvents only when necessary, preferring to apply cleaners like Simple Green.

Clean the underside of the hood before you start detailed engine cleaning to prevent water from dripping onto the clean engine. After cleaning the hood, dry it off so water doesn't drip on your head while you clean the engine.

As with every other part of detailing, always start engine cleaning using the mildest method. If the engine is not caked with grease, don't use a degreaser. Try a mild cleaner. Simple Green does not streak or cause corrosion. Mild dishwashing detergents have been used with good results, while heavy-duty industrial strength cleaners have faded paint and dried wiring.

Hood underside

The underside of the hood should be the last engine compartment item to clean. The reason is simple. If you washed it first, drops of water would fall on your head all the while you were busy cleaning the engine! Now, if the hood and engine both need lots of cleaning, do the engine first. Then, while the engine is still wet, wash the hood. Rinse the engine afterward to remove any residue.

During the detailed cleaning, since there will be little water use, clean and dry the hood first and follow with the engine. This way, you won't have to contend with residue falling off the hood and onto the perfectly clean engine.

Drying

To dry an engine compartment quickly after an initial cleaning, start it up and let idle. Check the water temperature gauge periodically to prevent overheating.

Large pockets of water on the intake manifold can be dried with a towel or a wet-and-dry vacuum. The air cleaner should be replaced, allowing it to dry also. Water spots will be noticeable afterward, but can easily be cleaned with a damp towel during detailed cleaning.

Operating the engine will force water out of hidden pockets on the front of the engine. This will also give the alternator a chance to dry, as well as all other engine components. The combination of forced air from the fan and normal operating heat should dry the engine compartment in about ten to fifteen minutes.

Detailed cleaning

Cleaning an engine and engine compartment to perfection will require water, Simple Green or other mild cleaner, SOS pads, a toothbrush, wash mitt and towels. Be sure to clean and dry the underside of the hood first.

Then, start by removing the air cleaner. To help reach every part of the engine compartment, remove the windshield washer fluid bucket, radiator over-fill bucket and battery. When disconnecting the battery, take off the negative lead first, positive last. These parts will be cleaned out of the car using Simple Green and water. If need be, they can be scrubbed with a soft plastic-bristled brush.

Cover the distributor and carburetor if you anticipate flowing water over the engine. Clean the carburetor first. If soap doesn't clean sufficiently, spray it with degreaser and agitate with a paintbrush. Rinse with low-volume water. Use the toothbrush around linkages and mounting screws. Concentrate your efforts on one spot at a time; don't get ahead of yourself. When the carburetor is clean, move to the intake manifold. SOS pads make quick work of removing caked-on grime. Use just enough pressure to get the dirt off and not scar the paint.

Next are the head and spark plugs. Remove only one spark plug wire at a time to guarantee

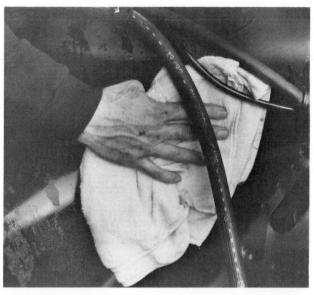

A towel is used to dry the inner fenderwell of a Pantera engine compartment. Large amounts of water can be quickly removed with towels. Towel drying also affords the detailer with a second chance to wipe away spots of dirt missed during cleaning. Be sure to clean hoses and wires on the bottom as well as the top and don't forget to clean metal areas under them, either.

An SOS pad works well to clean parts of this Pantera transaxle. Build-up along the ridges and in the corners was too tough for a paintbrush or toothbrush.

The very top of the carburetor is dirty because it was covered with a towel during engine cleaning. For carb cleaning, towels can be spread around the base to catch runoff and residue. Light cleaning with a paintbrush and a minimal amount of cleaner should loosen most of the dirt and filmy grease. Use a small rag to wipe clean.

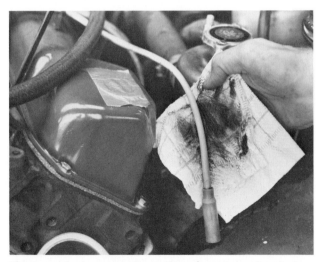

Clean spark plug wires by pulling them through a cloth or paper towel dabbed with solvent. Pull extra dirty wires off one at a time for cleaning outside of the engine compartment. Be sure to replace the clean wire before you pull off the next one to guarantee each one is positioned in its correct firing order.

replacement in the proper sequence. Clean as needed, using the toothbrush, SOS pads, paintbrush and cleaner. Spark plug holes in the head can be cleaned with the cable end of a battery brush. Greasy plug wires can be cleaned by dabbing a bit of solvent on a rag and wiping. Follow with a soapy rag to remove solvent residue.

At the front of the engine, use a wash mitt to clean fan blades and housing. Take pains to remove all signs of dirt around the thermostat housing and water pump. Use SOS pads on unpainted alternators and support brackets. Most bare metal parts, such as fuel lines and carburetors, will clean nicely with SOS pads. They can be polished later with Eagle 1 Mag & Chrome Polish or Happich Simichrome.

Chrome headers should be washed with soap and water, and polished with Simichrome or another comparable chrome polish. You can wax for protection, even though wax won't last long under the high heat headers produce. Stainless headers can be pol-

This small Pantera fan needed to be cleaned with a small cloth dabbed with a liquid cleaner. Best application is made with the fingers inserted in the cloth. A toothbrush can be used to remove build-up.

Buick hood hinges will require cleaning with a small brush and SOS pads. Lay a towel on the fender to protect paint and don't forget to lubricate the hinges after extensive cleaning.

Stubborn stains and grease build-up along the ribs on this Pantera transaxle required powdered cleanser and SOS pads for cleaning. Don't let cleanser suds and slurry dry, as they are difficult to remove. Frequent rinsing with low water pressure removes dirt residue and lets you see the progress being made.

Assure yourself of a quality engine compartment cleaning by taking the time to carefully check the engine compartment for lingering dirt and grease. This is especially important on engine blocks that are not painted because you won't be able to rely on a coat of paint for cover-up.

ished with Simichrome or Eagle 1 chrome polish. Painted headers are cleaned with soap and water. Touch-up is done with the appropriate color of heat-resistant paint, using paint blocks, towels and masking as needed.

Cleaning an engine that is not painted may require more work because you can't rely on paint to cover up tiny flaws. Use a toothbrush and SOS pads to reach into grooves and pockets formed by the engine design. Refrain from the use of harsh SOS pads on polished aluminum heads. For those, try lots of patience and a toothbrush with Simple Green. Stains can be polished out. A few detailers get good results using mag cleaner on aluminum engines. Although the cleaner quickly removes grease and stains, you must be concerned that it may cause corrosion on other parts, such as wires, hoses and electrical components. Protect them during cleaning.

Taking care of the battery box

Wash off battery corrosion with a fifty-fifty mixture of baking soda and water. Apply the solu-

Gentle use of an SOS pad made the aluminum tube on this Jaguar V-12 engine look great. The cleaning was followed by an application of chrome polish with excellent results.

tion freely, working it into corners with a paintbrush. Rinse thoroughly with water. Continue the process until the mixture doesn't fizz any more. Do not use any of the rags from battery cleaning on any other part of the car; acid residue in them can cause damage.

The area below the battery box also needs attention, as it suffers from the same corrosion. Clean threaded rod supports with the same solution. Clean them with a toothbrush and SOS pad. If the entire box is easily removed, take it off. You can clean, sand and paint as needed. It's best to use a good enamel or epoxy paint.

When the job is complete and paint dry, line the bottom of the battery box with a ribbed rubber mat. Be sure to make drain holes in the mat so that water doesn't puddle.

Engine painting

Auto enthusiasts have mixed feelings about painting engines. Wentworth prefers that an engine

After removing battery corrosion with a baking soda solution, clean the battery and surrounding area with soap and water, using a paintbrush or toothbrush as necessary. For extensive corrosion problems, always pull the battery out of the car and spend ample time cleaning the battery box. If the box is corroded, sand clean and repaint with at least two coats of a good epoxy paint.

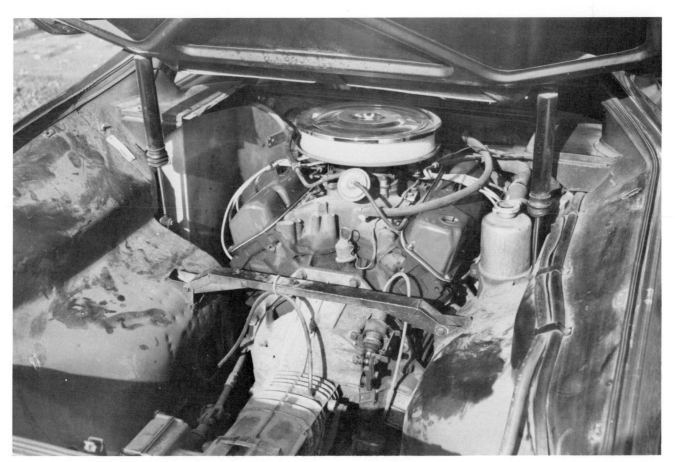

This is what the Pantera engine compartment looked like before it was detailed. The engine was coated with dust, dirt and rust to the point that it looked as though it had *never been painted. The valve covers and valve cover gaskets are new and were just installed.*

This is the Pantera engine compartment after detailing. Note the valve cover gaskets remain unpainted, as they came stock from the factory. The detailing was done in about six hours using Ford blue heat-resistant paint on the engine and semigloss black on the inner fenderwells and firewall. SOS pads, Comet, Simple Green and Gunk were the only cleaners applied, and the pressure washer was used sparingly.

Heat paint cans in a sink of warm water to improve paint flow and maximize aerosol pressure. Instructions on paint cans advise to keep them away from heat and below 120 degrees Fahrenheit. Warm water is designated as water that is not too hot for your hand. Never heat any aerosol or sealed can on the stove in a pot of water. This is truly a hazard as the can could overheat and explode, throwing pieces of metal in all directions.

look original. He doesn't care if a little paint is faded or chipped. Those kinds of flaws on a clean engine are authentic and give the impression of an engine that has been cared for over the long run.

Skiple, on the other hand, likes the block, heads and manifold to sparkle. Most agree, however, that a high-gloss detail conjures thoughts of engine neglect and a quick cosmetic fix to make up for it.

A happy medium may be thorough cleaning with judicious painting. Once again, you must make those determinations based on the purpose of the car you are detailing.

Engine paint is available at most auto parts stores. It comes in various colors, such as Chevy orange and Ford blue. The paint is specially formulated to withstand high temperatures of engine operation. Buy two cans if you intend to paint the entire engine. Warm the can of spray paint in a sink of hot water for about five minutes before starting to thin the paint and propellant for smoother application.

Warnings on cans of spray paint advise not to subject the can and contents to temperatures over 120 degrees Fahrenheit. Hot water used to warm paint cans should be from the tap and not hot enough to hurt your hand. The intent is that spray paint works much better at 80 to 100 degrees as opposed to 50 or 60 degrees Fahrenheit.

The engine, with air cleaner attached, should be allowed to idle to operating temperature before you begin. The warm engine allows paint to spread quickly and evenly, reducing runs and making for quick drying.

Take the air cleaner off and paint it away from the car. Gloss or semigloss black looks good. The wing nut can be painted bright silver. Paint them while still warm. Air cleaners not needing paint and those of odd colors can be waxed after the engine has been completed.

Before spraying paint on the engine, aim the can away from the car and test the spray pattern. Start

Polish and wax chrome parts, like this air cleaner, after the engine and engine compartment are finished. Wipe off wax residue with a clean towel. Carry and install chrome parts using the towel as a glove to prevent fingerprints from smudging the surface.

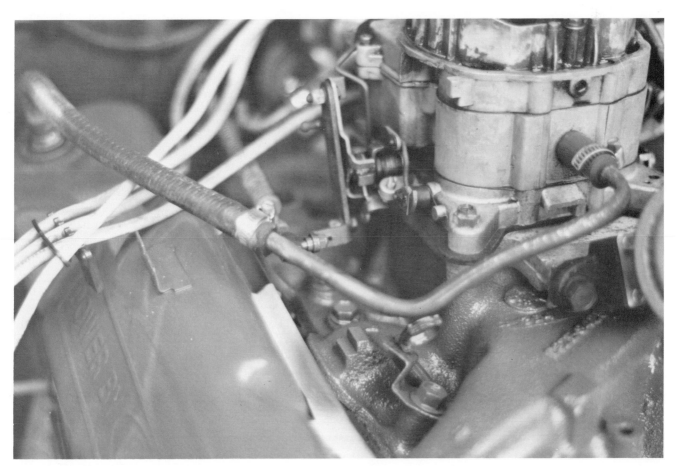

Use your free hand to hold springs, wires and hoses out of the way while painting. Remove springs that are easily taken off and replaced, pull off wires one at a time that are attached with clips and pull spark plug wire holders off valve covers to allow best accessibility. Always replace each item right after painting because you may forget them later.

The items masked on this Pantera V-8 were never painted. To remain authentic, they were masked before painting, even the small piece of intake manifold gasket in the bottom left corner. Masking tape extends onto the valve covers because they are new. Also note masking of the transaxle where it butts against the block.

Painting the heads around spark plugs is made easier by placing a piece of garden hose over each spark plug. Be sure the plug wire is out of the way.

painting the engine at the intake manifold. Disconnect throttle return springs and move wires out of the way. When that spot is painted, replace wires and springs; then move on to the next section. By doing a little at a time, disassembly will be minimal and reassembly will not be complicated. The object is to make the engine look its best without having to dismantle more than necessary.

Don't be overly concerned with small patches of overspray, as they will be removed with lacquer thinner and a rag later. At this point, be concerned about complete paint coverage on all parts of the intake manifold. Use a paint block to protect parts such as the carburetor, alternator and hose connections. Masking tape can be used to protect unpainted valve cover gaskets, fuel lines and anything else you desire.

When the manifold is done, move to the valve covers and down to the heads. Hold wires out of the way. Since the hot engine will dry paint quickly, lay the wires down after a minute or so. Maintain smooth, even strokes with each pass of the paint can. Each coat should be thinly applied, allowed to dry and retouched as needed. As you paint the head, pull plug wires one at a time, replacing before pulling another. The spark plugs can be removed, or you can cover them with short sections of garden hose.

Continue painting around the engine until it looks the way you want. The front of the block will pose some problems. Turn the paint can upside down to reach lower areas. If the can is running low on paint and won't spray in that position, use a new can. Use the paint block around fan belt, power-steering unit, radiator hose and anywhere else you need to.

Removing overspray

Lacquer thinner and a small clean rag will make short work of removing unwanted paint. Stick your finger in the rag and dab a bit of thinner on it. Rub the spot of overspray until it's gone. A droplight will help you see those spots quickly. It is very important that every bit of overspray be removed. Orange or blue paint on the carburetor, radiator hose clamp or fuel line is a dead giveaway that the engine has been detailed. If no overspray can be

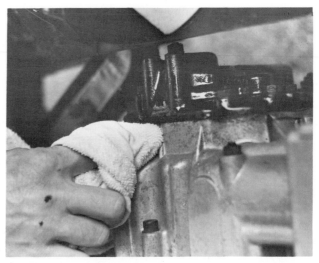

Paint overspray is removed from the back part of a Pantera transaxle with lacquer thinner. Removing overspray is most critical, as the slightest bit anywhere on the engine is a guaranteed giveaway that the engine has been detailed. Place your finger inside a rag, dab it with lacquer thinner and rub overspray off. Take plenty of time to thoroughly inspect every square inch of the engine to make sure all overspray is removed.

The Pantera engine has been painted and is looking better. Masking tape has done its job as noticed by the overspray on it. When the engine is done, the inner fenderwells and firewall can be painted.

Newspaper serves as a paint block while painting a Pantera linkage assembly. After painting this side, the linkage should be turned in order that the bottom can be painted also. Almost anything can be used as a paint block, from the bottom of a shoe box to an old towel.

detected, an admirer will notice that the engine has been well cared for and maintained.

It is best to mask stickers and emblems before painting. If, however, overspray has marred them, use paint thinner; lacquer thinner will erase all their printing. Paint thinner will not work as fast or as thoroughly, but it will preserve the writing on the

sticker—providing you do not use too much pressure while wiping.

Paper stickers are easily ruined. Lightly wipe them with a rag dabbed with paint thinner. Go over stickers a number of times, lightly. Continue until you achieve the desired results. You may try using the edge of a clean SOS pad to remove heavy overspray; remember to use very light pressure.

Engine paint on exhaust manifolds will be very hard to remove. Wiping with lacquer thinner alone will dull the spot. You'll have to use steel wool and thinner to completely remove the paint or let the heat of the manifold burn it off. Overspray on chrome parts can be removed with #00 or finer steel wool and wax.

Other engine parts

The best way to paint engine parts is to remove them from the engine, sand as needed, prime and paint. If you are inclined to make the engine look its best with the least amount of work, you can paint parts while they are attached to the engine.

Such parts would be the alternator, power steering and air-conditioning brackets, brake fluid reservoirs, battery boxes and fan blades. Use gloss or semigloss black paint. A paint block and towels work well to protect the engine, hoses and wiring from overspray.

The same paint can be used to rejuvenate exposed frame members, motor mounts, steering

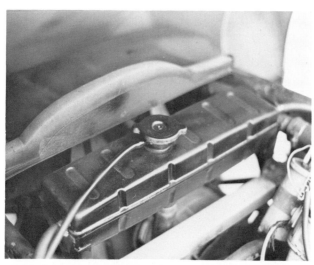

An inexperienced detailer painted the radiator cap black and failed to remove the overspray on the shroud in front of it. The radiator cap should have been painted bright silver and the painting done on a workbench away from the car. These kinds of minor details stand out for car enthusiasts and make them wonder what else has been tampered with.

The radiator cap should have been removed while the radiator and surrounding area were being painted black. The slight amount of overspray on the cap can be gently removed with #0000 steel wool without damage to writing. Note: The overspray is old, as this picture was taken before detailing was started.

box and radiator. Cleanup is the same as for engine painting.

Engine compartment

Do not attempt to paint the firewall and fenders unless they are in desperate need of paint and are black. The only way to professionally paint an engine compartment that is a color other than black is to remove the engine and start from scratch. Black is forgiving and won't emphasize minor flaws. Even at that, consider saving this type of paint job for a regular driver. Or paint as a temporary measure on a car slated for future restoration.

Mask the top edges of the fenders and cowling. Also mask the voltage regulator and other parts attached to the firewall and inner fenderwells. Cover the engine with newspaper or towels. Remove wiring from holders along fenderwells.

Start painting at the firewall and work your way around the compartment. Hold wiring out of

Although it is difficult to see through the layer of body shop dust, the inner fenderwells and firewall will need to be painted on Wentworth's 1970 GS 455. Note the dark black splotches on the firewall. Obviously, this is a "Before" picture.

The engine compartment of Wentworth's GS 455 after detailing. Job was accomplished using garden-hose water pressure, Gunk, Simple Green, SOS pads, paintbrushes, toothbrushes, Buick Red engine paint, semi-gloss black paint, lacquer thinner, Armor All and Meguiar's Car Cleaner Wax. The whole job took about four hours. Note that the underside of the hood needs a second coat of paint.

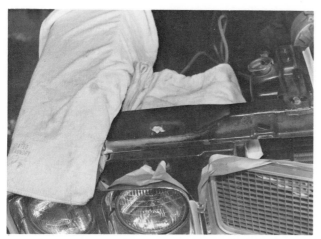

Towels are placed on the fender and over the battery to protect against overspray while painting the radiator and grille support members black. Note the masking material on top of the headlights and brightwork.

Brake fluid reservoirs are cleaned with SOS pads or small wire brushes and wet-and-dry sandpaper. The main body can be painted black. The top should be painted a stock color, normally bright silver or gold.

the way with your free hand, and protect other parts with the paint block. Apply paint with smooth, even strokes. Overspray can be removed with lacquer thinner.

Taking care of extras

The top of the brake fluid reservoir may be painted bright silver or gold. Take it off the car and paint separately. Valve cover caps are painted with the same paint used on the engine. They should be painted separately, as well. Silver parts like radiator caps, wing nuts, bolts and clamps should be

painted bright silver. Chrome parts should be polished and waxed.

Hoses and wiring will look new after applying Armor All or comparable dressing. First, clean as needed with a damp towel. Then, spray dressing on a clean cloth and wipe on. Remove the excess by wiping again with the dry side of the cloth. Do this on vacuum, radiator and windshield washer hoses, as well as ignition and other wiring, and any other rubber parts in the engine compartment.

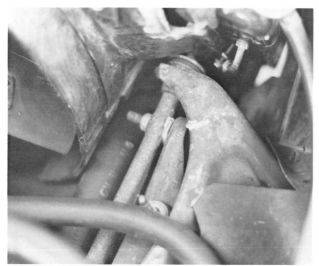

Suspension members should be painted black. Masking is optional except for special interest, show and concours cars. Use paint blocks and towels to prevent overspray problems.

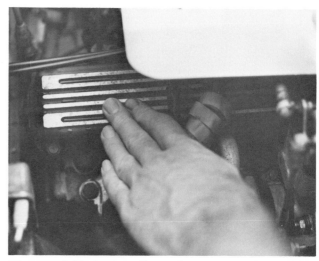

The top of this Jaguar alloy valve cover can be polished using a very fine (#600+) wet-and-dry sandpaper. A toothbrush will be used to get residue out of the slots.

Eagle 1 Mag & Chrome Polish can be used to bring back the shine on neglected parts like this deflector shield which rests below the hood louvers on a Jaguar roadster.

More than one application may be necessary to achieve mirrorlike results.

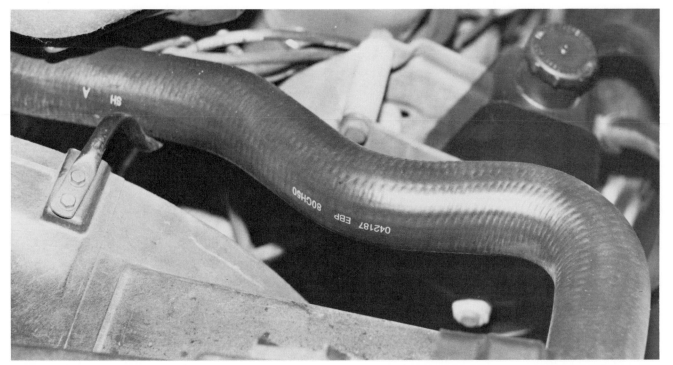

The radiator hose is rejuvenated with cleaning and a light application of Armor All or other polypenetrant. Apply dressing with a cloth to prevent overspray, and be sure to

dress the entire hose, not just the top. All hoses and wires can be made to look new with the same treatment.

If the firewall and inner fenderwells have good paint, consider waxing. I suggest using a one-step wax like Meguiar's Car Cleaner Wax. It goes on and comes off easily and does not leave a hint of powdery residue. This wax may even remove stubborn stains that you were unable to get off using soap and water.

Except for the areas around turbochargers and headers, most engine compartments don't get hot enough to immediately destroy wax protection on painted surfaces. You can expect a wax job to usually last a month or so, depending on weather and vehicle usage. Let your eyes be the judge. If the air cleaner, inner fenderwells and firewall look dull, polish and wax. The same holds true for wires and hoses treated with dressing.

Unless you have experience as an auto painter, I suggest that you paint only those hood undersides that are black. For those, mask off openings in the hood such as louvers and scoops. Place towels or newspaper over the engine, fenders, cowling and windshield.

Crystal clear lacquer

Many generic detailers spray the entire engine compartment with crystal clear lacquer paint after everything else is done. This paint will make minor dirt stains disappear, hoses glisten and wires shine. The whole compartment will look like new. But the look will not last because the lacquer will yellow and cause hoses and wires to become brittle.

True auto enthusiasts shudder at the thought of coating an engine compartment with clear. They would never do such a thing. Clear is just a quick fix designed to make ordinary, used cars look their best until buyers drive them off the lot.

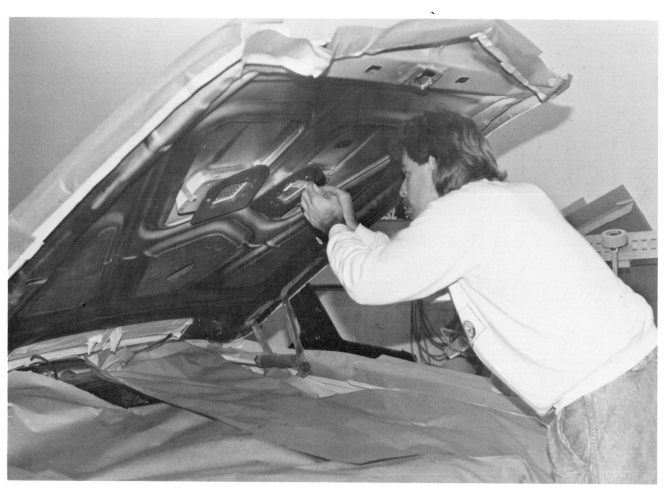

Properly mask the engine compartment with paper or towels, as well as hood scoops, before painting the underside of the hood. Unless you are a professional painter, I recommend you not paint this area any color other than black.

Chapter 4

Preliminary washing

Preliminary washing is the next step in a thorough detail job. If your automobile has been reasonably maintained, dirt and grease residue will be minimal. On the other hand, if you have just purchased a used classic, there may be years and years of accumulated road grime, dirt, grease and debris hidden in the fenderwells, doorjambs, trunk wells and engine compartment.

A complete day or two can be spent cleaning tires, wheels and fenderwells. Another day can be spent under the hood and another on the interior. Only you can determine the specific time needed to clean and polish various parts of your car. In this chapter, I am going to assume you plan to spend a full day on the preliminary wash, followed later with detailed cleaning, polishing and waxing.

Work area

For cars in clean condition, the wash can take place in your driveway with little worry of surface stains and dirt build-up. For the others, I suggest you try a self-serve car wash. As discussed earlier, their facilities are better equipped to handle the amount of dirt and grease that will fall off the car.

It is best to wash any car in the shade to minimize water spotting. Realizing this is not always possible, wash the shady side of the car first, saving the sunny side for last. Rinse frequently to prevent

Wentworth's 1970 Buick GS 455 convertible was reasonably well maintained before becoming involved in a traffic mishap. It will need extensive interior, engine and underbody cleaning after spending a couple of months at the body shop for a complete paint job. During that detail, the years of accumulated dirt and grease build-up can be removed along with sanding dust and other body-shop-related residue.

71

Older classics, like this fifties vintage Chevy pickup, that are maintained in super clean condition retain their highest dollar value. Regular cleaning can be done in the driveway or garage with little worry of grease residue.

Washing cars under cover with plenty of light is ideal. Other than that, wash the car in the evening when the sun is low or find a work site in the shade. Automatic car washes are not good for paint, as evidenced by the swirls and scratches on each side of the "testarossa" emblem. The dirt inside the emblem itself should be cleaned with a paintbrush and cotton swab.

Automobiles are designed for water to run from front to rear. Face your car uphill for washing. Dan Mycon's Blazer is in an ideal position: facing uphill with a water drain at the rear.

soap from drying on the body. If you must wash under a tree, be alert to tree and bird droppings. Wash them off immediately with cold water.

Art Wentworth likes to park his car facing uphill on the driveway when washing. He feels the car is designed to allow maximum water runoff from front to rear. During the frequent rinsing, water will flow in the direction intended and will run off moldings, trim, door drains and sunroof drains. Of course, water also will run off your car if it faces downhill, but why take a chance on moisture entering the car interior?

The temperature of the body is another consideration. You know what it feels like to jump into a pool of cool water on a hot sunny day. The paint on cars goes through a similar shock. If the car has been parked in the direct sun for over an hour, let it stand in the shade for a while until it cools. Feel the paint with your hand. It should feel no hotter than the ambient temperature. This will prevent "thermo-shock" and the creation of minute cracks that threaten the longevity of the paint. This is especially important for cars with new, high-tech and clear-coated paint finishes.

Dismantling

For super washes undertaken once a year or for the first time, you should pull the tires and wheels off the car. This will give you excellent access to the fenderwells and back sides of the tires and wheels. Do each wheel and fenderwell separately; you need not raise the entire car and do all four wheels at once. *Do not attempt this unless you have jack stands or other means to adequately hold the car*

Remove license plates and easily removed emblems before washing the car in order to wash behind them. Wash plates and emblems separately using a toothbrush as necessary. Wouldn't the 1988 tab on this license plate look better if it were applied in line with the other tab, instead of cockeyed?

with the wheel and tire off! If all you have is a bumper jack, forget it. You must block the car on a jack stand before you stick your head into the fenderwell. This book is intended to help you make your car look better, not get you hurt.

Take everything out of the trunk, including loose carpet or mats. You will need to wash the spare tire and jacking equipment. The carpet can be vacuumed, shampooed if needed. The mats should be washed, dried and dressed.

Interior ashtrays should be removed, allowed to soak, and then cleaned and dried. Unusually dirty dash knobs can be pulled off and soaked in the wash bucket. They can be cleaned later with a toothbrush. If the interior is in really bad shape, you should pull the seats out of the car. Necessary in extreme cases, removing the seats will give you more accessibility and working room to clean the interior thoroughly.

To prepare an automobile for its first Concours d'Elegance event, some owners will have the car dismantled to the frame. Each part will be cleaned, painted and polished to perfection. This operation can take years, even for professional shops. You will have to decide how far to dismantle your car. The more you take off, the better the detailing job will be, if care is given to each piece and if the pieces are reassembled correctly.

Stickers and decals

Some body emblems are easily removed. If this is the case with your car, take them off; it will make cleaning, polishing and waxing much easier. If they are not easily accessible, or are otherwise difficult to remove, leave them on. There is no need to chance damaging the emblem or scratching the paint. License plates and windshield wipers can come off too.

Bumper stickers are designed for bumpers, hence the name. Under no circumstances should a bumper sticker be placed on a painted surface—especially your trunk lid. The longer they stay on, the more paint will come off when you try to remove them. The paint underneath will not match the rest of the car and removing the blemish may require repainting.

If you just purchased a car that is marred by a sticker on a painted surface, use caution in removing it. Try a one-step wax first, like Meguiar's Car Cleaner Wax. If it isn't strong enough, use a product especially designed for sticker and decal removal. These products contain chemicals that are designed to loosen the glue used to adhere the sticker to a surface. Take your time, go slowly, peel a little at a time. Impatience will cause errors that may result in paint damage. Before you peel some of the material back using your fingernail, be sure the glue is loosened up.

Sometimes, glue on the outer edges will give way while glue in the middle of the sticker is still firmly attached to the paint. Spray more decal remover onto the exposed side of the decal. Let it stand for a few moments before continuing. Always, I mean always, read the instructions on the label of the product you use. The engineers who designed it spent many hours researching the effects of the chemicals. The instructions on the label are the results of their time spent developing and perfecting the product.

Stickers and plastic decals attach to surfaces by way of special glues. In most cases, it is safest to use a product designed to loosen these types of glue. Auto body paint and supply stores carry the widest variety of adhesive removers.

Hair dryers have been used to loosen glue to remove stickers. You must be very careful not to heat the paint to such a high degree that it is damaged.

Washing
Equipment

Always follow the instructions on the label of any product you use. Generally, car wash soaps recommend that you place the soap in the bucket first and use a heavy water spray to bring up foam. The label on Eagle 1 Car Wash & Wax Conditioner includes a usage guide. It shows how much soap per gallon of water to use for certain size rigs; for example, for large cars you need two capfuls per two gallons of water. This car wash product is advertised as one that safely removes road grime without surface abrasion, eliminates hard water spotting, renews wax shine and protection, and inhibits corrosion and oxidation. Meguiar's Professional Hi-Tech Wash #00, advertised as the perfect wash for maintaining optimum gloss on a continuing basis, is equally effective on high-tech and conventional paint finishes. Art Wentworth has had good luck using an inexpensive dish soap; others feel that dish soaps that claim to be soft on hands must also be soft on paint. Everyone has their own opinions. You shouldn't go wrong using a car wash soap; yet, if you have a favorite soap that does a good job, why change?

Fill the bucket about halfway with water, allowing foam to fill the rest. One bucket of soap

Use plenty of soft soap suds to wash the body. Rinse the mitt every time you feel it has collected even the smallest amount of grit. Note the straight, back-and-forth pattern this detailer uses for washing. I recommend you place your hand inside the mitt while washing instead of the method shown here.

and water will not do the entire job. As we work through the preliminary wash, you will note that the wash water will need occasional freshening. Washing lower parts of the car causes grit build-up in the bottom of the bucket. The grit will always find its way back to the wash mitt and ultimately to paint.

After the mitt has had a moment to soak up water, dip it in the foam. Use the foam for washing. This will reduce the amount of water and add cleaning agent to the mitt. It will also reduce the amount of water under the car while you wash the rear underbody. Periodically, dip the mitt in the water, rinse thoroughly and grab a new mittful of foam. If at any time you feel the mitt is impregnated with grit, use the garden hose to rinse completely. Empty the bucket and start fresh. Constantly keep in mind that you are rubbing on a precious surface, your car's paint. The slightest piece of grit in the mitt will leave scratches, requiring a rub-out and rewax.

Various types of cleaning brushes are described earlier in this book. The preliminary wash may require the strength of a plastic-bristled brush in

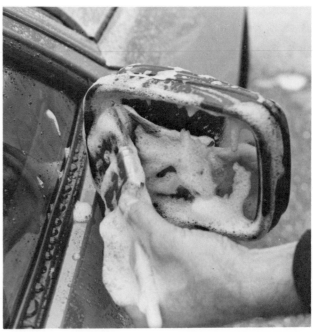

A paintbrush reaches deep into the edges of this Porsche side mirror. This is the quickest and easiest way to clean the edge of the glass, the slots between it and the mirror body.

A plastic-bristled brush is used to remove dirt and road film from the fenderwell lip on a Toyota MR2. Use this brush inside the fenderwell as needed, being careful not to extend to the body. Follow up with the mitt and thorough rinsing.

the fenderwells and on exposed underbody and tires. Paintbrushes work well on the grille, trim and mirrors, while a toothbrush can be used on lenses and rubber. Put the mitt and brushes in the bucket so they will be close at hand and not get kicked into the flower bed. If the bucket is too small, put them out of the way on a grit-free surface.

The garden hose is perfect for rinsing. Before you begin, always make sure the hose will reach all parts of the car. As discussed earlier, it is ideal to use a hose with the brass end cut off, allowing water to flow freely and in large quantities. You don't need pressure. Free-flowing water will run off a waxed car body in sheets, leaving the surface almost dry. Nozzle spray will result in thousands of water droplets, making drying more difficult.

If you are concerned about water conservation, put a shutoff butt on the end of the hose. Then, attach a small piece of hose to it, one with the brass coupling cut off the far end. You won't have to worry about the brass end scratching the paint, the free flow will remove soap nicely and the shutoff butt will prevent water waste.

Rear underbody

True car enthusiasts wash the entire car, including the visible underbody. Many like to start the wash job at the rear underbody. Because the car will be facing uphill, water will run toward the rear of the car. First rinse the entire underbody at the curb, let it drip dry and then relocate to a dry spot in the driveway. This will give you a dry surface to lie on. Use a systematic approach. Wash the rear underbody first because the ground will be dry and you won't get wet while crawling underneath. Then wash the side underbody and move toward the front. By the time you are done, the ground will be wet and you won't.

Fill the wash mitt with plenty of foam. Use the foam to wash the visible parts of the axle, shocks, fuel tank, trunk bottom and anything else in that area.

I advise you to use an old wash mitt for this chore. Use it for all the really grungy spots, saving the newer mitt for the body. This washing should loosen most of the dirt and road film that has accumulated since the last wash. If need be, wash

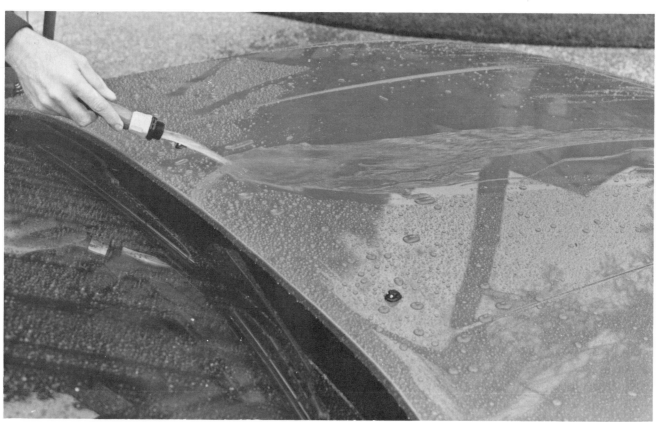

The hood of this 944 is almost dry immediately after rinsing with an open-ended garden hose. Free-flowing water falls off the car in sheets and doesn't leave the thousands of water drops common with nozzle applications.

the area twice before rinsing. Once you have rinsed with the garden hose, your work area will be wet and uninviting for you to crawl on.

I'm not quite sure how well it works, but some car people place a lawn sprinkler at the curb, turn on the water and drive the car over it to rinse the underbody. If you maneuver the car so that the sprinkler has access to all parts of the underbody, it should flush some deposits of road salt, mud and grime. You will have to drive over the sprinkler several times. I suppose this preliminary step could eliminate some elbow grease before serious hands-on cleaning.

Side underbody

The same "dry" philosophy holds true for washing side underbody areas after the rear underbody. Since the rear was done first, the ground under the sides should be dry, right? Get down on your knees, fill the mitt with foam and wash visible parts of the frame, exhaust and body. Use the plastic-bristled brush as necessary.

Accumulations of road tar can be removed using any number of tar-removal products, such as Turtle Wax Bug and Tar Remover. It is designed to remove road oil, tar, tree sap and bug residue. It is advertised as uniquely formulated to quickly and easily remove stubborn exterior stains. As with any other product, read the label before you put it on your car. Try it on an inconspicuous area first.

Although the lower sides of the car are hardly visible to you, take note of cars parked at stoplights and those on a used car lot. The rust-colored frame extending from the bottom of the side body is an eyesore. Imagine how much better your car, or truck, will look with this area cleaned and painted black. It adds a crisp gesture to the entire side of the automobile.

After a good cleaning using lots of foam, rinse with water. Start rinsing at the front, and aim the water spray toward the rear, leaving the area under the front end dry. This maneuver is designed to keep the detailer dry while cleaning under the front of the car.

If you have to go back and rewash a section of the underbody while the ground is wet, try kneeling

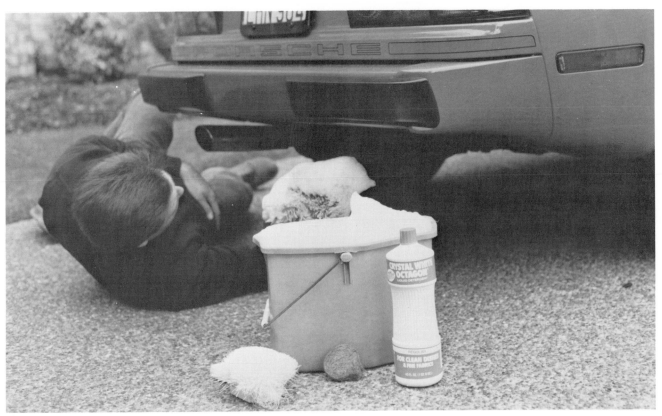

Wash the rear underbody first, while you have a dry surface to lay on. For a regularly maintained car, like Worthington's 944, you should only need the wash bucket and a mitt. Stubborn spots can be quickly cleaned with the plastic brush, and dirty chrome or metal with an SOS pad.

on the hose. This will help to keep your knee out of the water and your pants dry.

Front underbody

If the front of your car is equipped with a painted spoiler under the bumper, don't wash it with the same bucket of wash water used under the rear and sides; there will be too much grit in it. Clean the spoiler later when you wash the grille and bumper.

Under the front, use the same technique as above to wash exposed steering members, frame, radiator housing and such. If greasy parts on the engine block or oil pan are plainly visible, use a mild solvent or degreaser. Gunk in the spray can works well. Remember, if you are working in your driveway, don't get too carried away degreasing. The grease will fall on the concrete and make a mess. For large degreasing jobs, go to the self-serve car wash or other facility. Small jobs can be contained by placing rags under the greasy areas; cardboard and newspapers also work but can be more difficult to clean up. It's simplest to wet a rag with degreaser and wipe the part clean. Then wash with soap.

After rinsing, the underbody should be clean and your work area wet. If the job was done right the first time, you shouldn't have to kneel down on the wet ground again. The rest of the wash can be done in a standing or stooping position.

Wheels and tires

By this time, the water in your wash bucket should be dirty, with grit accumulation at the bottom. Take a few minutes to rinse the bucket, brush and mitt. Mix up a fresh bucket of soapy water.

As a later chapter is dedicated to wheels and tires, I will only touch the basics of tire and wheel washing in this section. That later chapter will discuss in detail the various ways to clean the many types of wheels as well as how to care for tires.

Some car people prefer to wash the wheels and tires last, theorizing that the water in the wash

Even though this Porsche wheel is in excellent condition, an old wash mitt is used for cleaning. Minute pieces of grit and brake dust can become imbedded in the mitt and will present scratch hazards should you use the same mitt to wash the body.

bucket will be dirty. Art Wentworth and Jerry McKee like to wash them after the underbody. This way, water doesn't sit on the body while the wheels and tires get done. Don't worry about the wash water. You should freshen the bucket three or four times during the wash and any other time you think it is dirty.

Rinse the fenderwell thoroughly. Dislodge accumulations of mud, leaves, road salt and pine needles. Remember, these pockets of debris retain moisture and are common spots for rust to grab hold. Afterward, rinse the tire and wheel.

Use the old wash mitt, rinsed and clean, to wipe off as much dirt and road film as possible. Rinse with clean water. The tires can be scrubbed with the plastic-bristled brush. Whitewalls can be scrubbed with a whitewall brush or an SOS pad, as both work well. For the most part, the soapy solution in the bucket should suffice.

If the tire is unusually dirty and stained, you can use any number of tire or whitewall cleaners. Most of them work quite well, although a few users feel some whitewall cleaners tend to fade the black after repeated use. SOS pads give good results as does powdered cleanser used with the plastic-bristled brush. You can also use Simple Green with the plastic brush. Keep in mind, the rougher the cleaning application, the more chance you take damaging the tire or wheel. Powdered cleansers contain a bleaching agent. Will that hurt the wheel on which the tire is mounted? Wentworth feels that it is much better overall to clean the tire three or

four times using a mild cleaner, than once or twice with a harsh one.

I don't know of many wheels that are prone to damage when cleaned with soap and water. Use paintbrushes to reach those areas around lug nuts and valve stems. Use them in the crevices and slots on special wheels. Toothbrushes work well on wire wheels and on those parts of the wheel which attract dirt build-up, like valve stems. Wheels designed with fins and slots are sometimes easiest to clean using your fingers. These handy little clean-

Tire cleaning products work well to remove dirt and stains from tires. Designed to be sprayed on and hosed off, this Eagle 1 product cleaned quickly without the need for scrubbing.

A plastic-bristled brush is very well suited for tire scrubbing. Car wash soap and Simple Green were used with the brush to break loose imbedded dirt on this neglected tire.

Cleaning around lug nuts is difficult. A soft paintbrush was used to clean this Porsche wheel with excellent results. Extra dirty wheels should be removed for thorough cleaning.

Chemical wheel cleaners are safe and do a good job of cleaning when properly applied. A mag cleaner could cause damage to the finish on this clear coated alloy wheel. A much better choice would be Eagle 1 Special Finish Factory Mag Cleaner.

ing tools won't scratch or wear out. The only hazard is sharp edges that may damage the tool.

Before you leave the wheel, take a look at the fender lip, that part of the painted fender that curls around to meet the fenderwell. Wipe it with the old

To thoroughly clean a wheel and tire, you will need a wash bucket with soap and water, a wash mitt, paintbrush and scrub brush. Chemical wheel and tire cleaners are an option generally saved for the most severe cleaning jobs.

mitt. It could be cleaned later while washing the body, but you take the chance of adding unwanted grit to the new wash mitt and soap bucket.

Always be sure to thoroughly rinse the wheel, fender lip and fenderwell before moving on. The clean rinse water will remove leftover dirt and soap residue. You can never rinse too much.

Body

At this point, I strongly recommend that you rinse out the wash bucket and start with a fresh mix of car wash soap and clean water. Rinse the mitt and brushes too. The old mitt can be set aside because you will want to use the newest mitt on the body.

You should have already removed the license plates, easily accessible emblems and anything else you wanted off the car. Start by rinsing the car first. Some car cleaning "experts" think high-pressure water is great for getting the big stuff off the body. Many others strongly disagree. They feel if the pressure is great enough to blow dirt off the car, it is apt to push dirt into the paint. High pressure can peel off paint and emblems, accentuate tiny paint chips and possibly cause tiny scratches.

Real car enthusiasts like to rinse with a soft flow of water and wash the body with a soft cotton wash mitt and lots of soft, sudsy soap foam. They treat the paint on their cars as if it were their own skin. They realize that paint is soft and any harsh treatment can result in a blemish.

Use the wash mitt in a straight, back-and-forth motion. Some car care product labels recommend application in a circular pattern. In some cases, the circular motion may cause spider webbing. Wentworth recommends the back-and-forth method, moving from front to back on the car. He washes, dries and waxes the car in this same pattern every time. Other car people agree. Massaging the body in this manner prevents swirls. In addition, airflow goes over the car in the same direction. It is conceivable that small dust and dirt particles in the turbulence flowing over the car are less apt to get caught in the tiny swirls of the paint if they are in line with the flow.

Start washing at the top of the car, washing one side of the roof first. Use the paintbrush to reach in the groove along the windshield and rear window trim. In the shade, on a cool day, you can wash one half of the windshield and rear window at the same time. Rinse with a soft flow of clean water. Wash one half of the hood, using the paintbrush along the gap between the hood and fender as well as around the radio antenna, hood scoops and windshield wiper blades. Rinse. Then wash the side windows, and use the brush along window trim, door post and mirror. Move on to do one half of the trunk in the same fashion. Be sure to remove all the soap each time you rinse.

Continue washing all parts of the car in the same manner. Use the paintbrush on every nook and cranny; it works very well. Dip it in the wash bucket frequently to rinse clean and gather foam. If wax build-up is a problem on emblems or light lenses, use the toothbrush. Freshen the mitt before washing each new area by briskly agitating it in the bucket. If at any time you feel the mitt is too dirty to continue, rinse it with the hose; rinse the bucket too because chances are that it is also contaminated with grit.

A common pattern for washing a car involves starting at the top, then going around the sides and ending up at the grille. The thought to keep in mind is completeness. Every part of the body must be cleaned. To do this, you need a method that guarantees that you touch every square inch of the body. Use any system you wish, as long as it works. The more you use a preferred pattern, the less likely you are to miss spots, and this will cut down the time you have to spend going over the car looking for them.

Very dirty cars should be washed twice. The first wash will remove heavy stuff, and the second will include a more detailed cleaning.

A paintbrush is a handy tool used to clean along the window trim of a Porsche 944. The soft bristles reach areas next to trim that a mitt cannot touch. Apply the brush after washing with the mitt to take advantage of the soap suds already in place.

After washing the windshield, take a moment to wash the wiper blades. Use the mitt, paintbrush and toothbrush as needed. Car wash soap is usually strong enough, although you can use Simple Green for heavy build-up.

Unusual cleaning problems like the outside vents on this Toyota MR2 are easily washed with a soft paintbrush. The heavy tape around the metal band of the paintbrush is a must when cleaning deep into painted surfaces. A toothbrush or cotton swab can be used to loosen stubborn build-up before application of the paintbrush.

During the wash, don't forget to bend over and clean lower body sections. The wash mitt will clean most of the residue and road film from the chrome strip running along the lower side section of this Corvette. Road tar and other debris can be removed later, using polish or a road-tar-cleaning product.

Grille and brightwork

This part of every car presents the detailer with lots of tight areas filled with dust and dirt. The wash mitt will only reach partly into them, leaving unsightly spots. Again, the paintbrush works superbly. Take your time cleaning and rinsing, assuring yourself of a thorough job. Use a toothbrush or cotton swab if necessary.

Stubborn bug residue can be removed with lots of water and a toothbrush. If you have to use a cleaner like Prepsol or Simple Green, remember to wax that area later. Clean surface dirt and road film from grille patterns and emblems as well as from behind the license plate, bumper and spoiler. Use the paintbrush around headlights and for reaching into recessed areas. Duct tape wound around the

Reaching inside the slots on the grille of this BMW is achieved with a paintbrush, toothbrush and cotton swab. This is the kind of dust and dirt noticed as a subtle difference between a clean car and a meticulously maintained vehicle. Cleaning it properly makes the front of the car look crisp.

A paintbrush is used to clean inside the fuel cap area on a 944. Clean the entire area, including hinges and the inside of the door. Rinse lightly to avoid forcing water past the fuel cap and into the tank.

metal part of the paintbrush prevents paint chips and scratches in these places.

Doorjambs

With the entire body washed and rinsed, you can use the old mitt and a paintbrush to clean doorjambs. There is no need to use a lot of water and soap. The damp mitt will remove dust; foam on the brush will remove more stubborn build-up.

Open vents on doors need not be cleaned at this time. They can be done later during the interior detail. Unnecessary water inside vents will filter down inside the door and become a source for rust deposits.

To rinse soap suds from the doorjambs, close the door and flow a small stream of water into the crack between the door and the body. You will be surprised by how well this technique rinses. Afterward, open the door and remove any remaining suds with the mitt. Do this to all the doors on the car.

If you are washing on a warm sunny day, don't forget to rinse the entire car periodically. This will help to prevent the formation of water spots.

After washing and rinsing the body, use the wash mitt to clean doorjambs. Use fingertip pressure to reach inside curves and lips and use the paintbrush as you see fit.

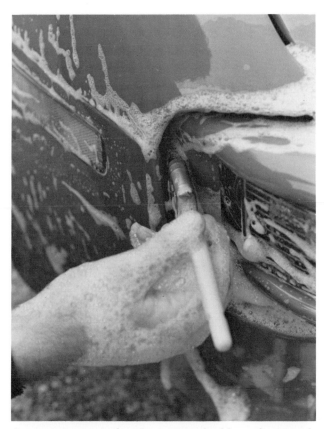

Once again, a paintbrush proves valuable to clean inside the gap between the fender and front bumper on a 944. Repeated applications may be necessary to remove the film of dirt left behind after driving on rain-soaked roads.

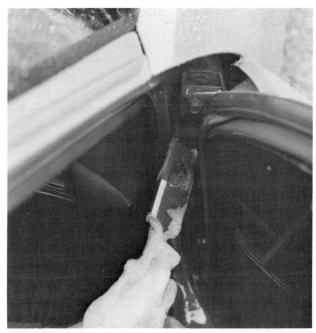

Front doorjambs collect the most dirt as lubrication products attract dust, dirt and lint. Use the paintbrush and Simple Green for heavy cleaning chores around hinges and bolts.

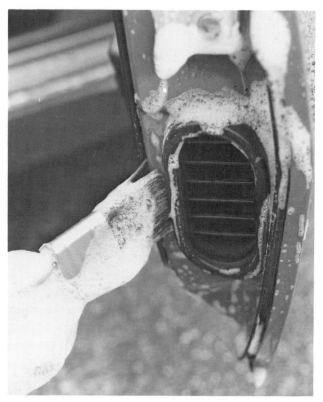

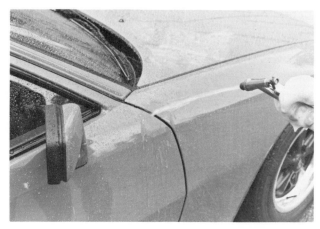

Vinyl tops and convertibles

This subject is covered in depth in a later chapter, so here I'll touch a few highlights.

Washing a vinyl top is no different from washing anything else, unless the top is terribly dirty with build-up trapped in the grain. If the wash mitt doesn't clean to your satisfaction, use a plastic-

The vent in the doorjamb of this Porsche will be cleaned later with a damp cloth and cotton swabs during interior cleaning. Refrain from washing these types of vents using lots of water, as moisture will collect inside the door unnecessarily.

Rinsing the doorjamb on this 944 is accomplished with the door closed. Rinsing with the door open permits moisture to enter the interior, sometimes in large quantities. Try using low water pressure, aiming the stream into the gap between the door and the body. You'll be surprised how well this method works.

A plastic-bristled brush used to work up a good lather on the vinyl top of a 1977 Porsche 911 Targa. Stout brushes work well to reach into the grain on vinyl tops, breaking up imbedded dirt.

84

bristled brush. Note that after such scrubbing, you must restore the vinyl with an all-purpose or vinyl top dressing. Scrubbing will remove most of the dressing already on the vinyl. Unless you apply a protectorant, bare vinyl will be more susceptible to the sun's rays and will dry out, aging the material unnecessarily.

Convertible tops present no unusual problems except for leaks and the delicacy of the plastic rear window. Ragtops are not watertight, especially around side windows. When washing, don't spray water directly at the tops of windows. Hold the hose at the roof line and let water flow down, preventing leaks inside the car. Use a minimal amount of pressure to wash and dry the rear plastic window. The material scratches easily. Eagle 1, Meguiar's, Turtle Wax and others make products designed to polish these windows and remove slight scratches. Don't rely on them to the extent that you are careless, however.

Extras

As you wash the car, take note of special items such as pop-up headlights, chrome exhaust tips and wiper blades. More than likely, the headlights on your Corvette or Porsche will be in the down position while it is parked. Wash the topside as you come to it. Then, before drying, hop in the car and pop up the lights. Use the paintbrush around the trim rings and housing; then rinse.

Extended chrome exhaust tips are cleaned with the mitt. If necessary, use an SOS pad to remove carbon build-up. Later, you can polish with Happich Simichrome, Eagle 1 Mag & Chrome Polish or #00 steel wool and wax. The same holds true for bumpers located directly above exhaust tips. The bottom edge of these bumpers takes a beating from exhaust. The heat and products of combustion cause chrome to rust and deteriorate. It is important to clean and wax the bottom side of these susceptible bumpers on a regular basis.

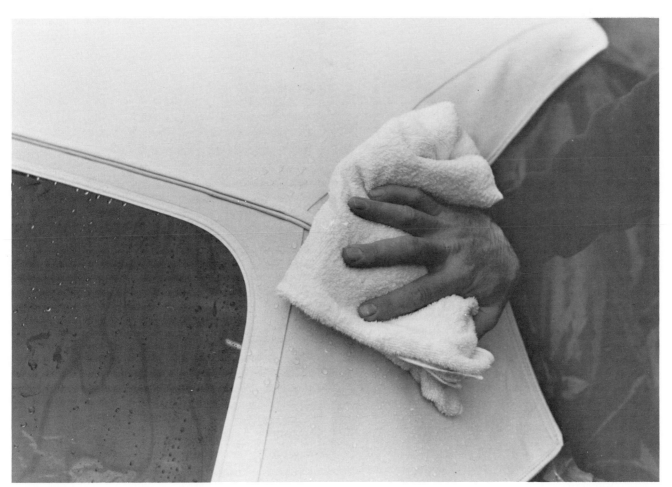

Clear plastic windows on convertibles are easily scratched. Carefully wash around them, as is being done *on this Corvette roadster. To wash and dry the plastic, use a thick soft wash mitt and towel.*

Pop-up headlights, familiar on Corvettes and some Porsches, can be easily overlooked. Remember to wash and dry them sometime during the course of the preliminary wash.

Windshield wipers are probably the most neglected part of any car until winter, when you really need them. While washing the windshield, take a moment to wash the entire mechanism with the mitt. Use the paintbrush to reach inside grooves. A toothbrush works well to remove bug residue. At the same time, look at the windshield washer nozzles. Frequently, they are clogged with wax. Use a toothbrush first. If the tiny hole is plugged, you can use a needle to clean it out, although it's best to

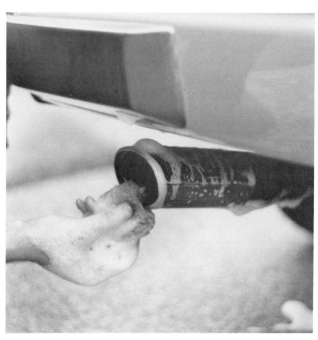

An SOS pad is used to clean the outside of a dirty Porsche chrome exhaust tip. The inside can be cleaned also, but avoid rinsing with water. Instead, remove soap suds and dry the inside with a rag.

disconnect the hose to the nozzle and blow out the nozzle with an air hose.

Every car has its own special features. It is up to you to notice and take care of them. Look at all the emblems and light lenses. These are very common spots for wax build-up. Use the toothbrush to remove wax. Check the edge of bodyside moldings. They catch a lot of debris, such as pine needles,

If these Pantera exhaust tips would have been cleaned, polished and waxed on a frequent basis, the chrome would have lasted longer. A short-term fix before replacement would consist of cleaning with an SOS pad, polishing with chrome polish and applying protective wax.

This windshield wiper blade is spotted with wax residue, dust and dirt. A paintbrush and toothbrush should be used to guarantee thorough cleaning. If need be, it can be removed for cleaning and touched up with black paint.

small leaves and lots of dirt. The paintbrush works well to remove that stuff. Also look at the edge of clear plastic mudguards. They tend to attract wax build-up that can be removed with the paintbrush.

Since the jacking equipment is out of the trunk, clean it after the car is dry. If your car is equipped with a tool kit, open it up. You may be surprised at the condition of the tools. Wentworth detailed Clint Worthington's perfect 1985 Porsche 944. He was ecstatic over the beautiful doorjambs, going on and on about the quality of paint and lack of service stickers. But the pliers in the tool kit were frozen. It took about thirty minutes to free them using WD-40, #00 steel wool and a toothbrush.

Clean the spare tire, too. Scrub the rubber if needed and wash the inside of the wheel. It is a good idea to wax both sides of the wheel and dress both sides of the tire, wiping off the excess. While you are

Wax build-up makes this Corvette emblem look old and worn. Scrubbing with a soft toothbrush will remove the wax, allowing the emblem to look crisp, clean and new.

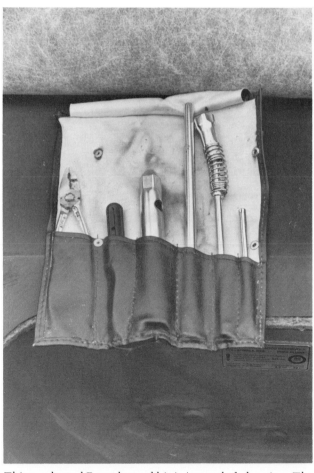

This neglected Porsche tool kit is in need of cleaning. The tools should be cleaned and lightly coated with a thin film of WD-40. The pouch should be scrubbed with a brush and cleaner, dried and dressed with a protectorant like Armor All.

This is the tidy trunk space in Worthington's 1985 Porsche 944. The clean jacking equipment and spare tire will not soil clothes when removed from the trunk and used to replace a flat tire. The black towel is part of the road kit and is wrapped around the portable air pump which came stock with the car.

Rubber floor mats are quickly cleaned with soap and water and a plastic scrub brush. Do this during the preliminary wash while all the cleaning equipment is readily at hand.

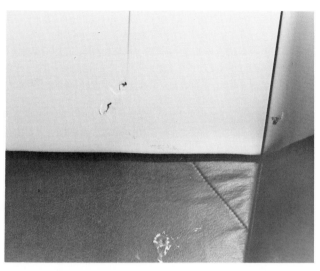

Remove bird droppings as soon as possible. The acidic nature of these substances can permanently mar paint. Use a soft cloth and plenty of water; paper towels or napkins work just as well, especially when that is all that is available.

at it, wax the jacking equipment and give the tools a wipe with WD-40. These measures will prolong the life of the equipment while it is stored out of sight, out of mind and in the dark of the trunk.

Common problems

Tree sap, bird and insect droppings are common problems. The best advice is to remove them as soon as possible. If after a wonderful dinner with a special friend you return to your car to find a gar-

Tree sap on the hood of this Nissan Z car must be removed as soon as possible to prevent paint damage. If caught early, within the first hour or two, cold water and mild rubbing should dissolve the sap. Cleaning sap that has been on the car for longer periods will require normal washing, and cleaning that starts with a one-step cleaner wax may have to be graduated to polishing compound.

gantuan sea gull has dropped last week's entire menu on your hood, clean it up. Go back in the restaurant, get some wet paper towels and clean it right off.

Tree sap can be removed with cold water. Gently rub the spot with cold water and a towel. After a while, it will dissolve. Try a glaze wax after the water, and eventually use polish if necessary. Insect droppings can be removed with cleaner wax. Don't wait a minute longer than you have to. The longer these acidic residues stay on your car, the more damage they cause. As always, a good wax job will help to prevent deep damage.

Automatic car washes

Every car enthusiast I have talked to has the same opinion of automatic car washes, especially for classic cars: they will hurt the paint and not do as good a job as you can by hand. The sole beneficiary of automatic car washes may be a regular driver—with an owner who refuses to detail—on the way to a trade-in.

Automatic car washes cannot remove wax build-up in emblems, decals and trim. Even the softest brushes scratch paint. Many car washes promise and provide a good job but cannot possibly guarantee the same quality as a thorough wash by hand. Although a car wash advertises scratch-free brushes, you must be concerned about grit that gets caught inside them.

Drying

Getting all the water off the car is almost as important as washing, especially if you live in an area that has unusually hard water. Water spots are unsightly and will require waxing for removal.

Jerry McKee likes to drive his Jaguar after washing. He believes that the movement of the car and the wind passing over it help to remove puddled water from all the nooks and crannies. Wentworth, on the other hand, doesn't like the idea because road grime easily adheres to the wet sides after being thrown up by the tires.

Ideally, you could dry the car with a soft towel and then drive it to remove hidden water. This would prevent water spotting on the body and remove puddles that might encourage rust.

Because water removal is so important, Wentworth likes to relate the following occurrence. A retired friend of his had a beautiful 1966 Buick Riviera. Although the friend seldom drove it, he washed it religiously every Saturday. After towel drying, he put the car back in the garage where it sat until the next Saturday. After a couple of years of this routine, he decided to take the car for a real

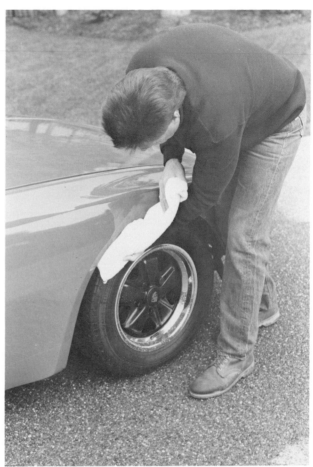

Drying the car after washing should not be taken lightly. Here, Wentworth uses a clean towel to dry the fenderwell lip on a Porsche after the main part of the body has been done. Don't forget to dry tires and wheels as well.

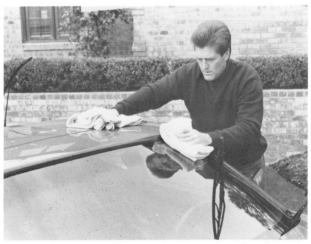

Use two towels to dry the car. The first will pick up the majority of moisture and the second will absorb any residual wetness. As parts of the towel become saturated, unfold to an unused side and continue drying, taking full advantage of all parts of the towel.

drive, not just down the driveway. To his absolute surprise, the brakes were nonexistent. The repeated washings without driving allowed water to sit on the brakes. After the prolonged period of time, the brakes were too rusty and corroded to function.

Drying is simple. Use two soft towels, folded in quarters. The first one can be used for primary drying and the second for picking up remaining streaks of moisture. As the towels become wet, refold to a dry side. Use the same wiping pattern as you did for washing: straight back-and-forth motions, from front to rear. Use folds in the towel to absorb water in tight spots around headlights, bumpers and the like. Don't forget to dry the wheels and tires.

Car people seldom use a chamois. They feel that it streaks and holds grit and dirt particles. They prefer large fluffy towels. After cleaning, they put the towels in the washing machine and clothes dryer to have them ready the next time that they clean the car.

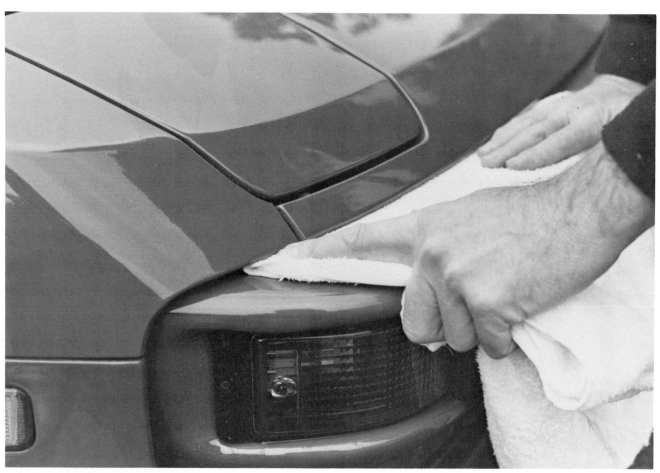

Use your imagination to reach hard-to-get spots. A fold in the towel is used here to dry the space between the bumper and hood on a 944.

Chapter 5

Interior detail

Detailing a fine automobile is labor-intensive, in some cases a labor of love. I doubt that you've seen many owners wash the outside of their cars with frequent use of a paintbrush. The same basic methods hold true for the interior. To produce a quality job and pamper vinyl, cloth and leather upholstery requires time and patience. Set a day aside, just for the inside of your car. If its present condition is good, you may complete the job in an afternoon.

It is a pleasure to admire the crisp and tidy interior of this 1955 Chevrolet convertible show car. Note the clean carpet edges and polished metal dashboard.

If possible, grimy handles and knobs should be removed for cleaning. Scrub with a toothbrush to remove dirt from lettering, allowing the white to stand out crisp and bright.

Interior dismantling

Cars need interior dismantling if they have sat in a body shop for extensive body and paint work or if their interiors have been neglected for lengthy

You may have to use a putty knife to remove heavy surface rust from floorboards. Follow with sanding, and remove dust and residue with a vacuum. Cover the finished surface with primer and then with a rust-inhibiting paint.

periods of time. Basically, this means removing the seats, easily detached knobs, consoles and rubber pads on brake and clutch pedals. Clearing the interior makes work easier and gives you more working room. It also allows easier and more thorough access to the detached parts for cleaning.

If the inside smells like mildew, you should pull the carpeting. Chances are that the carpet and padding are damp, and the floorboard is rusty. In this case, allow the carpet and pad to dry by hanging them in the sunshine. If the pad dries without an odor, good. If not, I suggest you replace it. Carpeting can be shampooed and dried. If it is still in good shape, the mildew smell should dissipate and you can reinstall the carpet.

A rusty floorboard should be cleaned, sanded and painted. The extent of rust damage will determine your course of action. If the metal is eaten almost completely through, you'll have to have a body shop repair the damage. If it is only surface rust, use wet-and-dry sandpaper to remove it and to expose a clean surface. Dry, and then protect with two coats of rust-inhibiting paint, allowing the first coat to dry before applying the second. You may want to check with a local body shop to see if they recommend a better method. Various climatic conditions may require special considerations.

For interiors in better condition, your concern will be dust and grime build-up. With the seats, console and knobs removed, you can vacuum every square inch of carpet, reach every nook and cranny on side panels, remove every speck of dust on the console, soak grime off knobs and scrub the seats entirely. You can also clean, repaint and lubricate seat tracks and floor shifts.

Vacuuming

A thought-out, systematic approach to interior detailing will save you time and result in a quality job. I like to begin with vacuuming. Removing the big stuff first provides a feeling of accomplishment and boosts my spirit to continue.

Most detailers use a crevice tool on the end of the vacuum cleaner hose. A plastic crevice tool is preferable because it does not pose the potential tearing hazard as a metal one might. The metal tool often bends and tears at the end, creating sharp edges. This is caused by extended use and the striking of hard objects. The crevice tool will reach into tight seams, around seat beads and under seats. Vigorous back-and-forth movement on the carpet brings up sand and grit. An old hairbrush works well to break loose pine needles stuck in the nap. On occasion, you can use a soft brush attachment. This works well for dusty dashboards, armrests and consoles.

Move the front seat to its most forward position. Start vacuuming the back seat first. Use your free hand to separate the cushion from the seat-back. You'll be surprised by the amount of debris that accumulates in this space. Spread the pleats to get at tiny bits of grit. Use the crevice tool around beads in the seat. You should be able to reach the entire seat from one side; if not, do one half and then move to the carpet in that area.

With the back seat vacuumed and the front seat still in its most forward position, reach under the front seat to vacuum as much carpet as possible. Briskly agitate the carpet, with the crevice tool, to bring up imbedded dirt. Sometimes, you can tap the carpet with the palm of your hand. This will cause grit to pop out of the nap and rest on the top of the carpet, making for easy removal. Black carpet requires the most patience. It seems that the more you vacuum, the more grit appears. Hang in there, the results are worth the work.

The crevice attachment works best for vacuuming upholstery. Spread the pleats in order to reach dirt and grit in seams, as demonstrated on this BMW leather seat.

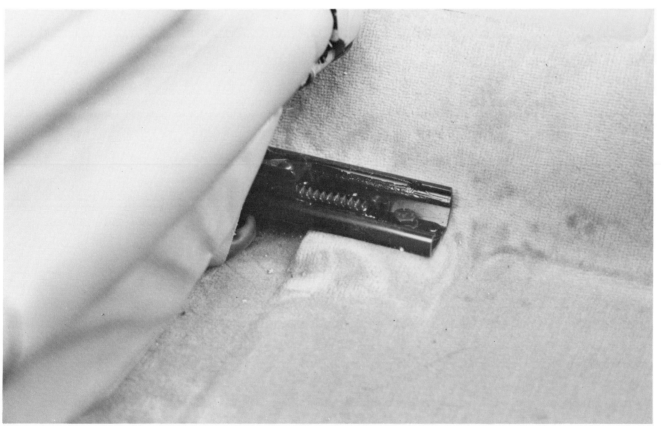

In order to reach as much carpet as possible, move the front seat to its most forward position before vacuuming *the rear seat area. Use the vacuum or a rag to clean the seat track.*

The pattern of holes on this Nissan carpet was caused by the bottom of the floor mat. Briskly agitate the crevice attachment to smooth the nap and bring up embedded grit from the carpet.

For light dust, this brush attachment works well to clean interior vents. Use a paintbrush along with this brush to reach deeper into vents and dislodge dust and lint.

After the back seat and carpet have been vacuumed, move the front seat as far back as possible. Vacuum the front seats and then the carpet. Use the same thorough approach. You should also vacuum wells in the armrests on door panels and the glovebox. If the dash is dusty, use a soft brush attachment to clean vents, gauges and grooves. Don't forget the center console and the carpeting surrounding it.

Some consoles include cloth pads. A toothbrush used in front of the crevice tool works well to loosen dirt along the seam between the cloth and plastic. The toothbrush also helps to break up dirt accumulations in gloveboxes, foot pedals and grooves in steering wheels and consoles.

Interior cleaning
Back seat area

When you are cleaning, the easiest way to reach most areas in the rear-seating compartment is to sit on the seat. If your shoes are wet or dirty, place a towel on the floor to protect the carpet. A clean, damp wash mitt will remove dust and lint. Excess water streaks from the mitt can be dried with a clean towel.

Start with the headliner above the seat. Then, work on the far side panel, the rear deck area, the near side panel and so on. Use a planned pattern, cleaning from the middle of the car toward the outside. Work your way out of the car by wiping the seat last. You can also easily reach the back side of the front seats. This will help you to maintain complete coverage and prevent the need to lean over a previously cleaned part to reach a dirty one.

For interiors in need of more than dusting, use a multipurpose liquid cleaner. Keep in mind that each time you use a cleaner, you will be removing some of the protection provided by the latest application of dressing or conditioner. Plan to reapply the appropriate conditioner after cleaning.

The liquid cleaner you use should be mixed with water according to instructions on the label. A spray bottle gives the easiest application. Before spraying headliner and side panels, fold a clean towel in quarters. Dampen one side with the cleaner, and wipe the area to be cleaned; use a dry side to remove residue. Spray directly on an area when it is so encrusted with grime build-up that a simple rub with the towel won't work.

Light bursts of spray on a seam or groove will help loosen dirt. Use the toothbrush as necessary. Place a towel below the work area to catch runoff. Take your time and aim the bottle accurately. Overspray will have to be cleaned, making more work for you. You can place the toothbrush on a towel and dampen the bristles with cleaner before using it to scrub a spot, minimizing overspray and runoff. By the way, a toothbrush works well to clean the rings on Corvette window cranks.

Your systematic approach should include the removal and cleaning of rear ashtrays. Small ones

A toothbrush is used to dislodge lint and dirt along the seam of this carpeted pad on the console of a Toyota MR2. The vacuum crevice is placed next to the toothbrush to remove debris as it is dislodged by the toothbrush. This method can also be used to remove debris caught at the interior base of windshields.

Pine needles and other such debris are difficult to remove with the vacuum alone. On this Corvette carpet, a brush is used to dislodge items caught in the carpet nap before vacuuming.

are easiest to clean using your fingers. I can't think of anything that works better. You can try a toothbrush, but the configuration of the smaller styles doesn't allow much work room. For ashtrays suffering from heavy encrustation, soak them in the wash

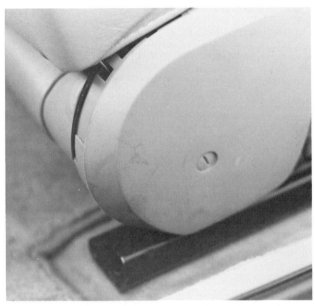

Check the lower parts of front seats for scuff marks. The light color of this BMW interior readily displays such marks. Use Simple Green or a household cleaner to remove marks from vinyl and plastic, and Lexol to clean leather.

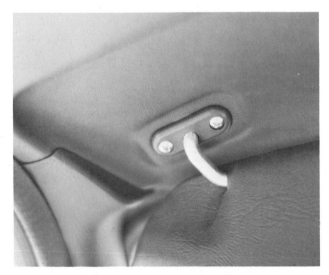

Sun visors and supporting brackets should not be overlooked while cleaning. This material is cleaned the same as upholstery. Screw slots and spots can be cleaned with a toothbrush.

bucket after rinsing with the hose. Later, they can be painted to look new.

Be sure to closely examine lower parts of the interior compartment. Scuff marks from shoes are common along side panels next to doorjambs and the bottom section of the front seat. Marks on vinyl and plastic can be removed by rubbing with the cleaner towel. For those marks unconquered by the all-purpose cleaner, try Eagle 1 Spot Remover and Cleaner or another brand of spot remover. The chemicals inside these powerful cleaners work very well, as long as you follow the directions on the label.

In essence, you should have touched every square inch of the back seat area before you move on to the front. Have you checked deep between the seatback and cushion, along the outer edge of the seat next to the side panel and under folding rear seats? Have chrome strips been polished, and has residue been removed from the grooves of Phillips screws? How about the lint on the rear deck and carpet from the cleaning cloth?

At this point, unless you plan to shampoo the cloth seat and the carpet, the back seat area should be clean. You will treat material with conditioner later.

Front seat area

Start with the headliner. Clean it as you did in the back. Clean the sun visors and the brackets holding them in place. Clean the back side of the rearview mirror, a commonly forgotten item. Use the toothbrush as necessary to clean around trim and to remove build-up in the exposed slots of Phillips screws. Seatbelt brackets for shoulder straps should be examined and cleaned also.

Metal dashboards, common in 1950s autos, can be polished and waxed. Meguiar's one-step Car Cleaner Wax is very well suited for this, since it doesn't leave a dry powdery residue. Use a small sponge for wax application. The square edges and small size make for easy maneuvering around gauges and trim. Be sure the surface is clean before polishing and waxing. Use spray cleaner and a towel to remove dust and dirt, a toothbrush along trim and screw slots. Remove residual moisture with a dry fold of the towel.

Once a year, Wentworth likes to soak vinyl dashboards with Armor All, using a paintbrush to force dressing into crevices and seams. A couple of days later, he wipes the dashboard with a cloth dampened with mild cleaner to remove the super high gloss and slippery feel. He believes that this way the conditioner will soak into the material

A paintbrush is used to work dressing into the vinyl on a neglected Corvette console. For the first-time detail on weathered vinyl, you can saturate the material with dressing and wipe off the excess. A few days later, clean the vinyl with a mild cleaner to remove the high gloss and slippery nature left behind by the excessive dressing application.

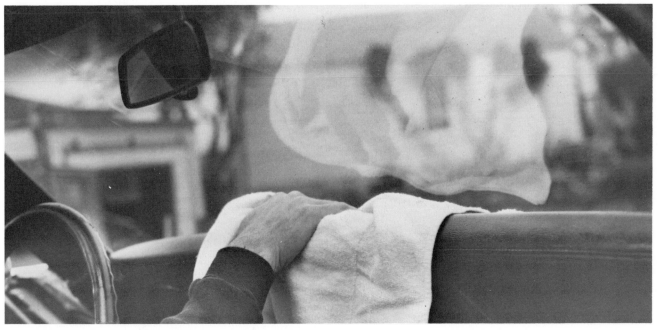

After dressing this Corvette dashboard, a clean towel is used to buff off excess and overspray.

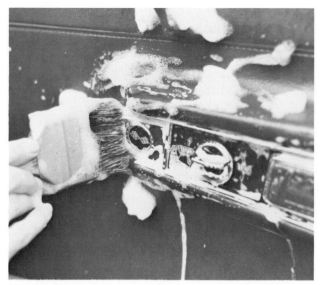

The paintbrush is used with soap suds to clean grooves and slots on this Corvette door. Using suds alone reduces the amount of moisture brought into the interior and cleans just as well as a heavy dose of soap and water. The area is dried with a clean towel and cotton swabs.

using soap and water or any number of vinyl cleaners on the market. Afterward, he applies a very light coat of Armor All.

Basic dashboard cleaning is simple yet time-consuming. Lots of grooves and slots along the face of the dash frequently collect dust. Knobs get dirty and sticky, and the new styles of steering wheels present the detailer with bumpy textures and grooves to clean.

Cotton swabs work best for grooves. Damp cotton will collect and retain dust much better than dry. Dip them in water and squeeze with your fingers to remove excess. To help remove dirt, dip them in soapy water. Use them in vents, too. For that matter, you can use these handy tools anywhere you think practical.

Dust in the tiny holes on the outside of stereo speakers is removed with the brush attachment on the end of a vacuum cleaner. Sometimes, a dry paintbrush is handy to help loosen stubborn dust. Speakers are delicate and you must use caution when cleaning. If the cover cannot be cleaned with the vacuum and dry paintbrush, consider removing it and cleaning it outside of the car with mild soap and water and a toothbrush. Be sure it is completely dry before reinstalling.

To clean sticky steering wheels and knobs, use cleaner on a towel and a toothbrush. Fold the towel as needed to reach hard-to-get areas. Use the edge of

deeper, last longer and keep future applications to a minimum.

Others, including Dan Mycon, disagree. They think that some detailers use dressing to cover up inadequate cleaning jobs, allowing dirt to build up even more. Mycon prefers to clean vinyl thoroughly,

A cotton swab is handy for cleaning and drying around the controls on a Corvette console.

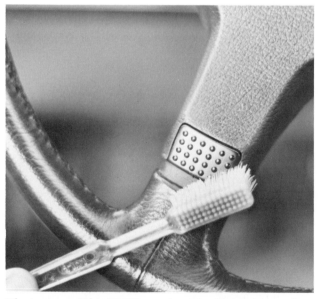

The texture of this BMW steering wheel is easiest to clean using a toothbrush. Sit in the driver's seat for comfort during cleaning and place a towel on your lap to catch soap suds runoff.

the towel along wide grooves on the center of the steering wheel. A toothbrush and cleaner can be used to scrub dirty materials featuring unusual textures.

The handle of the toothbrush placed inside the towel can be used to reach deep into dusty vents without fear of scratching. Some detailers like to spray the vents with liquid cleaner first, then remove dirt with the toothbrush-in-a-towel method. The liquid breaks loose the dirt, and the towel picks up the residue. Use a cotton swab to gather excess along the sides.

Clean the glovebox and console with towel, toothbrush and cotton swab. A paintbrush comes in handy to reach in grooves and deep corners of gloveboxes and storage wells on consoles. Be imaginative. Use the tools at your disposal to clean whatever needs to be cleaned. Always use the simplest and mildest methods first.

Gauges

Clear lenses over gauges can be cleaned with water or glass cleaner. Removing dust from the

Cotton swabs made quick work of cleaning the dusty vents on this BMW dashboard. Some detailers prefer to use cotton swabs dry; others spray dust cleaners, like Endust, on the swab for better absorption.

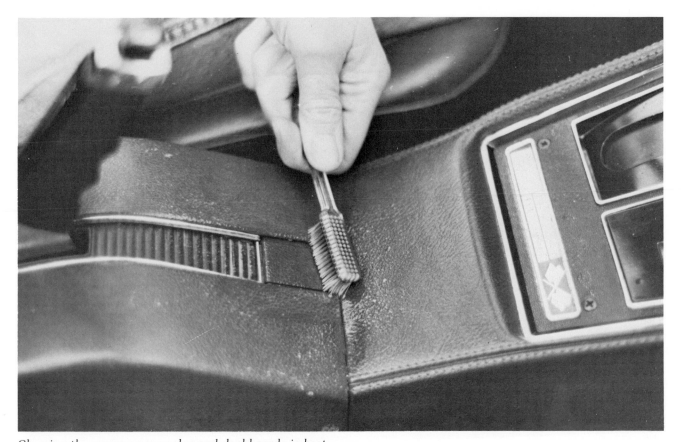

Cleaning the seams on consoles and dashboards is best achieved with a toothbrush. Follow with a clean towel to pick up residue and moisture.

This Corvette window crank displays a ringed design which is easiest to clean using a toothbrush. Door handles and window cranks presenting slots and grooves are also easiest to clean using a toothbrush. Spray the bristles of the toothbrush with cleaner before scrubbing instead of spraying the part to be cleaned. This will minimize cleaner usage and runoff.

inside of gauges will require dashboard dismantling to remove the gauge. Then remove the lens from the gauge itself. Unless you know what you are doing, you may want to seek help from a certified mechanic.

If the lens is scratched, try polishing. Jerry McKee likes to use Eagle 1 Plastic Polish on the plastic rear window of his Jag roadster. This product is described by the manufacturer as "A unique non-abrasive cleaner and polish for plastic, plexiglass, window tint film, porcelain and other hard surfaces." If the glass or plastic lens is scratched and you are determined to fix it, try this first while the gauge is still in place.

Door panels and jambs

Now that the inside of the car is clean, you can clean the door panels and jambs. The panels are cleaned the same way you cleaned the side panels in the back seat area. Vinyl can be scrubbed, if necessary, to remove shoe scuffs and other marks. You can also try spot removers such as Simple Green or Turtle Wax's vinyl cleaner as necessary. Leather material is cared for a bit differently; this will be described in the section about leather seats. Use caution around imitation plastic chrome strips. Vigorous scrubbing can cause the thin plastic film

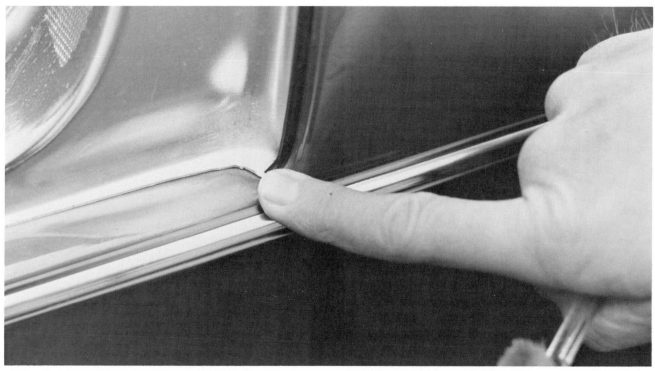

Dirt was overlooked in the rear corner of the front door-jamb on Mary Jo Wertheimer's BMW. Easily cleaned with a damp towel or toothbrush, check spots like this that were missed during the preliminary wash.

to peel away from the plastic trim base. Thoroughly clean door handles and window cranks, using the toothbrush as needed. Be sure to clean and dry the wells on armrests and the grooves on speakers.

The doorjambs were cleaned when you originally washed the car. At this time, use a damp wash mitt to pick up any missed spots. Clean both the front and rear jambs, as well as the top and bottom of the door. If the damp mitt doesn't do the trick, try the towel and cleaner. Use a paintbrush, dipped in the wash bucket, to reach difficult spots. Dry the entire door frame with a towel. Painted surfaces look great when they are wet. Once they are dry, you can easily detect flaws. Clean again as needed.

Most car doors are equipped with drains. They are nothing more than holes in the bottom of the door frame. You have to get your head below the door and look up to see them; it is recommended you look at these drains a few times a year. Should they plug, you run the risk of giving rust a start in the bottom of the door. These drains can be cleaned with a pipe cleaner.

Moldings around doors serve a very useful purpose. Clean them with the towel and look for any sections that may be coming loose. You can condition them with an all-purpose dressing such as Armor All or Meguiar's, and reattach bad spots with proper molding glue such as 3M's glue.

Check the owners manual for your car, or check with a body person, to see if the hinges and latching mechanisms require special lubrication. If not, it is

Dirty Corvette front door hinge should be rinsed with water, sprayed with Simple Green and cleaned with a paintbrush. A light coat of WD-40 applied after cleaning and drying will keep the hinge lubricated.

This is the bottom edge of a Lamborghini Countach passenger door. The four holes next to the right-hand edge are door drains, common with most auto doors. Use pipe cleaners to keep these holes clean and open in order that water will drain from the door.

101

a good idea to lubricate with WD-40 after complete cleaning. WD-40, sprayed through its plastic tube nozzle, works well inside key holes on the doors. An occasional shot will keep the key mechanism working freely and allow for easy key turning.

Service stickers on the doorjamb are unsightly to most car buffs. Use your fingernail to gently remove them. If at any time you think they are about to damage the paint, stop. Use a sticker and decal remover to loosen the glue, then peel as necessary. To remove residual glue, put some removal product on a rag and wipe. Meguiar's one-step Cleaner Wax also removes glue residue.

You can wax the doorjambs now, or wait until you wax the rest of the car. There is no big secret to waxing. The best advice, however, is to take your time and concentrate on applying wax where you want it. Use the rectangular sponge as an applica-

tor. Its straight sides are great for cutting an edge along vinyl and rubber trim and molding.

Seatbelts

Seatbelts should not be overlooked. Pull them out of their cases to check for dirt and proper rewinding. Use the crevice tool on the vacuum cleaner to remove dust and dirt from the case. If the return mechanism is squeaky or unusually slow, clean and lubricate with a light coat of WD-40.

Clean seatbelts with soap and water using a toothbrush or plastic brush as needed. You can lay a towel on the seat and clean the belt on top of it to prevent runoff residue getting on fabric or carpet. Check the owners manual if you question proper soap usage. Allow the belt to dry before returning to its case. To keep seatbelts stretched while drying, tie one end of a string to the end of the belt and the other end to the steering wheel, door handle, sun visor bracket, or what have you.

Seats
Vinyl

Since they won't absorb water, you can scrub dirty vinyl seats with soap and water and the plastic-bristled brush. This is not necessary on those seats that can be easily cleaned with a towel and an all-purpose cleaner such as Simple Green or a vinyl cleaning product such as Turtle Wax or Meguiar's.

This Porsche door vent was not cleaned with soap and water during the preliminary wash in order to prevent water from entering the inside part of the door. Here, the vent is cleaned with a damp towel, using tight folds to reach inside the vent openings.

Scrubbing vinyl seats, like this Corvette bucket seat, is done with a plastic brush and a bucket of soapy water. Use mostly suds from the top of the bucket as opposed to bringing in a brush full of soapy water.

Spray liquid cleaner on a section of the seat, starting on the backrest and working down. Use the brush in a circular pattern to break loose the imbedded dirt from the grain. Reverse the direction for better coverage. Use the brush along seams and pleats, adding cleaner as necessary to maintain a foamy base. Place towels anywhere you want to prevent overspray or splattering.

Dry with a towel. You can also use a wet-and-dry vacuum to remove suds and moisture, followed by towel drying. The crevice tool works well to remove moisture and dirt caught in seams and along beads. Be sure to dry any residue left on armrests, side panels, chrome strips and deep creases in the seat.

Scrub one section of a seat at a time. For instance, do one half of the backrest of the rear seat, then one half of the bottom. Move to the other side and do the same. Then, move the front seat to its most backward position and do the passenger side,

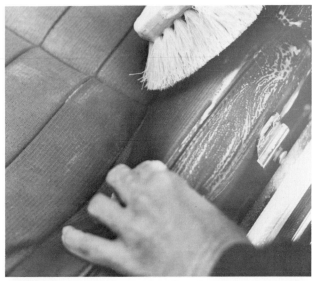

Spread the pleats on seats to allow bristles to reach into seams and along beads, dislodging debris and removing dirt.

Vinyl seats can be dried with a clean towel. You can use a wet-and-dry vacuum first, if available, and follow with a *towel. Use folds in the towel to dry areas along seams and pleats.*

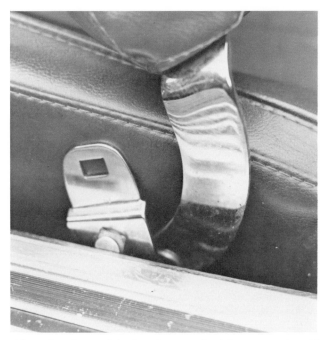

After cleaning and drying the seat, don't forget to wipe off seat brackets. Chrome seat brackets and seatbelt mechanisms, like these Corvette items, are cleaned with a towel and then polished as necessary.

then the driver's. This pattern assures good coverage and prevents soap from drying on the vinyl.

Stubborn stains left behind will have to be removed with a vinyl spot remover. Most of these products advertise the same qualities and do the job very well. Be very, very cautious about using solvent, paint thinner or lacquer thinner. These harsh

This Corvette bucket seat looks like new after scrubbing and drying.

chemicals may remove the stain, but also damage vinyl. Try repeated applications of vinyl spot removers on vinyl before using solvents or thinners.

Cloth

The fabric used for cloth seats is similar to some fabrics used for household furnishings. The exception may be those seats especially treated to reduce flammability. Many have had good luck cleaning them with upholstery shampoo purchased at the supermarket. If you decide to shampoo, use a wet-and-dry vacuum cleaner to remove water and suds from the upholstery, which will help prevent mildew.

Turtle Wax Vinyl/Fabric Upholstery Cleaner is easy to apply and remove. Other fabric cleaners are available too. It is tough to recommend one over the other, since various car people have had luck using different brands. If you don't have access to a wet-and-dry vacuum cleaner and don't want to rent or use one at the self-serve car wash, you will have to use a product designed to be removed with a dry vacuum cleaner. Be sure to follow the instructions on the label before application.

The pattern for shampooing cloth seats is no different from that for scrubbing vinyl. Fill a spray bottle and a small bucket with shampoo mixed with water according to instructions. Spray a small section of seat first; then dip the clean plastic brush in the bucket and start scrubbing. The shampoo on the upholstery makes a rich, foamy mixture. Scrub in a

A wet-and-dry vacuum will be needed to help dry cloth seats after shampooing. Without the vacuum, moisture will sink deep into the seat and become a source of future mildew and odor problems. This Toyota cloth bucket seat will be scrubbed with suds from a mixture of upholstery shampoo and then immediately vacuumed using the crevice attachment.

circular direction, reversing it occasionally for added cleaning power.

Vacuum each section immediately after scrubbing. This will prevent shampoo from drying on the surface and will remove moisture before it is allowed to soak in any more. Use a clean towel to dry things such as chrome strips and seatbelts.

After the detail has been completed, park the car outside with the windows open to help dry the seats. During winter months, open the doors and place a fan at the opening, allowing air to blow over the seats and hasten the drying process. Some detailers use small portable heaters to speed drying. You risk the danger of placing the heater improperly, which may result in the melting of some plastic parts or, worse, starting a fire. For those reasons, I advise against their use.

To remove stains on cloth seats and carpet without shampooing, try Turtle Wax Spot Remover or any other product designed for the same use. These products spray on wet. The outer edge dries first, resulting in a white ring around the stain. The remover dries to a white powder. Use the bristled cap to brush powder and stains away, and vacuum

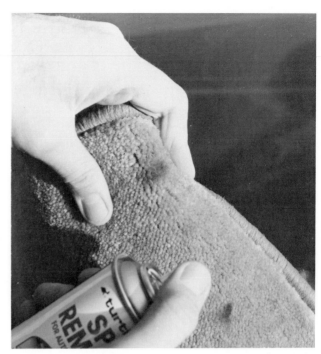

Spread the carpet nap to allow deep penetration of the spot remover. In this instance, Turtle Wax Spot Remover is being applied to spots on a BMW carpeted floor mat.

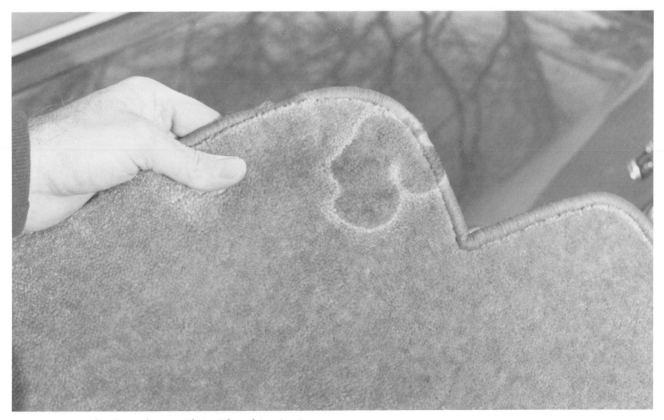

Spot removers dry from the outside in. The white ring is a sign the outer edge is drying.

105

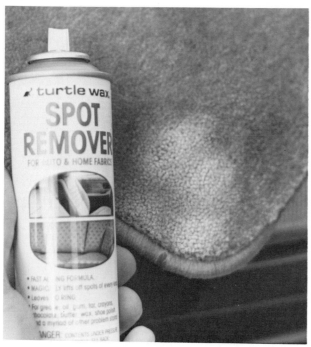

The white powder on the surface of the carpet shows that the spot remover is dry and ready to be removed.

The spot remover's white powdery residue can be brushed away with the brush-like cap provided with the product, or can be vacuumed with a dry vacuum cleaner. The residue on this carpet mat was brushed away with the brush-like cap.

any residue. As always, follow the instructions on the label.

Thick debris can be scraped with a dull knife and then blotted with a rag dabbed in cleaner. Scrub the remaining residue with a toothbrush and shampoo. Use a wet-and-dry vacuum cleaner in the direction of the grain. Speed drying with a hair dryer.

Contact an auto upholsterer or professional detailer for unique upholstery, including expensive crushed velour, suede or any exotic fabric installed on a custom basis.

Leather

Leather seats are expensive, beautiful and comfortable. Wipe with a clean, damp towel first; then dry. Never use heavy cleaning products or cleansers on leather.

For seats that need a real cleaning, the car enthusiasts I spoke to preferred Lexol-pH Leather Cleaner. Application is simple. Just apply a small amount to a wet sponge or cloth and scrub in an easy motion. Reapply as necessary for extra dirty areas. For spots, dip a toothbrush into the cleaner and scrub gently. It is best to go over a stubborn spot a number of times with soft pressure rather than once with too much. If that just doesn't work and the seat is still filthy, you can try saddle soap.

When you have completed a section, use a clean, damp towel to remove residue. Use your hand to

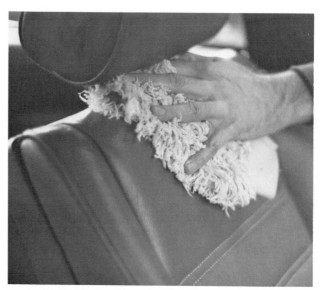

Dusty leather seats do not need to be cleaned with cleaner or soap. A simple wipe-down with a clean, damp wash mitt is enough. This mild cleaning method will remove dust and preserve any conditioner that is still imbedded in the material. Vigorous cleaning will remove conditioner, which will require that a new treatment be applied.

spread the leather, stretching folds in the material to assure complete coverage. Be sure to clean and dry under buttons, along seams, beads and headrests.

After cleaning, protect the leather with an application of Lexol Leather Conditioner and Preservative or Hide Food. Both have been used successfully by many car enthusiasts.

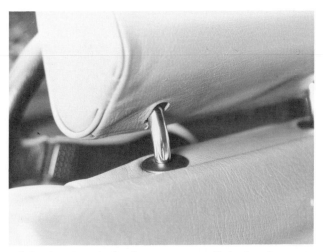

While cleaning the back seat area, pull the headrests up on the front seat. Remove dust and dirt with a towel and use a toothbrush to remove build-up around posts and washers.

A toothbrush is used to remove a spot on a BMW leather rear seat. Repeated applications may be necessary to remove tough spots. In the long run, it is much easier on the material to gently go over a spot a number of times than to harshly scrub one or two times.

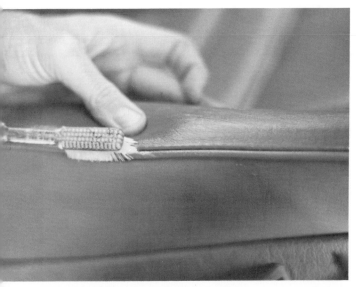

Use a toothbrush and Lexol cleaner in seams and along beads to remove dirt from leather upholstery. Follow with a clean towel to remove residue.

Leather needs to breathe; a trait which helps make it so comfortable. Use only those conditioning products designed for leather. One such product is Lexol, another is Hide Food. A little goes a long way, so use sparingly.

107

Shampoo carpet with vigorous agitation of the plastic brush. Spray stubborn spots with carpet shampoo from the squirt bottle for added cleaning strength. The brush can be used in a circular or a back-and-forth pattern. Reverse the pattern periodically to guarantee complete coverage over the entire carpet nap.

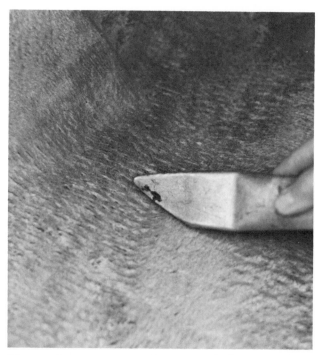

The crevice vacuum attachment works best for pulling shampoo and water out of the carpet. Push down on the tool to squeeze water out of the carpet nap. Go over the area a number of times in an attempt to remove as much moisture as possible.

Carpet shampooing

Many dry carpet cleaners are available at supermarkets, variety stores and some auto parts stores. Turtle Wax Carpet Cleaner and Protector claims to remove heavy dirt and also provide a dirt-resistant silicone shield; it works. These products are designed to be rubbed into the carpet with a sponge. When dry, removal is done with a regular vacuum cleaner. .

With a wet-and-dry vacuum cleaner handy, you can shampoo carpets using any number of carpet shampoo products. Supermarkets carry an assortment of brands, some with specific uses. You will have to read the labels to determine which will work best for you. A few detailers have had good results using Woolite as a carpet shampoo.

The process is similar to shampooing cloth seats. You will need a plastic-bristled brush, spray bottle, small bucket, towel and wet-and-dry vacuum cleaner. It is best to thoroughly vacuum the carpet first, removing loose debris. Start in the back seat area, on one side of the car. Spray shampoo mix from the spray bottle on heavy stains and spots as needed. Next, agitate the brush in the small bucket and bring up foam and suds. It is not necessary to use lots of water and shampoo with the brush; suds and foam work just as well and prevent carpet from becoming soaked. Scrub the carpet in a circular pattern, reversing the direction occasionally. Bring up a good lather. Heavy stains can be sprayed again with shampoo for added cleaning power.

When the section has been scrubbed to your satisfaction, use the wet-and-dry vacuum cleaner and crevice tool to remove suds, dirt and moisture. Press the tool against the carpet while vacuuming. This will help to force water to the top and allow suction deeper into the nap. The vacuum cleaner will sound different when it is picking up water; you will easily notice the tone. After two to three passes, it will sound as though nothing is being taken in. Continue vacuuming for another four or five minutes. Although the majority of water has been removed, additional vacuuming will assure drying small pockets of moisture that were missed, as well as help the rest of the section dry a bit faster.

Afterward, use a towel to wipe off splatter on seats, panels and trim. When the carpet is com-pletely dry, fluff the nap using your hand or a clean, dry brush.

Shampooing is not often necessary. Simple stains can be removed with dry spot removers. It is not good to soak carpets with water and shampoo, as moisture can remain in the padding for a long time, especially in cold, wet weather. The best time to shampoo is during warm weather when you can park the clean car outside with the doors open to aid drying. For those carpets that need it, I recommend that you try frequent maintenance with dry cleaners, saving shampoo for once a year.

Carpets should not be dyed a different color. If faded, renew carpet with a light coat of dye that is the same tint as the original. Apply as directed in the instructions, and then rub it in with a sponge to prevent a crust forming on top.

Cloth protectorants

Scotchgard is a familiar product. It is designed to help cloth resist stains and liquid absorption. It

Scotchgard is a familiar fabric protector. Other such products are available at auto parts stores. Use towels to protect against overspray and use your free hand to spread the material, assuring deep and complete coverage.

works well on cloth seats and carpet. Application is very easy. There are other brands available, and you'll have to decide which one is best for you.

Scotchgard comes in a spray can. To apply, you simply spray it directly on the clean, dry fabric. I

Dried, weathered and neglected Corvette dashboard is receiving a bath in Armor All. Not every detailer agrees with this technique. However, a one-time dressing soak, followed a few days later with a mild cleaning, leaves otherwise dried-out vinyl looking rich and rejuvenated without the high gloss and slippery surface so common on excessively dressed surfaces.

suggest you use towels to protect windows and side panels from overspray. Use your free hand to stretch the fabric tight. Spray in a uniform pattern, following the instructions on the label. If a powdery white residue appears after drying, simply brush or vacuum away. This is caused by overapplication. On the other hand, if water drops fail to bead on the treated cloth, you must repeat the application.

This product is recommended for all types of fabric except leather, vinyl and imitation suede. Applied correctly, it will help to prevent stains on your cloth seats and carpet. Its lasting quality is not certain. Once every couple of months, test its strength with a few drops of water. If the water soaks in, it is time for a new application.

Dressings

Multipurpose dressings can bring life to faded interior vinyl. In this case, too much is not too good. We have all experienced the slippery feel of vinyl seats conditioned with too much dressing. It is better to apply a thin, penetrating coat than one heavy dose.

The exception may be those interiors that have been neglected for an extensive period of time. On those, apply a heavy spray and work it in with a soft brush. Let it sit for a few minutes, and then wipe off the excess with a clean towel. A day or two later,

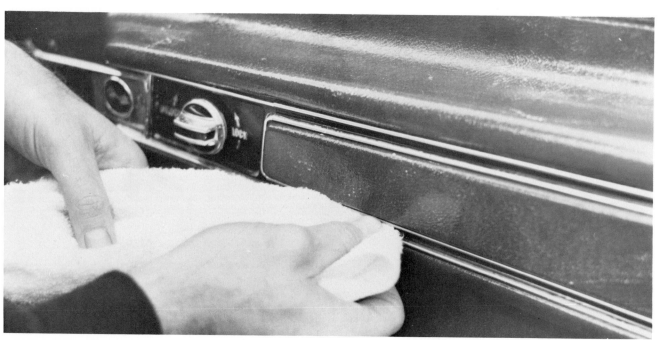

After soaking this dried-out Corvette interior with Armor All, excess dressing is removed with a clean towel. Here, a fold in the towel is used to remove dressing from a slot *along the passenger door panel. A few days later, the entire interior will be wiped down with a cleaner-dampened towel.*

gently wipe the dressed parts with a towel dampened with a mild mix of all-purpose cleaner and water. This should remove excess dressing and get rid of the extra slippery feel of the material, while leaving the vinyl with a rich, rejuvenated appearance.

Wentworth has one small towel he uses exclusively with dressing. Preferring Armor All, he likes to spray the vinyl first and then buff off the dressing. The towel seldom gets dirty because he only dresses clean parts. For tight areas, he wipes with the towel only. In many cases, this towel is so impregnated with dressing that he doesn't have to spray Armor All—he just buffs with the towel.

Rather than spray dressing on a surface directly, other detailers like to spray the towel and then wipe on the dressing. They feel this lessens overspray and allows them the chance to put the dressing where they want it, as opposed to where it lands.

Eagle 1, Turtle Wax and Meguiar's all make products similar to Armor All. It is impossible to

Dressing is most commonly applied to a cloth first, and then wiped onto vinyl. This assures controlled application and allows you to put the dressing where you want it. Use one certain cloth for all dressing applications. The surfaces to which you apply the dressing should always be clean, and therefore, the cloth should remain clean. In those cases where only a dab of dressing is required, the residual dressing in the cloth is generally enough.

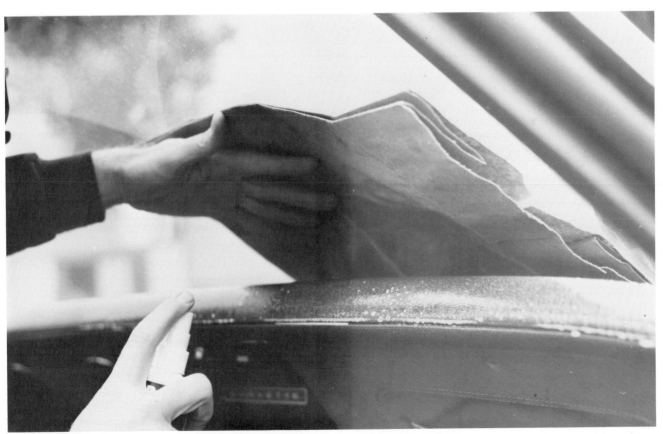

The paper bag being held up to the windshield protects glass from dressing overspray during a one-time Armor All soak. You can use paper bags, towels and cardboard as overspray blocks to protect glass, metal and upholstery.

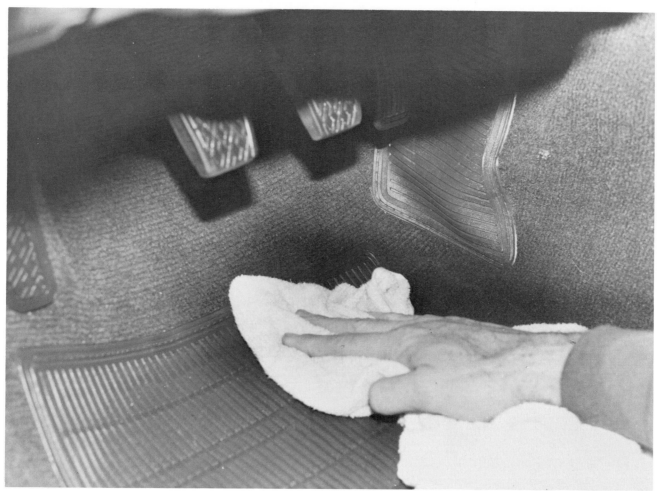

Rubber floor mats can be lightly dressed. Buff the mat with a clean towel after applying dressing to remove all excess. It is important for this area to remain dry. Too much dressing on the mat will make your shoes slippery and could cause them to slip off of the brake or clutch pedal.

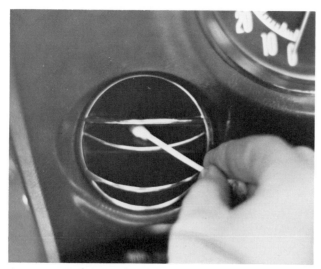

A cotton swab is used to remove dressing overspray on a Corvette vent. Use the fold of a towel first to remove the big stuff. The cotton swab will pick up the remainder.

recommend one over the others; I suggest you talk to other car buffs to see what they like and why. McKee bought one brand and used it all. Then he bought a different one until he had tried them all. He prefers Armor All and notes that since he keeps his cars in such clean shape, they seldom need more than a very light coat to maintain a rich appearance.

Spray dressing on a small, clean towel. Using a folded edge of the towel or your fingers, guide the application carefully. Only vinyl and rubber need be dressed. Dressing on plastic and metal parts does not look good and is unnecessary. Start in the middle of the back seat area and work your way out of the car, just as you did when cleaning. For tight spots, put the handle of the toothbrush inside the towel. As the towel dries, spray a little more dressing on it.

Vinyl dashboards present unique problems during dressing application. There are many nooks, crannies and obstacles in the way. Use your fingers as a guide. For tight spots, spray a little dressing on a cotton swab and make the application with it. Wipe off the excess with a clean towel.

Leather should be treated only with a leather conditioner and preservative, such as Lexol or Hide Food. Leather needs to breathe. It is this breathing quality that makes it so comfortable. Vinyl dressings are advertised as safe for leather. Some detailers believe that these dressing are all right but tend to plug pores of the leather, reducing its breathing ability.

Foot pedals and rubber mats can also be dressed. For these parts, apply only a very thin coat and be certain all the excess is removed. If too much dressing is applied, your feet may slip off the pedals and cause you to have a driving accident.

Rubber moldings can be wiped with a cloth dampened with dressing. They will look new. The same holds true for all rubber and vinyl parts of the

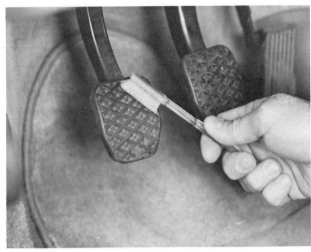

Foot pedal rubbers are best cleaned with a toothbrush and an all-purpose cleaner, like Simple Green. Lay a towel on the carpet below the rubbers to prevent dirt and soap residue from staining. In extreme cases, take the rubbers off of the pedals and clean outside of the car.

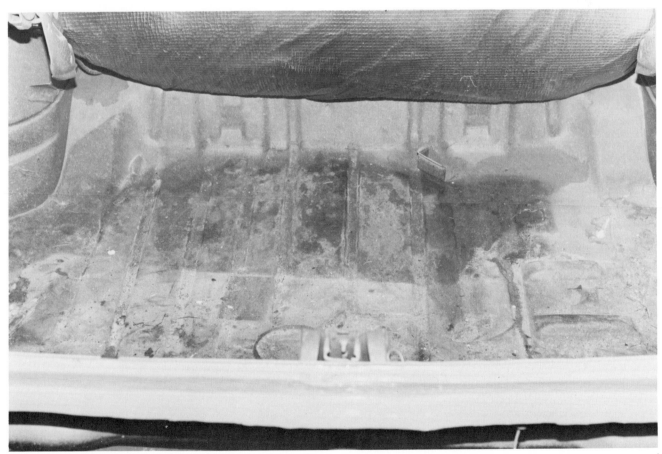

This is the neglected trunk of Wentworth's 1970 Buick GS 455 convertible before detailing. During cleaning and detailing, care must be given to the soft fabric at the front of the trunk so it does not become wet, torn or sprayed with paint. Surface rust will have to be removed and all dirt and grease residue cleaned off.

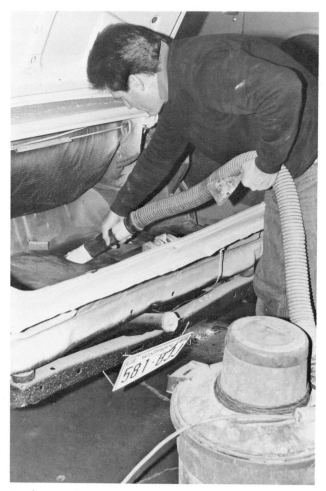

interior. Using the same pattern you did when cleaning, assure yourself of complete coverage and rewipe any spots that were missed.

Trunk cleaning

When you washed the car, you emptied the trunk, right? The jacking equipment, tools, detachable mat and anything else that was in there have already been cleaned.

If the trunk you are about to clean is dirtier than anything you have ever seen, consider pulling the rubber drain plugs and using plenty of soap and water and the plastic-bristled brush to scrub. You will have to dry it afterward. A wet-and-dry vacuum cleaner helps, along with a few towels. Use caution with the hose. Don't get the fiberboard or back part of the rear seat wet.

Sometimes you'll find the floorboard of the trunk in rusty condition. In extreme cases, you may

For heavy cleaning chores, like removing the rust from this Buick trunk, use a wet-and-dry vacuum. It has excellent suction strength, the ability to pick up large pieces of residue, and can remove water from wells and other low spots.

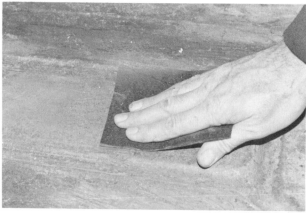

After the heavy surface rust was scraped off with a putty knife, wet-and-dry sandpaper was used to clean the trunk on Wentworth's Buick. It is essential that all rust be removed before any paint is applied.

A plastic brush is handy to loosen up dirt and other build-up. It can also be used with cleaner to remove stubborn stains and debris.

114

have to use a putty knife or wire brush to scrape off the big stuff. Then, use a fine-grit sandpaper to remove remaining rust. A damp towel and vacuum cleaner will pick up residue.

For trunks in good shape, use a towel sprayed with Armor All. Follow up with a folded towel, damp with clean water on one side and dry on the other. Give the trunk a close inspection and clean all of it, including the locking mechanism, brackets for the taillights and bottom side of the trunk lid.

Trunk rejuvenation

Nicely painted trunks, such as those on Porsche 944s, should be waxed. You just can't go wrong cleaning and waxing any painted surface.

Vintage American cars are generally complemented with large trunks. Many have been painted with spatter paint, a slightly rough coating that consists of gray paint dotted with white specks. For such trunks, especially the ones that required rust

The first coat of protection applied to a trunk that has been cleaned to bare metal, should be primer or a paint like Rust Magic that helps to prevent rust. Two coats are usually sufficient. After that, you can repaint with a different color or use a spatter paint designed for trunks.

Once again, the crevice attachment works best for picking up dust, dirt and rust residue. The style of this tool allows the greatest suction power and the size of the opening permits rather large pieces of debris to be removed.

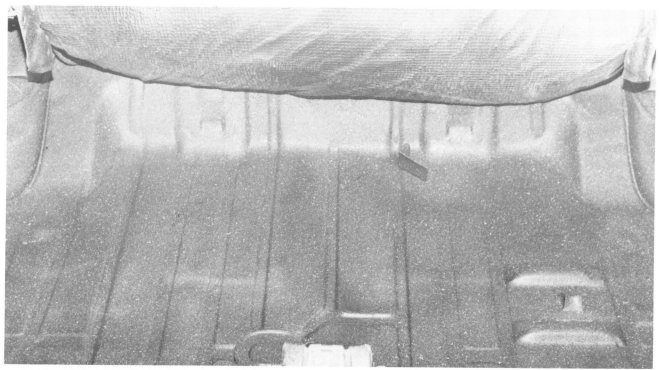

The trunk of Wentworth's Buick GS 455 convertible after detailing. It was cleaned and painted with two coats of Rust Magic. Then, it was coated with two cans of Zolotone, a trunk spatter paint.

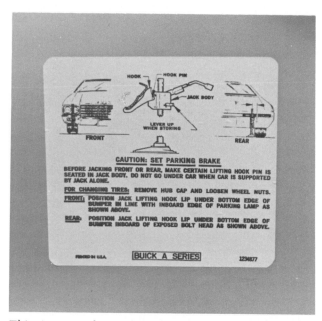

This is a stock Buick jacking equipment instruction sticker for the trunk of Wentworth's 1970 Buick GS 455. Since the original trunk lid was destroyed in an accident, a used one was repainted and used in the restoration. To keep as original as possible, this new sticker was purchased through GM. If you need stock stickers, emblems or lettering, check with your local dealer's parts department. If they can't find one for you they may be able to suggest an alternative source of supply.

removal, I suggest you clean and sand as needed. Then, apply two coats of a rust-inhibiting paint such as Rustoleum. Allow to dry, and then apply a coat of Zolotone or other trunk spatter paint. These paints come in different colors and are available at local auto parts stores. Mask as needed, using masking tape, newspaper and towels as you see fit. The end result will knock you out. The trunk will look brand new.

If you don't like the spatter paint, use whatever you want. Be sure the surface is thoroughly sanded and smooth. If not, flaws will be noticeable.

Follow the directions on the paint label, and wait the appropriate time to let paint dry before reassembling the trunk. If you have forgotten how the spare tire and jacking equipment are supposed to fit in their prescribed spot, check the instruction sticker on the trunk lid. If it is missing, look at the pictures you took before you started or use the trial-and-error method.

Believe it or not, many of the trunk stickers are available for purchase. Check with local auto parts stores and dealerships to see who carries them. Wentworth had extensive body and paint work done on his 1970 Buick GS 455, and Mycon was able to buy new stickers for the trunk and engine compartment, as well as the GS emblems for the front quarter panels and plastic center caps for the wheels.

Many car people wrap jacking equipment in towels before stowing it in the trunk. Towels protect the tools and lessen road noise by preventing vibration. McKee carries a road cleaning kit, a tool kit with some minor engine parts and a car cover in the trunk of his 1970 Jaguar V-12 roadster. Clint Worthington likes to wrap his tool kit in a towel before placing it in the trunk of his 1985 Porsche 944. The towel keeps the tools quiet and comes in handy to remove moisture from windows and surprises deposited by uncaring birds.

Last little details

After spending an entire day or two detailing the inside of your automobile, you will have developed a keen eye for perfection. You might even be able to go to a car show and note small flaws in some of the exhibitions. The more you clean the interior, the more attentive you will become to the details. Before you know it, you will automatically clean all those little spots so commonly missed by less enthusiastic detailers.

To complete the interior detail, there are some final chores. Line up all the vents on the dashboard so they point in the same direction. If seatbelts are not automatically retracted into holders, fold them neatly across the seat or fold them into a tight roll and gently tuck them into the space between the seatback and the cushion. Line up the rearview mirror so it is in its proper position and square with the top of the windshield. Replace worn mats with new ones and be sure the straps for sheepskin seat covers are properly attached and not hanging loose.

The molded tool kit McKee carries in the trunk of his Jag prevents tools from rattling. Properly stored, road kits and car covers are protected and don't take up any more room in the trunk than necessary.

After cleaning and dressing, take a few minutes to tidy the interior. Seatbelts can be folded or laid neatly across the seat. Hanging threads can be cut from upholstery and carpet, and a lint brush can be used to remove tiny pieces of lint left by cleaning and dressing towels.

117

The used plastic ashtray is out of a Chevy S-10 and the metal one is out of Jim Yocum's Calypso Coral and Cream 1972 Ford pickup. Restoring the plastic ashtray is done with cleaner and a toothbrush, followed with a coat of crystal clear lacquer. Yocum's ashtray will require cleaning with a toothbrush and a small wire brush to remove the years of accumulated build-up.

Plastic and metal ashtrays after cleaning and painting. Plastic ashtrays clean easily and the clear lacquer paint makes them look new. Apply two light coats as opposed to one heavy coat. Yocum's metal ashtray cleaned up quite nicely for a regular driver. A small wire brush, wet-and-dry sandpaper and bright silver paint were used.

While checking the interior for flaws, look behind the gas pedal for lint, threads or dirt. Slowly look at every part of the interior for the slightest imperfection. Use a systematic approach starting with the headliner and working down to the floorboard.

Clean metal ashtrays can be painted with bright silver paint to look new. Clean plastic ashtrays can be painted with crystal clear lacquer, making them look unused. Foot pedal brackets can be carefully painted with semigloss black, using towels to protect against overspray. Floor shifters can also be painted and chrome-polished. Plastic consoles can be polished with Pledge or any other furniture polish by applying the polish to a clean towel first and then wiping and buffing.

Minor tears in upholstery should be repaired as soon as possible. The longer you wait, the worse the tear will get. You can buy vinyl repair kits and do it yourself or go to an auto upholsterer. Sometimes, it is better to have the entire seat section replaced.

The little things are what makes the difference between a good detail and a great one. Are there any dead moths lying in the bottom of the dome light? Do sun visors complement each other by lining up in the same position? Are the bottoms of door pouches clean? Does the glovebox look like you just threw a bunch of stuff in it, or does it look neat and tidy when you open the door?

Deodorants

Car people have told me they don't use deodorants inside their cars. Rather, they prefer the smell of clean. This can be maintained if you clean the inside on a regular basis. If not, a deodorant can only attempt to cover up, not remedy, the cause of the odor.

If you want to use a particular scent, it is perfectly OK. As discussed earlier, there are a multitude of such products available at variety stores and auto parts houses. Solid types can hang from a knob or can be placed under the seat out of sight. Liquids are also available, in a variety of scents. Follow the directions on the label and don't use too much! Start out with just a hint of the scent, gradually increasing it to please your nose.

Some car buffs clean the interior with lemon-scented Pledge. The lemon scent stays with the car a long time, generating a pleasant aroma. They also dust vents using cotton swabs dampened with it. Others like to put a little Lysol in cleaning solutions and carpet shampoo to get similar results.

Chapter 6

Exterior shine

When you wash your car, does the paint rub off on the wash mitt and drying towel? If so, the paint can be considered severely oxidized. If not, the paint may still suffer from moderate or light oxidation. You need to determine your problem—the degree of oxidation—and work toward a solution—restoring the shine. On the other hand, you may be fortunate and need to maintain, not restore, the shine.

Oxidation

Oxidation starts on the top layer of paint, which dries out and becomes chalky. Paint should never really dry. Wax protects it from the sun's ultraviolet rays and the elements, and also helps it to retain certain oils that paint needs to stay healthy. With little or no protection, layers dry out, lose oils and therefore lose the ability to shine and

Art Wentworth's 1970 Buick GS 455 convertible was involved in an accident. The only way to bring the exterior of this car back to life was a complete paint job. Note the amount of disassembly to assure excellent paint coverage and the plastic cover to protect the convertible top from sanding dust and overspray.

bead water. Under an electron microscope, oxidized paint looks like the floor of the Mojave Desert in the middle of summer: cracked, dry and lumpy. Fresh paint appears smooth and even.

Solutions that shine

There are three ways to make the exterior of your automobile shine like new. First is a new paint job. A good paint job is expensive but may be your only option. This depends entirely on the paint's present condition. If it is oxidized to the point that primer shows through, paint it. Get a number of estimates first, asking each painter to explain just exactly what you'll be getting. Will the painter remove small parts such as emblems, door handles and trim? Does he or she plan to sand? Will small dents be repaired?

These things, and others, should be agreed upon before the job starts. Have them included in the written estimate. The type of paint used is up to you. Enamel is most common, while lacquer and urethane jobs are more expensive and require much more preparation and finishing work, but last much longer and resist rock chips much better.

The second way to make a paint job look new is to buff it or have it buffed by a professional detailer. This process requires the use of a buffing machine in conjunction with certain buffing pads and various polishes and waxes. You can do this yourself, although you run the risk of paint damage. I'll describe buffing later in this chapter.

Your third choice is to polish and wax by hand. For oxidized paint, this is a labor-intensive operation—but well worth the effort. On the other hand, paint that has been maintained should polish and wax easily.

Polishing removes the top layer of dead paint and exposes good paint. If oxidation is not too severe, you can save the paint with polish and wax.

An excellent paint job requires the removal of all items attached to the exterior of the car, such as door handles, emblems, bumpers and lights. Make sure this type of preparation is included on paint and body work estimates.

Painters must plan in advance for areas subject to overspray. Masking paper and tape protect the area at the base of the windshield. Paper has been removed from the windows to allow the driver to see while the car was moved to a different area for sanding.

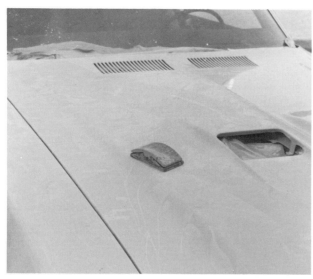

After this Buick was painted, detailed sanding removed minute flaws and slight imperfections. Good auto paint shops spend much more time sanding than painting.

Terry Skiple's ultimate hand-applied paint treatment includes two applications of polishing compound, two passes with sealer/glaze and two to three coats of pure carnauba protection wax. The paint was so smooth after applying that treatment to the driver's side of this 300ZX hood that it was difficult getting the towel to stay in place for the picture.

A power buffer polishes a car much faster than by hand. Be sure you use a glaze or sealer wax designed for machine application. The amount of wax spread on the top section of this Nissan 300ZX is just right, as is the size of the area to be buffed. Because the detailer will have to lean on the side of the car to reach all sections of the roof, it is important his or her clothes do not contain hard buttons or other objects which might scratch. The buffer's electrical cord could be placed over the detailer's shoulder to prevent it from dragging on the roof edge.

If, however, polishing doesn't bring up the shine or you find yourself polishing into primer, it is too late—the car needs a new paint job.

Introducing polishes and waxes

Determining the correct product to use for restoring shine is not always easy. For the most part, there are rubbing and polishing compounds, sealers and glazes, one-step cleaner waxes and protecting waxes.

It is hard to find two car people who agree on any specific product. An individual will find one product that works best and refuse to try anything new. You will just have to try different brands until you find one that suits your needs.

To help solve this dilemma, consult the table below as a quick general reference. In the following pages, we will discuss the use of each type of product.

Problem	Solution
Heavy oxidation	Try a sealer and glaze first. If results are not satisfactory, use polishing compound or Meguiar's Professional Cleaner #4. Follow with sealer and glaze to remove swirls; then wax for protection.
Moderate oxidation	Use liquid polish for a quick fix, or one-step cleaner wax. Best results are with sealer and glaze, then wax.
Light oxidation	Use one-step cleaner wax or sealer and glaze, then wax.
No oxidation	Use one-step cleaner wax or plain wax.

Doing the job by hand
Compounds

Two compounds are available: rubbing and polishing. These products come as a paste and are designed for hand application. They contain grit that removes dead paint, wipes out stubborn stains and removes the toughest of paint blemishes. They are used as a last resort before sanding.

Since rubbing compound is so very strong and gritty, I cannot see why or where you would ever

Apply polishing compound in a straight, back-and-forth pattern to prevent unnecessary swirls. Every time you touch the car with a wash mitt, drying towel, wax applicator or wax removing cloth, always move your hand in this same back-and-forth pattern.

have to use it. Polishing compound is strong enough for any job you should come across. Use polishing compound *only after* you have tried a glaze or one-step wax. You see, the objective here is to renew the paint while doing the least damage. Polishing compound will remove more paint than sealer and glaze or one-step cleaner wax. Why remove more paint than necessary?

If glaze or one-step cleaner wax doesn't work, apply polishing compound according to the instructions on the label. When rubbing on the car, use a back-and-forth motion as opposed to a circular one. Circular movement causes swirls that will have to be removed later and require more work. Do a small section at a time, one half of the hood, for instance. Let dry, and buff with a clean cloth. One application

is generally enough, but don't be afraid to try again if results are not satisfactory.

The same method works equally well to remove deep scratches. Concentrate on the scratch, and then work on the area around it to blend the surface and color together.

Polishing compound does not fill small cracks in newly exposed paint. Glazes and sealers fill cracks and scratches, which helps to make the surface shine and feel smooth. Polish is not a wax, either. It will not protect the paint against sun and weather. To accomplish these goals, you must apply coats of sealer and glaze and then protecting wax after using compounds.

Liquid polishes

Eagle 1 Car Cleaner & Conditioner, Turtle Wax Color Back and Meguiar's Professional Cleaner #4 are liquid polishes designed for hand application. These products use cleaning solvents to remove dead paint and imbedded dirt not removed by washing. They are advertised as safer than rubbing and polishing compounds for removing oxidation and water spots. I'm not convinced they work as well, or last as long, as an application of polishing compound for severely oxidized paint. For lighter oxidation problems, though, they work fine and are quick and easy to apply. As with polishing compound, you must understand that these products do not protect the paint. You must apply wax afterward for protection.

I would use one of these products for a quick fix on a regular driver. Application can be made in about an hour, followed by a quick wax with a one-step cleaner wax.

One-step cleaner waxes

For those cars with good paint, a one-step cleaner wax is quick and easy to use. It usually comes in liquid form. You can remove slight oxidation, hide swirls and give paint some protection, all in one application. These products are perfect for people who like to maintain their ride on a consistent basis, waxing at least once a month.

Meguiar's Car Cleaner Wax works very well; Wentworth refuses to use anything else. In addition to waxing, he uses it to remove everything from road tar to sticker glue. To maintain good paint protection, he waxes a different part of his car with every wash, which is once a week.

You cannot expect a one-step cleaner wax to do the same job as a two-step polish and wax, nor can you expect it to last as long. But, to reach a high level of shine with protection in a short amount of time, you can't beat a one-step cleaner wax.

One-step cleaner waxes are good for those car enthusiasts that wash and wax their cars on a frequent basis. They also work well to remove slight scratches and marks left by moldings. Paste waxes can harden if improperly stored for lengthy periods and could cause scratches if applied in that condition.

Note the straight back-and-forth pattern in which Meguiar's Car Cleaner Wax was applied to this 944 roof.

This wax dries to a haze and does not present the powdery residue so common with most waxes.

While waxing, use body lines and seams as guides to divide the body into sections. Here, a small rectangular household sponge is used to apply wax along the seam of

a Porsche sunroof. Be careful not to get wax on the molding surrounding the sunroof; it is difficult to remove and adds unnecessary work to the process.

Meguiar's Professional Sealer & Reseal Glaze is just one of a number of polish and wax products available. This product is designed to remove swirls and minor oxidation and is great for the car which is often maintained but has been let go for a couple of months. Follow this with a good carnauba protection wax for long-lasting results.

Apply this wax in the same manner as any other, in a back-and-forth motion as opposed to a circular one. Always apply it in the shade, making sure the temperature of the paint is no higher than ambient temperature. The label on Meguiar's Car Cleaner Wax states that the entire car can be waxed in one application or one section at a time. The choice is yours. Most car folks like to wax a section at a time, removing dry wax from one section before applying fresh wax to another.

Complete and uniform application is most important. Set a pattern for yourself before you get started. Do one half of one side of the hood first, then the other. Split the front quarter panel at the center of the wheel. Use ridges in the body design as dividers, as well as cracks at the doors and trunk lid. This system will help you maintain equal and complete coverage.

Sealer and glaze polishes

Polishing compound is needed for severe oxidation. Liquid polish relies on chemicals to remove oxidation and shine paint. One-step cleaner wax is

Eagle 1 Ultra Glaze & Sealer did a fine job on this side of a neglected 300ZX hood. It quickly and easily removed the residue of tree sap and bird droppings after washing and brought back a deep, lustrous shine.

good for light oxidation and swirls. But what about moderate oxidation and scratches?

In this case, use a sealer and glaze, such as Meguiar's Professional Sealer & Reseal Glaze #7. Once again, this is a polish, which will require application of a protective wax after the glaze's application and removal.

Sealer and glaze is recommended for a deep, long-lasting, swirl-free shine. The fine grit inside the polish removes oxidation, fills cracks and works out minor blemishes and scratches. Eagle 1 Ultra Glaze & Sealer is another such polish intended to shine paint that is basically in good shape.

Before using polishing compound, I recommend you try one of these sealer and glaze products first. The fine grit removes less paint and allows gradual polishing, as opposed to compound's immediate polishing and heavy paint removal. If you are forced to use polishing compound because of the condition of the paint, plan to polish again using a sealer and glaze. It will remove all swirls, fill microscopic scratches left behind after polishing and leave the paint in perfect, or near perfect, condition. Follow up with wax.

Protective waxes

Good paint needs wax to help keep it oily because paint never really dries. Paint also needs to breathe, and wax helps keep pores open. Paint was originally put on cars to keep them from rusting; wax preserves the paint, inhibiting oxidation.

It is difficult to recommend one brand of wax over another. Most car people agree that any product that highlights carnauba wax as the base ingredient is good. Meguiar's Yellow Paste Wax and Eagle 1 Carnuba Paste Wax clearly note on their labels that they are specifically intended for use on cleaned and polished surfaces. Two coats of wax are better than a single heavy one. Application is the same as for polish—use a back-and-forth motion on small sections.

The lasting quality of wax varies with climate, sun exposure and temperature. By far, carnauba-based waxes last the longest, generally three to six months, depending on such factors as weather, parking conditions, car cover use, maintenance and car wash soap. In summer, the roof, trunk lid and hood need the most protection. This is due to the penetrating rays of the sun and high temperatures. In winter, the sides take a beating from road grime, salt and sand. It is a good idea to keep this in mind and concentrate more frequent waxing on those areas affected during each season.

Carnauba-based waxes can be difficult to remove during cold weather and may leave streaks and clouds. You will have to experiment with them. Ideally, wax in a heated garage or shop to minimize problems. If not, you may have to settle for a one-step cleaner wax during those times.

Liquid waxes containing carnauba generally last as long as the pastes. Spray waxes may not last as long because the contents must be thinned to allow the formula to flow out of the tiny nozzle opening.

Automobiles should be waxed four times a year. A cleaner, or cutting, wax is recommended twice a year to remove old and yellowing wax. Newer cars with high-tech paint jobs need wax specifically designed for them.

The ultra wax job for paints other than high-tech is two applications of polish, two of cleaner wax and three of carnauba. It will probably take two days to do the job, but the results will be brilliantly noticed.

Carnauba-based waxes offer the longest-lasting protection. You can generally count on them to last at least three months under moderate conditions. In severe conditions, such as summer desert heat, plan to wax once a month for optimum protection.

Polysealants

New car dealerships are famous for offering polysealant treatments to customers purchasing a new car. Polyglycoat and similar products combine polymers, silicones and waxes into a single treatment that is supposed to last up to a year, as long as it is rejuvenated according to schedule (sometimes every six months). For the most part, they can outlast regular wax, even carnauba, if conditions are right.

Some car people wonder about the effects this type of sealer has on paint. They believe paint, especially lacquer, has to breathe and should not be covered with anything but carnauba. Others wonder about the silicones in polysealants and their effects on future paint jobs or touch-ups. Can the silicones penetrate body fillers and metal, making a new paint job or touch-up difficult? Mycon dislikes silicones because they cause fisheyes in new paint.

It is generally accepted that polysealants might be good for those car owners who do not intend to wax their cars with any frequency.

Special products for high-tech paints

Clear coats and urethane paint finishes need special polish and wax. Meguiar's Professional Hi-Tech Cleaner #2 is designed to remove oxidation and harsh scratches and to restore color on clear coats and urethane paint finishes. Since the instructions recommend that you follow with Meguiar's Professional Hi-Tech Swirl Remover #9, you know that this cleaner is intended to remove heavy oxidation. Try the less abrasive swirl remover Meguiar's #9 first to see how it works. If it does the job, fine; forget the cleaner. If not, use the cleaner, and follow up with the swirl remover to polish the finish to perfection.

Complete the job with a nonabrasive carnauba-based wax, such as Meguiar's Hi-Tech Yellow Wax #26. The end result will be a deep paint finish as smooth as silk and as clear as glass.

Wax applicators

The best wax applicator I have come across is a small rectangular sponge, measuring about 3 by 4½ inches. These are commonly found in supermarkets in bags of four or more. Wentworth has used them

A small rectangular sponge is great for waxing inside the seam of a 944 sunroof. The size and shape of the sponge allow excellent control in tight spaces.

for years. He likes them because of their handy size, their low cost and their straight edges that allow controlled wax application around emblems, trim, rubber moldings and vinyl tops. As they get dirty, simply rinse with water. Throw away the torn or damaged; they are cheap to replace.

You can use other applicators as you wish. Soft towels, baby diapers and old cotton shirts work fine. Fold the cloths into workable sizes. As they become soiled, refold to a clean side. Some waxes come with applicators. These are fine too, as long as you keep them clean.

Putting wax or polish on the car requires no great skill. There are some things to keep in mind, however. Again, more is not better. Two light applications are much better than one heavy one. This is what "Use sparingly" means on the label. Always try to use the same straight, back-and-forth motion whenever rubbing on the paint. This reduces the chance of spider webbing and swirls.

When applying polish or wax, slow down around emblems and trim. Wax, smeared on these and other obstacles, makes more work for you later during removal. If this wax is not removed, the car will not look as good. If you apply wax with a cloth, use your finger to guide around emblems and antenna bases.

Doing the job with a machine

Many professional detailers use buffing machines to polish paint. In a sense, they have to. Polishing by hand is time-consuming. They cannot afford to spend that much time on each car and expect to make money. Because of the workload and the competition, they must detail cars as quickly as possible while keeping quality at its best. Hence, the reason for special equipment like the buffer.

Buffer, pad, polish and wax

Buffers can be purchased at hardware and tool stores for about $175 or rented at a rental yard for

A good wax job will cause water to bead. The lack of wax permits water to lay flat. Some car people judge the need for waxing by the way water beads on the car. Tight beads that are well rounded at the top denote good wax protection. Beads that have flattened out usually signal a need for wax.

around $10 a day. Either way, you'll have to buy buffing pads; rental yards will not rent used pads.

Before choosing a buffer, consider the rpm it delivers. For a novice, I recommend a buffer with no more than 1750 rpm. The slower pad speed is more forgiving than buffers producing up to 3000 rpm. The slightest mistake using a buffer will result in paint burns, dislodged moldings, broken windshield wipers or a broken radio antenna. You'll have to decide if the potential time savings is worth the risks of using a buffer.

Two types of buffing pads are available: a cutting pad and a finishing pad. The cutting pad is used with a fine sealer and glaze liquid polish to remove oxidation and scratches. Results, especially on dark colors, will look great but include fine swirls. After buffing with the cutting pad, you should buff again with the soft finishing pad and a nonabrasive liquid

wax. The end result will be nearly perfect, with no sign of swirls.

The polish you use with the buffer should state that it is recommended for machine application. Meguiar's Professional Machine Cleaner #1 is specifically designed for machine use on paints with severe oxidation, scratches, water spots and other serious paint problems. Meguiar's Professional New Car Glaze #5 can be applied by machine or hand and is designed for paints with less than severe oxidation. The difference between the two is the amount of grit in them. Cleaner #1 obviously contains more than Glaze #5. As explained earlier, it may be a good idea to try the less gritty polish first, in hopes that it will get the job done and remove less paint.

Wax for the finishing pad should also be in liquid form. I have had good luck using The Treat-

One half of this Pantera top is about as big an area as a detailer should attempt to buff in one pass. The amount of wax spread on the top is good and the detailer is wearing a sweatshirt which presents no scratch hazards. The buffer should be maneuvered from front to back gradually mov- *ing closer to the edge. Three passes over the entire half of the top should be sufficient. Note that a cutting pad is attached to the buffer to remove light oxidation and some minor scratches.*

ment and other carnauba-based liquid and cream waxes like Meguiar's Professional Hi-Tech Yellow Wax #26. The combination of soft, nonabrasive wax and soft finishing pad removes minute swirls and leaves paint with a deep luster and mirror finish. For added protection, apply a final coat of carnauba wax by hand. The results will be stunning.

Using the buffer

If you have never used a buffer but are determined to give it a try, practice on a friend's old beater before tackling your classic Ferrari. Immediately understand that if the buffer is improperly placed on top of a fender ridge or pressed too tightly in a door handle pocket, you will buff paint down to the primer in a split second. This is called a paint burn.

Polish, like Meguiar's #1, comes in a plastic bottle with a spout cap. Spread three lines of polish over the two-foot-by-two-foot section you intend to buff. I have had good results starting on the back

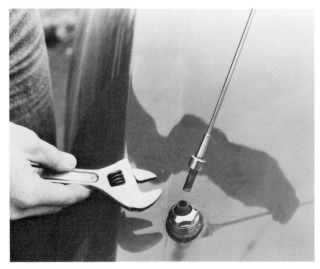

The high speed of the spinning buffing pad can damage radio antennas, wiper blades, emblems and lettering. Remove obstacles, if possible, like this Corvette radio antenna before buffing.

After buffing with the cutting pad and a sealer/glaze, buff again with a finishing pad and a soft swirl-removing wax or a creamy carnauba wax. This process will remove swirls and leave the paint in mirror-like condition, even in the sun.

Three to four lines of wax are plenty for any section to be buffed. The position of the buffing pad is correct for moving from right to left as you look at the picture. Tilt the left side of the pad up when moving toward the left, and the right side up when going right. Letting the pad sit flat takes away control. The angle of this pad is just about right; it could be let down slightly and should not be raised any higher than what it is.

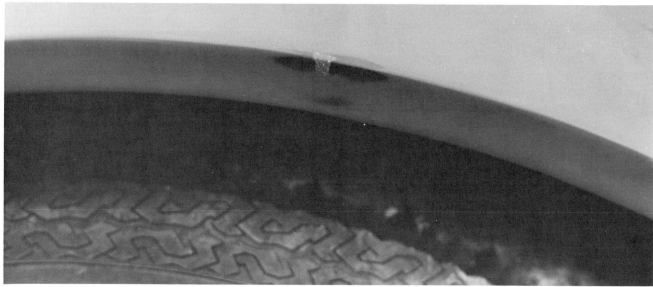

This is a paint burn caused by the buffing pad resting directly on top of the fender ridge. The paint has been buffed away, exposing primer. Buff up to ridges and never on top. To buff the section under the burn, throttle the buffer on and off quickly to reduce the pad speed and move gently over the area applying very little pressure, if any. The size of this paint burn requires the expertise of a professional paint shop. If only the light-colored area were exposed, you could mask off everything around it and apply a number of coats of touch-up paint. When dry, you could sand with #600 or lighter wet-and-dry sandpaper, with masking tape in place. When the top of the new paint was almost even with surrounding paint, you could use repeated applications of polishing compound to smooth and blend the spot to match the surrounding area.

half of the hood, driver's side. Then move to the front half of that part of the hood, to the front fender, roof, driver's door and so on around the car in a counterclockwise direction. I am right-handed, which may have a bearing on this pattern. Buff a section at a time, using body lines, ridges and trim as guides. Buff until the wax is gone and the paint shines, usually about three to four passes over the entire section.

Keep the machine moving at all times. Allowing the pad to spin on one spot will surely result in a burn. Buff up to ridges, never on top. Stay away from bodyside moldings. If the pad catches the trim in just the right spot, it will tear it loose from the car. The same is true for windshield wipers and emblems. Use extra caution around the radio antenna. More than one detailer has been struck on the side of the face by the whipping action of an antenna that

This is an improper way to buff. Resting the buffing pad on top of this ridge will surely cause a paint burn, possibly along the entire section of the ridge. Buff up to the ridge with the back of the pad while buffing the top of the fender, and up to the ridge with the front of the pad while buffing the side of the fender. Buffing on top of the ridge does absolutely no good.

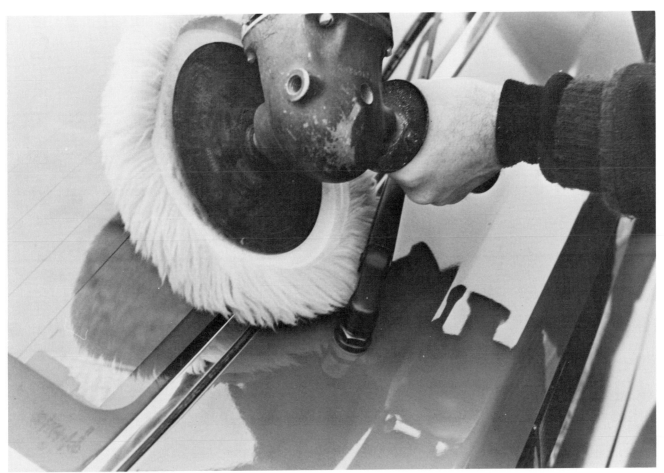

The buffing pad can be easily ruined and the rear wiper blade on this 300ZX damaged with improper buffing along this area. Throttle the buffer on and off to slow pad speed while buffing paint in these types of close quarters. Plan your approach and trigger the buffer on for only a

fraction of a second to get the pad spinning. Then, let the pad free-spin without power. The pad speed will be significantly reduced and there will be no torque from the machine pushing or pulling the buffer into the obstacles.

has been touched by the fast-spinning pad. It is best to remove the antenna (if easily accessible) as well as the trim, emblems and windshield wipers.

Buff a section more than once when results are not satisfactory after the first attempt. This may be prevalent when you start by using a mild polish. If results are no better after the second pass, try a polish with more grit. This common occurrence is the reason why most professional detailers have an assortment of polishes on hand. Many have special blends they have experimented with over the years. Still, even the professionals like to start with a mild polish, graduating to a grittier one as needed.

The electrical cord on the buffer generally isn't much of an obstacle. You may notice a problem with its dragging on the fender while you buff the hood. In this case, drape it over your shoulder to keep it off the car. Also drape it over your shoulder while buffing the roof and trunk lid.

Once the buffing pad makes contact with the polish, you will quickly notice the polish splatter.

Tiny spots of polish will eventually cover you, the car and nearby walls. Be prepared. If you are buffing in the tight quarters of your garage, you may consider covering tools and other items within six feet of the car. For you, I suggest an apron and glasses.

Periodically, the pad will cake with polish. Use a pad spur or dull screwdriver to clean it. Carefully, lay the buffer down while maintaining a firm grasp on the handle. Reposition your hand on the handle so your thumb can activate the trigger. Turn on the machine, making sure your grip is still secure. Gently press the spur, or screwdriver, into the pad, starting at the outer edge and moving toward the center. You will see the color of the pad change from the color of the car (removed oxidation and paint) to its natural off-white. Do this about three times, and the pad should be clean. During the buffing procedure, you should clean the pad three or four times.

Buffing the sides of the car is the most difficult, because of the awkward position you'll be working

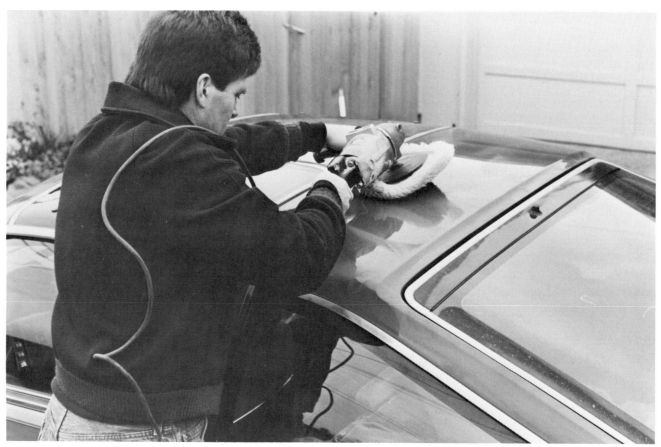

To prevent the electrical cord from rubbing against the edge of the roof while buffing, drape it over your shoulder and out of the way. The position of the buffing pad denotes that it is going from left to right. This is a good angle for the pad.

in. When bending down, I am most comfortable if I reverse the position of my left hand, the one holding the handle extension. Instead of grasping the handle with my thumb next to the buffing head, I hold the handle with my little finger next to the head and my thumb away from the head. I also rest my left forearm on my left knee. This works especially well while buffing the lower sections of the sides. Find a comfortable position for yourself, always keeping in mind the hazards near emblems and trim.

When buffing is complete, your car will shine nicely. It will also be covered with fuzz from the pad and polish splatter. You can clean it up with a soft cloth such as a diaper or piece of flannel. Buffing

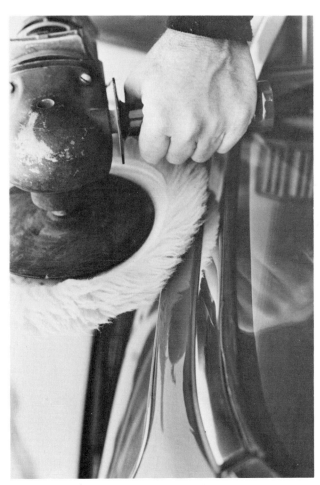

Use the same technique for buffing along narrow strips as you would around obstacles. Throttle the buffer on and off to reduce pad speed and apply little pressure. Use the edge of the pad for optimum results.

Buffing pads become clogged with wax as you buff. Special spurs designed for pad cleaning are available at auto body paint and supply stores. In lieu of the spur, you can use a dull screwdriver. With the buffer securely held in the position demonstrated, turn it on and gently press the screwdriver into the nap. You will note lint and wax residue coming off the pad. Do this about four to five times during the buffing, or whenever the pad becomes caked with wax.

This is a comfortable position for a right-handed person to hold the buffer while buffing the lower side sections of the car. The left hand has been reversed with the thumb toward the outside of the machine as opposed to being on the inside during other buffing.

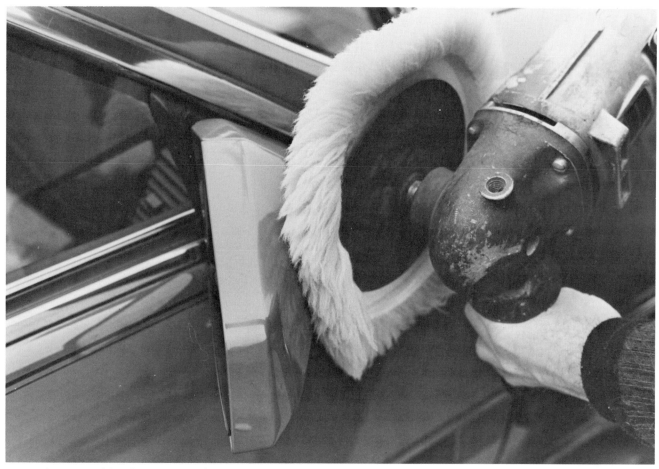

Painted mirrors, like this 300ZX side mirror, may need buffing. Use the buffer lightly and throttle it on and off to *reduce pad speed and help you maintain complete control. The edge of the pad works best in this awkward position.*

with the finishing pad and wax will not be as messy. For the easiest final cleaning, hand wax the entire car with a liquid or cream carnauba product.

Color sanding

Color sanding is done with very fine wet-and-dry sandpaper (#600 and finer) and lots of water. Auto painters use this process to smooth paint to perfection, removing orange peel, fisheyes and other blemishes. This can only be done on cars that have enough paint to spare, as a lot of it will be sanded off.

I feel color sanding is a much too drastic method of polishing—just as using rubbing compound is. It is just too easy to sand through to the primer. In special cases, done by an experienced paint person, color sanding can save a paint job. As with using polishing compound, a color sander must go over the car again with sealer and glaze and then wax, more than once.

I suggest you stick with the reliable method of polish, sealer and glaze and wax.

Removing polish and wax

Just about everybody knows how to remove wax once it has dried on the car. You use a soft cloth and wipe off. Simple enough. The cloth you use should be very soft and absolutely nonabrasive. Car enthusiasts use old baby diapers, cheesecloth, discarded cotton T-shirts, bath towels or plain, white flannel purchased at the local fabric store.

Whichever cloth you use, cut it into manageable two-foot squares (if need be) and fold it into quarters. Use one side to remove the bulk of the wax and follow with a clean side to pick up anything left over. Don't try to get more out of a side than practical. As the cloth soils, just refold. If need be, get another one. You have spent almost an entire day polishing and waxing your car, don't fudge now. As with washing and waxing, use the same back-and-forth motion—don't rub in circles.

A one-inch paintbrush with the bristles cut to about one-half to three-quarters of an inch works great for removing wax from emblems, decals, mirrors, light lenses, louvers and antenna bases. Use it as you wipe off wax. The stubby soft bristles have the strength to remove even the most stubborn wax build-up. You might lay a piece of duct tape around the metal band securing the bristles. This will help to prevent accidental paint chips while you are busy removing wax from tight spots.

Fixing paint blemishes and chips

The best way to protect paint is with a good coat of wax. The rule of thumb is to wax when water stops beading on the surface. That rule is OK, but many think waiting for water to stop beading is too late. They prefer to wax when beads of water start to flatten out, losing the firm round shape that they maintain on fresh wax. Others prefer to wax once a month with no regard to water beads.

Paint blemishes

Bird and bee droppings, splattered insects, road tar and tree sap all blemish paint quickly. A good coat of wax helps, but removing these hazards as soon as possible is the best way to prevent paint blemishes. Cold water and a towel should be sufficient to remove most of these problems. The harder ones can be removed with one-step wax.

If a bird dropping has been allowed to sit on your car for days, you may have to polish and wax to remove the blemish. You may have to go over the spot a number of times to remove the mark and blend the blemish into surrounding paint. Use a fine-grit polish like sealer and glaze three to four times before breaking out the polishing compound.

Paint chips

Cars that are driven are subject to paint chips; there is no way of avoiding them. You can apply a clear plastic guard along the bottom of the rear quarter panel, designed to protect paint. These are standard items available at auto parts houses.

Minor paint chips can be repaired using touch-up paint. Most touch-up colors are readily available at auto parts stores. If not, a paint store can mix a quart matching the stock color of your car by using the color code from the vehicle identification number. They can also mix custom paints as needed. Old-school car buffs used the bottom end of a cardboard match stick to apply touch-up paint. I suggest you purchase a fine artist's paintbrush. Apply more than one coat of paint, allowing each to properly dry before the next coat. The painted area should stand higher than the rest of the finish around it.

When the paint has dried according to the label (generally about a week), mask it off and sand with a very fine grit of wet-and-dry sandpaper, #600 or higher, and plenty of water. Masking tape around the painted chip protects surrounding paint. When the bulk of paint has been reduced to the level of the

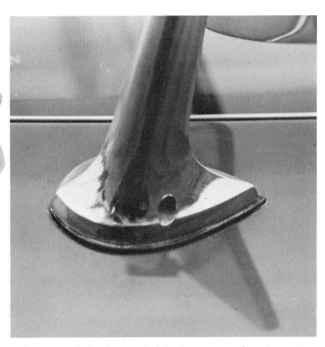

Wax around the base of this Corvette side mirror is a subtle item that prevents the car from looking crisp. Use the cut-off paintbrush to remove such wax residue from the base, as well as the slots of any mounting screws.

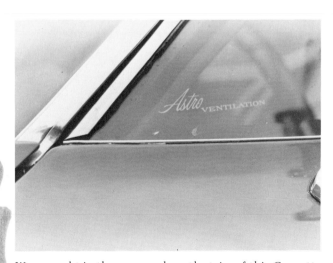

Wax caught in the groove along the trim of this Corvette door glass is another subtle item that unnecessarily detracts from the overall appearance of an otherwise fine automobile. The cut-off paintbrush or a toothbrush will quickly remove this kind of an eyesore.

finish, remove the masking tape and follow up with a couple of light applications of sealer and glaze. Don't worry about waxing for about a month. This will give the paint plenty of time to cure. For chips and blemishes that have become major paint problems, consult a reputable body and paint shop.

Waxing new paint

New paint jobs don't need waxing immediately. The painter should advise you about waxing when you pick up the car. If not, ask. For the most part, you should wait at least a month before applying wax to enamel jobs, much longer for high-tech finishes.

Racing stripes and pinstripes

Painted racing stripes and pinstripes are cared for the same way you wash, polish and wax body paint. Tape-type stripes can be waxed along with paint. Be sure to apply wax in the direction of the stripe to minimize wax build-up along the stripe's edge. Residual dry wax is removed from edges with your thumbnail inserted inside a towel or a cut-off paintbrush.

Special accessories

Special accessories like air dams, spoilers and wheel flares are maintained the same as comparable parts. Namely, painted accessories can be washed with car wash soap, polished with sealer and glaze and waxed with a carnauba-based paste or cream. Rubber and vinyl accessories are cleaned the same and protected with a light coat of dressing.

If you doubt the use of a dressing or wax on a particular part, apply the product on an inconspicuous spot. If the results are satisfactory, so be it. If not, try a different product or consult an auto body paint and supply store or a professional detailer.

Rock chips are unsightly, especially on dark-colored vehicles. Clear plastic guards along lower body panels protect paint and work well to prevent rock chips. These stand-ard items are available at most auto parts stores and are custom-made for various makes and models.

Chapter 7

Underbody

Next time you drive by a used car lot, look at the fenderwells and visible underbody of cars on the front line. Do they look dirty? Does the back of the front fenderwell complement the wheel and tire? Is the visible frame running under the doors in fine condition? Cleaning and painting these areas freshen the entire automobile.

Squat down and look at your car from ground level. Notice the parts that catch your eye. Frame, exhaust pipes, mufflers, suspension and fender-

Skiple's De Tomaso Pantera looks great—except for a few subtle items. The fenderwells would look much better painted black, as well as the exposed exhaust. Transaxle parts need to be cleaned and painted, and the chrome exhaust tips need to be polishing. The license plate frame is a perfect size and blends well with the chrome "detomaso" and Pantera emblems.

The lower side body of this Pantera is black and needs detailing—note how it detracts from the overall appearance of the car. Cleaning and repainting will improve the area and enhance the entire side view of this fine automobile. The light-colored horizontal strips extending past the front and rear parts at the bottom of the door are strips of masking tape.

Doesn't the rocker panel look much better cleaned up and painted? Just a few minutes' work got rid of the light-colored eyesore and helped make the entire side of the car appear crisp and sanitary.

wells don't have to be unsightly and draw your eye away from the rest of the car. Clean, paint and shine those items so they add to the overall appearance of your fine automobile.

Thorough rinsing

During the preliminary washing, you did your first cleaning of the underbody and fenderwells. Let's refocus on these areas. Fenderwells are constantly bombarded by road hazards thrown up by the tires. During winter driving, salt, sand and mud are splattered throughout fenderwells and open areas close by. These include steering and suspension parts, wheel hubs, frame and bumpers. Pockets of grime will retain moisture and give rust a start; this is why body cancer generally starts at the rear bottom of quarter panels, just behind fenderwells.

Thorough rinsing isn't just a quick spray with a garden hose. It is a concentrated effort to wash away every loose bit of grit, sand, salt and road grime. The most effective method requires raising the car, bracing with jack stands, pulling wheels and flushing completely. You should do this at the end of each winter driving period. This is also a great time to wash the wheels, front and back.

The inside lips of fenderwell edges are prime spots for dirt build-up. Feel for this with your fingers, break loose with a brush and flush with water. The top of the front wheel support bracket is another likely place to find dirt and grime build-up. Inside bumpers, on tops of axles and frame are also areas exhibiting build-up.

Cleaning

Normally, garden hose pressure through a nozzle is sufficient. A power washer is better, although you must spray cautiously to avoid paint and undercoating damage. The plastic-bristled brush

Fenderwell areas need to be rinsed thoroughly. Access to the front fenderwells on McKee's 1972 Jaguar is easy with the tilt-up hood. Use plenty of water with nozzle pressure to dislodge dirt, grit, leaves, pine needles and any other debris caught in the various cracks and crevices. Foreign material will absorb and retain moisture which can lead to a starting place for rust.

A toothbrush is used to clean the inner lip on the front fenderwell of a Jaguar tilt-up hood. These kinds of ridges are found on most inner fenderwells and are very susceptible to dirt and road salt build-up. Every time you wash your car, you should maneuver the garden hose inside the fenderwell to remove dirt and road salt from these areas. Scrub the area with a brush once a month and plan to repaint or undercoat at least once a year.

does a good job of removing stubborn build-up, especially when combined with a cleaner like Simple Green. This brush can be used on the inside of the fender lips without much risk of scratching exterior paint. Use a toothbrush to clean slots on screws attaching trim to fender lips.

The visible frame under doors should also be cleaned with a brush, soap and water. The chapter on preliminary washing describes a pattern for side frame cleaning that helps you maintain a dry working surface during the process.

The underbody below rear bumpers is another spot that needs cleaning. Corvette designs allow that part of the car to be most visible. Use an old mitt and scrub brush to remove dirt and unsightly grime. This includes muffler, visible shocks and axle housing.

The once-a-year or first-time cleaning may require more than brushing. The front fenderwell of Wentworth's newly acquired 1970 Buick GS 455 had never been completely cleaned or detailed. Dirt on the A-frame was caked an inch high. A putty knife had to be used to remove the heavy stuff and

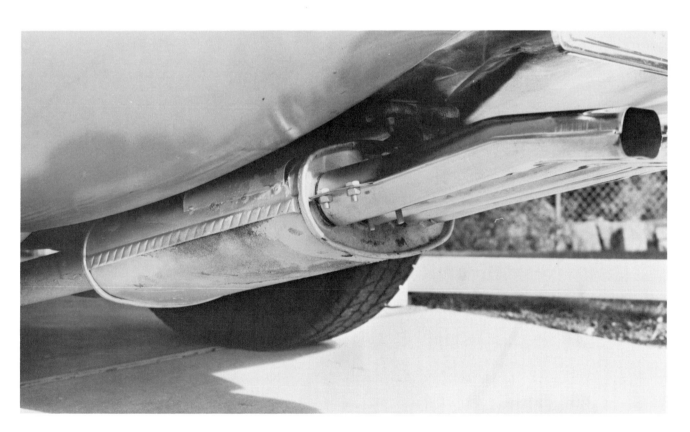

This highly visible Jaguar muffler has been painted with heat-resistant silver to help it blend with the bottom of the car. Use a paint block to protect body and chrome parts while painting. Note how cleanly the underbody is maintained. The painted underbody should be waxed just like any other painted part of the car.

lots of brushing with cleaner was needed to reach clean metal.

Clean everything inside the fenderwell. Brake lines, bleeder valves, light buckets and wiring come clean with soap and water. Use a toothbrush in tight spots and a plastic brush on flat surfaces. Slight rust formations are cleaned with #00 steel wool and WD-40. Along with rust prevention, cleaning prepares those surfaces for paint.

Sanding should not be necessary, unless building a show car. In those cases, consider removing unsightly, nonoriginal undercoating and every speck of dirt. You may have to dismantle front end parts to have them sandblasted, painted or buffed.

Fenderwells
Masking before painting

Front fenderwells vary with each car. Some include open areas to the engine compartment, exposing the block and exhaust manifold. Others are fairly tight, exposing only struts and steering assemblies. All have brake, fender lip and hub parts that need masking.

Front end and steering assemblies, as well as drum brake housings, can be painted semigloss black. Two or three coats are sufficient. Mask lugs, brake fluid bleeder valves, grease fittings, brake lines and everything you don't want painted. Three-quarter-inch masking tape is a good workable size.

Use newspaper for large masking jobs around wheel hubs and openings to the engine.

Chrome-trimmed and painted fender lips should be masked, even though controlled painting will prevent overspray. Wide masking tape covers these thin surfaces with one pass. You can also try four-inch strips of newspaper and masking tape. Mask mudflaps too.

Older classics may have years of accumulated grease, grime and road dirt built up on front end suspension parts. Use a putty knife, if necessary, to remove the layers of goop. Afterward, spray the area with an all-purpose cleaner and scrub with a brush. Rinse often and continue the process until all parts are clean.

The use of heavy-duty lift and jack stands made it easy to clean, paint and undercoat the fenderwells and visible underbody of Wentworth's 1970 Buick GS 455 convertible. Never work on a vehicle with a wheel removed unless it is properly secured on jack stands. Trusting bumper jacks is a giant mistake.

This front Jaguar fenderwell looks good. Its condition has been maintained with frequent cleaning and touch-up painting. The dark solid color helps to accent the chrome spoked wheel, raised-white-letter tire and silver body.

After this Buick front fenderwell was cleaned, the fenderwell lip, grease fitting and lugs were masked in preparation for painting and undercoating. Mask as necessary to keep fittings and threads clean and to allow silver parts to stand out in contrast.

Black fenderwells look good compared to rust-colored ones. The real difference is noticed in detail work. To break the monotony of solid black, allow grease fittings, brake connections and the like to remain unpainted; it adds color to the area.

Painting

The type of paint to use on fenderwells is debatable. Use a semigloss with rust-inhibiting agents, such as Rustoleum. Of equal importance is surface cleanliness. Most paints will not adhere to grease and will fall off with painted dirt as it is vibrated loose.

It's preferable to paint in warmer temperatures. Heating the spray can in a sink of hot water expands the propellant and thins the paint. This helps paint go farther and you can apply smoother coats. *Never heat a can of spray paint in a pot of water on the stove. The added heat can cause the propellant to expand too much, bursting the can and possibly resulting in injury or a fire.*

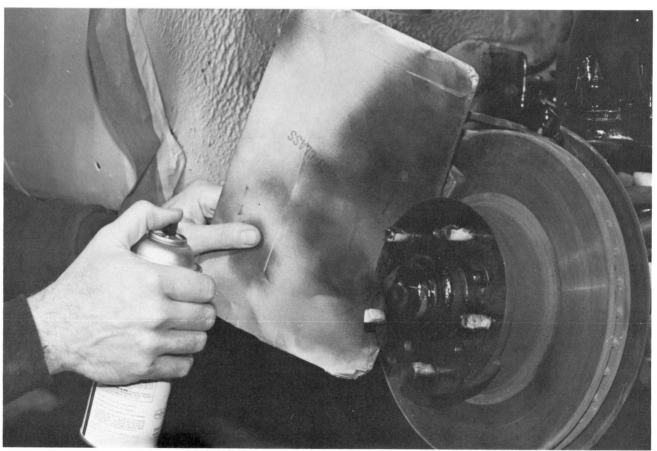

A manila envelope is used as a paint block to protect the brake disc while painting the hub. A paper bag could have been opened up, slit in the middle and placed over the hub to cover the disk in one piece. Using the thumb to operate paint can nozzles is a preferred method with some detailers. They feel this position is more comfortable and allows better control of the spray.

Since most spray cans carry a warning not to expose can or contents to temperatures over 120 degrees Fahrenheit, hot water should be from the tap only. At no time should it be too hot for your hand. The objective is to warm paint, as it flows and adheres much better at 80 to 100 degrees Fahrenheit than at 50 or 60 degrees.

Follow the directions on the can and spray with even strokes. Continue with additional coats until reaching the desired effect. Always let the first coat dry before applying the next. Remove accidental overspray with glaze wax on painted surfaces, lacquer thinner on others.

Undercoating

Many times, car people prefer to use undercoating on fenderwells instead of paint. Paint looks good on front end and suspension parts but flat on previously undercoated fenderwells. You will need two spray cans to adequately undercoat all four fenderwells.

I suggest you heat the cans first by immersing in a sink of hot water for about five minutes. Apply the undercoating as you would spray paint. You will notice the spray immediately bubble once it touches the fenderwell surface. Overall results will be good, and fenderwells will look new.

Undercoating is not a rustproofing agent. It is intended to deaden road noise. True rustproofing requires a much more detailed process. The part has to be completely cleaned down to bare metal, and properly prepared with primers. Afterward, a rustproofing material is applied which never seems to dry or harden. Consider rustproofing for an automobile scheduled for complete dismantling and restoration. Regular drivers, and those classics intended for good weather driving, easily survive

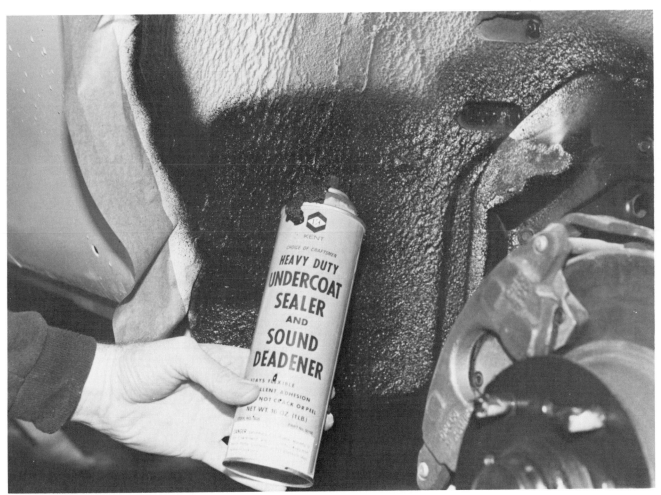

A fresh application of undercoating will make this Buick front fenderwell look new. When using undercoating, be sure to mask surrounding parts, as the pattern of the splatter spray is not nearly as confined as regular spray paint. Apply undercoating to the fenderwell and paint to suspension parts.

Masking tape and newspaper are used to protect the green Pantera body while painting the rocker panel black. Newspaper was placed over the panel with the door open.

When the door was closed, the newspaper was raised to expose the panel and guarantee complete masking protection.

This rust-colored exhaust tip should be painted with black heat-resistant paint to make it less visible and help it blend with the bottom of the car.

with fenderwells that are frequently cleaned and undercoated or painted.

Painting visible frame members

Many times, it is quite easy to paint visible frame members using a paint block instead of masking. You have to go slowly, making sure the hand that sprays the paint doesn't lag behind or rush ahead of the one holding the block. To be on the safe side, mask rocker panels with newspaper and masking tape. Again, semigloss black goes on in smooth coats and looks good.

Combating rust

Paint was originally put on cars to keep them from rusting. Salt is a predominate factor, as evidenced by severe corrosion problems on cars driven on salted roads and those in close proximity to bodies of saltwater. Pockets of dirt, leaves and other debris also retain moisture and should be removed from the car as soon as possible. Look for rust wherever moisture collects: floorboard, trunk, lower door sections, rocker panels, fenders and battery boxes.

Once you notice rust coming through paint, it is too late. That section of the body will have to be repaired at a body shop. The best way to combat rust is by not giving it a chance to start. Frequent and thorough washing is a good beginning.

While cleaning the fenderwells and underbody, closely check seams and joints for evidence of rust. Remove surface rust with a soft wire brush or sandpaper. You can also use acid-based chemicals like Oxboe to kill rust. Be sure to follow the instructions carefully. After you have removed the hazard, dry the area completely and cover with two coats of good primer paint. Afterward, paint again with semigloss black or undercoating.

George Ridderbusch likes a product called Extend. It is a one-step product that kills rust and coats metal at the same time. Extend turns rust black and dries to a rubbery texture. Being a water-based product, it does not adhere to metal as well as primer paint. Therefore, it is a good idea to recheck the area frequently and recoat metal as necessary. Ridderbusch uses it on fenderwells, frame members and around batteries.

Rustproofing products are available at most auto parts stores. Sealant sprays come in aerosol cans. They are equipped with small hoses designed for application through drain holes in doors or other holes allowing access to open cavities. The entire area must be coated and any holes made for access must be covered. Its main purpose is to prevent moisture from coming in contact with metal.

Undercoating is not designed as a rustproofer. If water is trapped between it and the metal, rust will occur. As with Extend, if it peels loose or chips off, moisture will come in contact with the metal and pose the same rust problem again.

Tailpipes

Exhaust tips and mufflers are best cleaned with SOS pads. Use heat-resistant paint in the color most appropriate, generally bright silver or black, to help the part blend with the car or truck. Exposed mufflers, like those on Corvettes, Lamborghinis and Jaguar roadsters, are plainly visible, and anything you can do to help them blend with the bottom of the car is an improvement.

The insides of tailpipes can be cleaned with rags and SOS pads. Do not use much water to rinse. If you think water has entered the pipe, simply start the car to blow it out. The inside can be painted a flat black using heat-resistant paint.

Front fenderwells present a lot of places for dirt and debris to accumulate. By rinsing fenderwells every time you wash the car, and after each lengthy drive on salted roads, you will stand a better chance of staying on top of build-up accumulations and keep rust problems at a minimum.

Chapter 8

Glass, trim and moldings

Glass

Have you ever noticed how much better an automobile seems to perform when the windows are clean? More importantly, have you ever considered clean glass to be a safety factor? Operating a motor vehicle on a rainy night, in heavy traffic, straining to see through a dirty windshield blurred by the smears of worn windshield wipers should convince you.

Removing stickers and decals

Unwanted stickers and decals should be removed before cleaning is started because you may have to use adhesive removers to loosen and dissolve glue residue. The sometimes messy process

Most window stickers are unnecessary and detract from the car's overall appearance. To remove them, try using your fingernail to loosen an edge and then peel off. Glue residue is removed with paint thinner or adhesive remover. The residue from this sticker was removed with Meguiar's Car Cleaner Wax. Stubborn stickers can be loosened with adhesive remover and as a last resort, with a razor scraper.

can smear clean windows and cause you to wash them a second time.

Stickers and decals are easier to remove from glass than paint because glass is more resistant to scratching. Try to peel them off with your fingernail. If that doesn't work, moisten a towel with sticker remover and soak the sticker to loosen the glue. Peel off as much as you can. Use the remover to take off the remaining glue. Meguiar's Car Cleaner Wax also removes glue residue quickly and easily.

As a last resort for stubborn stickers, carefully use a razor scraper. Don't try to remove the entire sticker in one swipe. Gently ease the blade into one corner of the sticker, and slowly turn it a little at a time. Use your wrist to apply pressure and not your arm. Controlled pressure is necessary to prevent the blade from slipping off the sticker and cutting into paint or upholstery.

Glass cleaners

Just as in choosing car wash soap, cleaners and wax, no two car enthusiasts can agree which window cleaner is best. Skiple sells GM products and swears by GM's glass cleaner. Mycon likes those which include ammonia, and Wentworth prefers

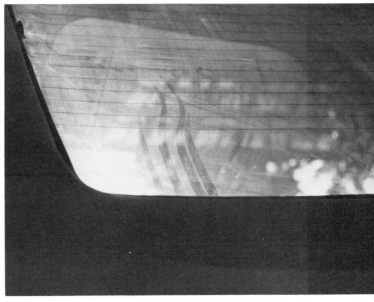

Dirty windows will make an entire vehicle feel dirty. The film on the inside of this BMW rear window was not noticed, until viewed in the sunlight at just the right angle. After cleaning, it is important to inspect each window in the sunlight and from various angles in order to spot imperfections.

This is a small assortment of glass cleaners found at an auto parts store. Some cleaners contain polish, others come with ammonia. Many detailers prefer to use clear water for glass cleaning and polish afterward with a household glass cleaner like Windex.

149

plain, clear water. I have talked to some who like TSP and to others who use liquid soap, rinse with plain water and dry with newspaper. Many car show people clean with plain water and then polish with glass cleaner. Once again, you'll have to experiment to determine which method works best for you.

Glass cleaners in spray form work fine. The only problem may be overspray. It is difficult, at best, to direct these cleaners on the inside of the windshield without spotting the dash. You may have better luck spraying one side of a clean towel, wiping the glass with it and then drying with the other side. Most glass cleaners, like Windex, are fine. Those containing ammonia tend to streak less. Sometimes, however, they tend to push a dirty film around the window causing smears. Two or three applications may be necessary.

Liquid soaps will clean, but you must go over the glass with clear water to remove the film they generally leave behind. Consider this for extra dirty windows, those used as fingerpaint canvases for small artists with sticky fingers. Keep in mind that glass cleaner will do the same job—and neither leave the same soapy film nor present the potential of etching glass.

Although TSP is a good general cleaner, it is not widely considered a glass cleaner. As such, I would be concerned about tiny grains not fully dissolved in the water. Picked up by the wash cloth, they become a scratch hazard. That, and the extra steps involved in mixing the solution, may not be worth the effort.

Clear water with a clean wash mitt is simple and easy. There is not much worry about residual films or smears. A couple of swipes with the mitt, followed by a dry towel, is sufficient in most cases.

Many detailers mix ammonia with water for glass cleaning. The ammonia cuts through grease and helps water to evaporate quickly. Not much is needed, about a capful per half bucket of water.

Regardless of what glass cleaner you use, prevent the solution from dripping on painted surfaces or upholstery. If need be, lay a clean towel over the paint, dashboard or seat, just for protection.

Glass polishing

Many car people wash windows with clear water and dry immediately with newspaper. The paper absorbs water and picks up the dirt, while the ink works as a very fine polishing compound. Be careful around light-colored cloth interiors, as the ink can rub off the paper and stain cloth door panels and seats.

Eagle 1 makes a glass cleaner and polish. It is designed to dissolve road grime, dirt, tar and oil, as well as remove film caused by cigarette smoke and vinyl vapors. Apply it like wax: pour a small amount on a damp sponge or cloth, and wipe on a

Spraying glass cleaner on windows will result in some overspray landing on other parts. It is easier to spray cleaner on one side of a towel, wipe the glass, and use a dry side to pick up moisture and residue. Hard-to-reach areas, like the lower sections of rear glass, are easier to clean using the back of your hand, as opposed to your palm.

A clean wash mitt rinsed in clear water is used to clean the lower section of a BMW windshield. Clear water works very well to clean glass and doesn't just push a film around the window like some glass cleaners tend to do. After cleaning, dry glass with a clean towel.

thin coat in a straight back-and-forth motion. Let it dry to a haze, and remove with a clean, soft cloth. It wipes off without a dusty residue.

Paint overspray and dried insect residue can be removed from glass in a few ways. First, always try water and a soft cloth. Bird droppings and the like will dissolve with water and elbow grease, and you won't have to worry about scratching the glass.

For more persistent residue, tar and paint overspray, try a glass cleaner polish such as Eagle 1. If that doesn't work, use #00 or milder steel wool and glass cleaner. Then, clean the glass again, and flush with water, using a mitt to pick up any remaining steel wool fibers and residue. Polish afterward with glass cleaner or water and newspaper. Note: Steel wool may scratch acrylic glass on newer cars. For those, use Meguiar's plastic cleaner or plastic polish.

Windshield and headlight wipers

Windshield wipers work best when the rubber is in good shape and the glass is clean. Wash front and rear wiper blades at the same time as you wash the glass. Use a paintbrush and toothbrush to remove bug residue, wax and any dirt or grease build-up. The toothbrush works well to clean rubber. This holds true for headlight wipers, as well.

Although dressing helps most rubber parts maintain a rich dark color, wiper blades should not be treated. Dressing will quickly wash off and under light mist conditions could cause smears. The best overall treatment is frequent cleaning. This will help prolong their usefulness.

No amount of cleaning will make them last forever, however. When they become faulty, worn and dried, replace with a new set. A once-a-year replacement is normal for windshield wipers and most rear window wipers. Headlight wipers may last longer.

Removing build-up from window edges

More than likely, a close inspection will reveal build-up of dirt in the corners of glass, next to trim.

Substances like tree sap can be removed from glass using a glass cleaner and #00 or finer steel wool. Newer automobiles may feature acrylic glass which can be damaged with steel wool. For those, use glass cleaners and polishes only.

This is especially prevalent along the windshield, rear window and fixed glass. Remove this caked-on stuff with a toothbrush and cotton swab. Whether it be on the inside or outside of the car, lay a towel at the base to catch drips and splatter.

Spray the toothbrush with window cleaner or dip it in water; shake off the excess. Scrub along trim and molding to break loose the crud. Use the fold of a thin towel to reach into the seam and remove debris. A cotton swab can be used in tighter spots. If a toothbrush isn't strong enough to break up the build-up, you can gently slide the blade of a razor scraper along the glass and under the dirt. Carefully raise the back of the scraper to loosen the dirt. Follow with the toothbrush and towel.

Special care should be given the use of a razor scraper. Inserting it too far into molding may cause leaks; a slip could end in a scratch or tear; while pushing it along an inside curve of a window, the square edges can scratch glass. Use this tool as a last resort.

Defogger strips on rear windows are not always imbedded in the glass. For those windows with strips on the surface, wipe in the direction they run, not against them. Never use the razor scraper near them either. This same caution applies to areas in the molding where the defogger strips exit the glass. Slipping the razor blade into these areas may sever the tiny wires coming out of the glass. The slightest break in the continuous strip will render the defogger useless, requiring replacement.

Cleaning windows

During the preliminary wash, you cleaned the exterior glass, removing heavy grime and any droppings. The windows got dirty again during the exterior shine, whether you buffed or not. Now, armed with your favorite glass cleaner (a cleaning product or water and a mitt), you are ready to make the windows invisibly clean.

Start with the driver's door. Roll the window down about an inch or so. This will allow access to the top part of the glass hidden in the upper groove along the frame. Clean and dry this part first. Then, roll the window back up and clean the rest of it. Take note of the corners. This is where most of the smears will wind up. Take your time and inspect each window before moving on. Don't forget mirrors.

Rear windows are the most difficult to clean. Use the back of your hand to guide the towel or mitt. If necessary, unfold the towel and use a corner of it for more manageability.

The inside windshield is easiest to clean from the passenger side. The steering wheel won't be in your way, and you can easily reach across the full length of the window. Go slow around rearview mirrors glued to the windshield. Bumping into them with your hand, at just the right angle, will knock the bracket loose from the glass. Having done this before, I've found that only those glues made specif-

A toothbrush is used to clean trim along the bottom of the rear window on a 300ZX. The dirty soap suds indicate deep cleaning in an area that has been long neglected. Car wash soap works well, although you may have to use a mild cleaner on stubborn areas.

The tops of windows are frequently overlooked during cleaning because they rest inside the track. Roll the window down a few inches and clean this part first.

ically for windshield-mounted mirrors are strong enough to keep the mirror in place. Super glues won't work.

Cleaning etched glass

Some parts of the country are burdened with extremely hard water. So hard, in fact, it can etch and waterspot glass. For this special problem, clean the glass first with water. Gradually increase the strength of cleaning methods, using cleaner, glass polish and #00 or finer steel wool. If the problem persists and you are contemplating glass replacement, try polishing with a very fine sealer and glaze by hand or with the buffer. In some cases, the glass is so deeply etched replacement is inevitable.

Cleaning window tint film

Very common with passenger vans, window tint film is a thin sheet of Mylar applied to the inside of glass to prevent folks from seeing inside the vehicle. To clean, use mild cleaners and water. Deep scratches cannot be repaired; the entire sheet must be removed and replaced.

Film-tinted windows that are extra dirty can be cleaned with nonabrasive cleaners designed for plastic windows on ragtops. One such product is Eagle 1 nonabrasive Plastic Polish. It comes in a spray and is safe for use on plastic, plexiglass and window tint film.

Antennas

Radio and telephone antennas should not be overlooked. Those in moderately clean condition are washed with the mitt at the same time you wash the part of the car where they are located. Those with accumulations of dirt and grease can be cleaned with a paper towel sprayed with WD-40 and followed by a quick buff with a clean cloth. Extra dirty antennas can be gently scrubbed with an SOS pad making sure you rinse away all pad residue from the antenna and car body. Clean antenna bases with a paintbrush or toothbrush.

Chrome antennas can be polished with chrome polish and then lightly waxed. Electric antennas should be wiped with a cloth sprayed with WD-40. The light coat of lubricant helps them to extend and retract smoothly, prolonging even operation.

Trim
Cleaning

Trim includes those metal strips surrounding glass, headlights, taillights and vinyl tops, as well as the straight strips that run the length of some cars. They are attached to the car by means of screws, clips or double-backed tape. Regardless of the means of attachment, dirt finds its way into, behind and along the edge of trim.

The easiest way to clean most trim is to use a paintbrush during the preliminary wash. The skinny bristles reach into grooves on the face and seams to break loose dirt, pine needles and wax residue. Gently use a toothbrush to clean screw slots and stubborn wax and dirt build-up along seams and edges.

Direct a stream of water behind side trim to dislodge and float away dirt caught between it and the car body. Lower rocker panel trim may have to be cleaned with bug and tar remover to get rid of road-tar blemishes. One-step wax may also do the trick.

Chrome

All chrome—which may include bumpers, mirrors, door handles, fender moldings and hood ornaments as well as trim—may be polished and waxed. Happich Simichrome works very well, as do most chrome polishes. As with paint, don't polish unless it is necessary.

Heavily rusted and pitted chrome can be cleaned with an SOS pad or #00 steel wool with wax. Follow this with a mild chrome polish. Afterward, apply a thin coat of car wax. Use a soft cloth to remove polish and wax. The cut-off paintbrush is great for removing build-up around carriage bolts and screw slots.

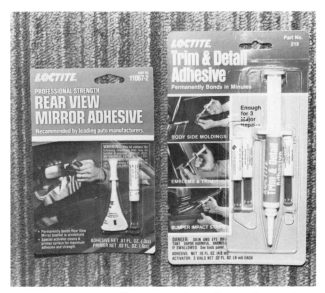

Rearview mirror adhesive is the only product I have found that keeps a mirror attached to the windshield. Super glues may work for a few days, but that's all. Adhesives designed for automotive use work better than all-purpose products.

153

Pitted chrome parts must be rechromed at a rechroming shop; they cannot be permanently repaired in any other way. To make those parts look decent in the interim, clean and buff with #00 or finer steel wool and polish as described above. Before applying wax, clean the part again with Prepsol or another wax removing cleaner. Then, using a toothpick or fine artist's paintbrush, dab a bit of bright silver paint into the exposed pits and other areas where chrome has peeled away. At a distance, the part will look fine, depending on the size of the touch-ups.

Black trim

Many new cars are featuring black trim. Most of this newer trim is plastic, although many pieces are made of rubber or anodized aluminum.

Plastic trim is cleaned with a wash mitt, paintbrush and toothbrush using mild soap. Solid textured, smooth plastic can be waxed along with the rest of the car. Textured plastic cannot, because wax will adhere to the grain and be almost impossible to remove. Lightly dress those parts. Rubber trim is cleaned the same way but treated with a light coat of dressing applied with a cloth. If you are in doubt whether to wax or dress, test a small inconspicuous section first to determine product compatibility.

Anodized aluminum is fragile. The sun is its worst enemy as it beats down and fades the black color. Harsh rubbing and scrubbing will also quickly remove the thin, coated surface. Wash with a clean soft mitt and paintbrush using mild car wash soap. Once or twice a year, apply a very light coat of protective wax. Never use polish, as the slightest grit will surely remove anodization.

Trim detailing

Chrome trim is common on older cars. To polish, use Happich Simichrome or other chrome pol-

The bottom of this Jaguar chrome bumper has deteriorated from extensive exposure to exhaust vapors. At this point, it needs to be rechromed. Frequent cleaning, polishing and waxing may have protected the chrome better and allowed it to last longer.

ish. The hazard lies in scratching the paint while polishing over the trim. To minimize this hazard, you can mask off the paint or remove the trim to polish it. Nonabrasive polishes like Never-Dull work very well too, especially for softer metals like aluminum.

Trim suffering from paint loss can be repainted. Wentworth repainted the red strips along the lower rocker panel trim on his 1970 Buick GS 455 convertible with excellent results. He acquired the proper paint from an auto body paint and supply store, and used a fine-bristled artist's paintbrush to apply. A steady hand helps, but masking is the surest way to guarantee straight lines. Emblems can be repainted the same way.

Be sure to use a good paintbrush. Artist's brushes are available at hobby shops and stationery stores that carry artist's supplies. When you are done with the brush, clean thoroughly and then apply a thin coat of petroleum jelly to the bristles. This helps them to retain their shape.

If your car has plastic trim on the interior with a thin chrome film that is falling off, try this. Peel off all of the film. Sand the trim smooth, and paint glossy black. You lose the chrome look but save the cost of new trim.

Rubber and vinyl

Rubber and vinyl trim is cleaned in much the same way as metal. You'll work more with a tooth-

Rubber moldings are cleaned with soap and a toothbrush. Paint overspray and other stains can be removed with paint thinner; in some cases, you may have to carefully use lacquer thinner to remove deep paint stains. Use extreme caution with lacquer thinner as it can quickly mar any paint or plastic surface it drips on.

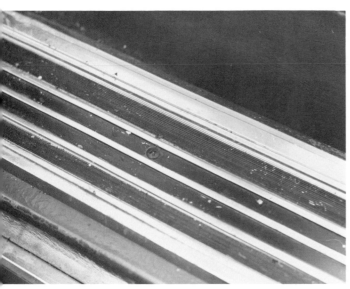

Clean trim with soap and a toothbrush. Repaint with a fine artist's brush using quality paint from an auto body paint and supply store. It is best to remove parts like this rocker panel for painting. Screws can be inserted into a piece of cardboard to hold them steady while painting the tops.

Dry exterior rubber can be rejuvenated using a three-step process. First, wash rubber completely, using a paintbrush and toothbrush as needed. After drying, apply a liberal amount of dressing, working it in with a paintbrush and without worrying about dressing on other parts of the car. After the dressing has had a chance to soak in, wash the car with car wash soap and a mitt. Excessive dressing and extra high gloss will be washed off, leaving the rubber looking like new.

After rubber moldings have been cleaned and dried, apply a light coat of dressing. This will help them look new and maintain elasticity. Easiest application is made by wiping with a cloth dampened with dressing. Spray just a spot of dressing on the cloth so that nearby metal is not smeared.

Removing paint overspray on this rubber collar covering a Pantera bumper mount will require the careful use of lacquer thinner. Removing the collar for cleaning is the safest method. If done on the car, surrounding areas should be masked to protect against damage due to the lacquer thinner.

brush because dirt is trapped more readily in the pores of rubber and vinyl.

To keep rubber and vinyl trim looking their best, treat with a dressing like Armor All. Use caution during application so that dressing goes on the trim and not on paint. A good method is to clean and dry the trim first. Then, apply a liberal coat of dressing, using a paintbrush to work it in. Afterward, wash the entire car, including the trim. The dressing's high-gloss finish will be gone, as well as any smudges on paint.

Moldings

Rubber moldings are located around doors, trunk lids and windows. These items should not be overlooked during a detail. Clean them with soap and water. A toothbrush can be used for stubborn spots.

Paint overspray can be removed with lacquer thinner, but be extremely careful. The slightest drop of lacquer thinner will blemish paint. Just put a dab on a rag, and wipe the molding. It is best to make a number of gentle passes instead of one heavy swipe. Gentle pressure is also advised, especially for the soft molding along doors.

Pickup trucks display a heavy rubber molding around the rear window. It is very common for this to be laden with dirt. Use plenty of soap and water to clean, using a small brush as necessary.

After rubber moldings have had time to dry, rub on a thin coat of dressing. This will improve their appearance and prolong elasticity.

The inside parts of rear window moldings on pickup trucks are easily cleaned with a toothbrush and cleaner. Place towels under the work area to prevent runoff from staining carpet or upholstery.

I.D. badges

I.D. badges, like the Porsche or Lamborghini crests, are cleaned with a soft toothbrush and mild soap. Those suffering exceptional build-up can be gently scrubbed with a toothbrush and mild polish, all the while using very gentle pressure so as not to polish away the thin film of paint on the various adornments. Use a carnauba-based wax for protection and a very soft cloth for buffing. Wax residue along the tiny ridges is removed with a soft, cut-off paintbrush.

If you have to touch up paint on badges or crests, use a fine artist's paintbrush. They can be purchased at any artist's supply store and most stationery stores. Buy paint at an auto body paint and supply store. Many times, they carry small vials of paint for such intricate touch-up work.

Painting around badges requires masking. Clean and wax the badge first so masking tape won't adhere too strongly or remove paint when peeled off. Carefully apply tape to the badge, overlapping strips to assure full protection. When the badge is completely covered, use a sharp knife, like a razor-bladed X-Acto knife, to trim the tape along the edges. Use the knife at a slight angle in order to cut the tape at the very base of the badge and prevent overspray on its side.

License plates

License plates should be removed from the car for cleaning the front and back once a year. They are cleaned with a mitt, paintbrush, toothbrush or plastic brush as needed.

Should the plate become oxidized, you can gently shine it with a mild polish. Excessive polishing could remove paint from the letters and numbers, so go easy. The plate can also be waxed for protection.

When it comes time to install new tabs, take the license plate off the car and bring it in the house. Wash it in the sink, and towel dry. Allow the new

Dressing application using a cotton swab along the rubber molding on the front part of a 300ZX driver's door window. By lightly spraying the tip of a cotton swab, you can maintain excellent control while dressing in extra tight spaces. Excessive dressing can be squeezed out of the cotton tip with a cloth pinched between your fingers.

tabs and plate to warm to room temperature. This makes application of the plastic tabs easier and assures their best adherence. Take pains to get the month and year tabs on straight and even with each other.

Plastic light covers

Scratches in plastic light covers can be polished with plastic cleaner and plastic polish. You can carefully do this with the part on the car; however, the job turns out much better when you remove the part. Wash thoroughly inside and out. Then polish. Be sure to check the condition of gaskets before you replace the light cover.

Chapter 9

Vinyl and convertible tops

Vinyl and convertible tops can present unique cleaning problems. By far, the easiest method of maintenance is to clean frequently. Just like any other material, vinyl has a certain life span. Longevity is encouraged by regular upkeep and common sense preventive maintenance.

Vinyl tops
Cleaning

The grainy and porous nature of vinyl tops attracts dirt build-up. Warm weather causes the material to expand, opening pores and creating pockets for dust and dirt. During summer, unpro-

The grainy nature of vinyl tops attracts dirt and grime build-up. Using a good cleaner with a plastic-bristled brush is about the only way to safely clean neglected vinyl tops. After vigorous cleaning, application of a quality vinyl top dressing is essential to restore moisture and protection against weather and sunlight.

tected vinyl slowly soils, resulting in dark lines of dirt running through the deeper crevices of the grain. Removing the build-up requires lots of scrubbing.

Start the project with car wash soap and a plastic-bristled brush. The wash mitt will remove surface dust, not imbedded dirt. Plan to rinse frequently, especially the car body, to prevent water and soap spots. Look closely at the grain; is it getting clean? If not, try again. Concentrate on a small section, while graduating from one cleaning method to the next.

When little or no results are achieved with car wash soap and the brush, try a stronger cleaner like Simple Green. Terry Skiple has used upholstery cleaner on vinyl tops with good results. He says that it cleans and leaves a sheen when the vinyl dries. Spray a small section, and let it soak in for a minute. Scrub in a circular pattern, reversing direction from time to time, letting the bristles attack dirt from different angles. Rinse thoroughly, including the body. You must realize that stronger soap solutions

To avoid scratches on painted surfaces, use the brush in a controlled manner. The type of brush used here was purchased at a supermarket in the household section. The straight sides on this brush make it easy to scrub along a trim line without touching paint.

The vinyl top of a 911 Targa is being cleaned with car wash soap and a small plastic-bristled brush. Car wash soap works well for moderately dirty tops. A circular brushing pattern, reversed occasionally, assures complete coverage and allows the bristles to dislodge dirt deep in the grain.

may have adverse effects on body paint and glass, hence the importance of frequent rinsings.

If results are not satisfactory at this point, consider using a product made for vinyl top cleaning. One such product is Turtle Wax Vinyl Top Cleaner, a foam formula designed to be applied with a soft-bristled brush. Without damaging the vinyl's protective top coat, these products are intended to open pores and allow the soft bristles to loosen dirt. In most cases, vinyl top cleaners work quite well. Follow the directions on the label to get the most out of them.

If you have a white vinyl top that has been neglected, and none of the milder cleaning methods have removed the crud still sitting in grain crevices, try a powdered cleanser such as Comet. Since most of these products contain bleach, you will have to be on your toes to keep it from drying on paint, trim and glass. Frequent and plentiful rinsing is generally sufficient.

Sprinkle the cleanser on a wet section of the top. Use the plastic brush to work up a good lather. To avoid scrubbing over trim or paint, move the brush back and forth along edges, instead of in the normal circular pattern. Rinse thoroughly.

A towel is used to protect a Targa windshield from dressing smears while application is made to the vinyl top. A number of car enthusiasts have used Armor All successfully for years as a vinyl top conditioner. It must be noted that these enthusiasts dressed their car's vinyl tops on a consistent basis. Dressings made specifically for vinyl tops last much longer and are available at auto body paint and supply stores.

You can use a powdered cleanser and brush in a self-serve car wash and take advantage of the high-pressure washer. Save this method for only the most stubborn jobs. Together the brush, cleanser and high water pressure do a good job of removing stubborn grime. Use the high-pressure wand in a very controlled manner. Keep it away from seams as the pressure can force them apart. Stay away from edges, too. High-pressure spray can force material loose from trim, requiring a trip to the top shop for repairs. It can also penetrate molding and cause unwanted leaks. Rinse the body from a distance to prevent paint and emblem damage.

You must also plan to apply a protective dressing on the vinyl before the day is done. Scrubbing with cleanser will remove dirt and any protection the vinyl had. Unprotected, vinyl will fade and deteriorate rapidly.

Cleaning extreme cases

White vinyl tops that have been sorely neglected can sometimes defy the most vigorous cleaning. As a last resort, try lacquer thinner. Too much emphasis cannot be placed on the cautions needed during this application. Lacquer thinner is unforgiving and will eat through just about anything. One drop will mar paint and ruin plastic. Try this only after trying everything else and just before you drive down to the top shop for a new vinyl top.

Don't use a lacquer thinner in a closed garage near a hot water heater. It is very flammable, and the vapors can be easily ignited by a pilot light. Apply in an open area with plenty of ventilation. Have a garden hose and wash bucket handy to dilute spills, and immediately clean any spot on the body or glass splashed with thinner.

As a precaution, lay towels along the windshield and rear window. You may consider protecting all areas surrounding the top. Away from the car, pour a little thinner on a folded towel. Make absolutely sure there is no thinner dripping from it; if there is, you have poured entirely too much thinner on it. Carefully, put the towel on the top and wipe. Do a very small section first, about one square foot. Rub in the thinner for about thirty seconds. Then, wipe the same area with a dry side of the towel. You will notice the vinyl soften up, maybe to the point of being sticky. This is not good for vinyl, but as a last ditch effort this procedure should remove all imbedded dirt.

If the results are satisfactory, continue cleaning small sections at a time. Before each application, check to see that windows, paint and trim are protected. Plan your moves before you work along edges and trim. If you can't clean close enough to the edge without risking damage to plastic trim, leave it. Work on those parts later with a toothbrush and cleanser.

Dressings

Lacquer thinner will remove everything from a vinyl top and you will have to apply a vinyl top dressing after cleaning. Most auto parts and auto body paint and supply stores carry an assortment of vinyl top dressings and top coats. If you choose to use a simple dressing like Armor All, Clear Guard or Meguiar's, allow it to saturate the top for a day or two before buffing.

In different parts of the country, detailers use different brands and types of vinyl top dressings and top coats. Some have access to thick, syrupy liquids that are applied with a paintbrush, others rely on liquids. You will have to check with the auto parts store and auto body paint and supply store in your area to see what is available.

For exceptional jobs, seek advice from a professional detailer or vinyl top installer. Lacquer thinner and vinyl dressing may not be the solution to your top's specific problem. Talk to more than one detailer and top installer to compare restorative methods and cost. Afterward, you will have a much clearer understanding of the problem and may be better off having a professional restore the top or replace it altogether.

Regular maintenance

The drastic cleaning using lacquer thinner may have to be done once, if at all. Future cleaning should be done at least once a month, using a soft brush and car wash soap. You can also clean with a vinyl cleaner and conditioner, such as Meguiar's #40.

After cleaning, apply a thin coat of dressing. You can use Armor All, Eagle 1 Tire Dressing & Protectant, Turtle Wax Vinyl Top Wax or any brand of vinyl dressing. The important thing is not so much what you use, but that you do use something. Dressing will help vinyl maintain internal moisture and repel those elements that can cause drying, fading and cracking. It will also keep the top looking new and enhance its natural luster.

Turtle Wax Vinyl Top Wax is just one of a number of products designed specifically for vinyl top protection. Auto body paint and supply stores carry the largest selection, while auto parts stores may display just a few. Instead of vinyl dressing, use one of these products for tops that have been long neglected or vigorously cleaned.

Turtle Wax Color Back Vinyl Restorer and Protector is used on vinyl that is severely dry and has faded. It will help bring back the original color and provides some protection against weather and sunlight.

Vinyl repair

The quickest way to lose a vinyl top is to let a small tear go unchecked. As soon as you notice a problem, take care of it. The local top shop can fix it, or you can buy a vinyl repair kit at the auto parts store and tackle the job yourself. For loose seams and edges, have a professional do the job.

Most car enthusiasts recommend you not change the color of vinyl tops. For those in which the color has faded, however, you can apply a vinyl top coating (dye) of the original color. Application is easily made with a sponge applicator. Trim should be masked and towels can be taped to glass for splatter protection. The best assortment of products and colors is found at auto body paint and supply stores.

Vinyl dye

Vinyl tops can be dyed. The process is simple. Clean as directed, mask the edges and apply the dye. There are a variety of colors, and you use a spray can, a spray gun or a sponge applicator. Talk to the people at the auto body and paint supply store. They can help you select the proper color and decide on the best application technique for your needs.

Convertible tops
Cleaning

Although not as porous as vinyl, ragtops can collect plenty of dirt. Always start by employing the mildest cleaning method first. If the wash mitt and car wash soap do not do it, try a soft-bristled brush with soap. Then try a cleaner and brush, and so on.

Convertibles present two unique areas of concern: the rear plastic window and leaks. While washing, avoid direct water spray at the windows. Hold the hose up and let the water flow down. Because the rear plastic window scratches so easily, stay away from it as much as possible. Wash it gently with a clean mitt full of suds.

If cleaning with a cleanser is necessary, consider covering the car with plastic. This is done rather simply on convertibles. Use two pieces of plastic. Place one under the rear part of the top up to the seatback. Keep this plastic in place by securing the top with its proper latches. Put the other piece in

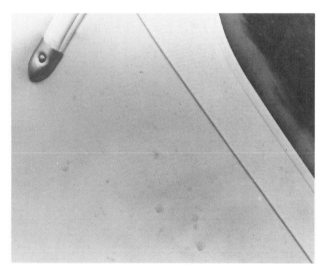

This is a dirty convertible top on a Corvette roadster. Mild cleaning is required and should be accomplished using car wash soap and a soft plastic brush. A toothbrush will do well along the trim piece in the top left corner and along the seam.

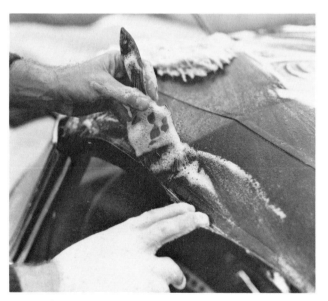

A paintbrush works well to dislodge and remove dirt in the drip seam along the side of this Jaguar ragtop. The brush is perfect for loosening light dirt and dust along seams and around windows.

front: fit it under the top and over the doors. The plastic will protect paint from harsh soap suds.

For harder cleaning jobs, Terry Skiple prefers to use SOS pads instead of powdered cleansers. He feels that the bleach in cleansers does more harm than good. The pad works well for removing dirt build-up along seams and beads. It is not necessary to exert great force while scrubbing with the pad. Be extra careful around the rear plastic window. One swipe with the pad will surely scratch it.

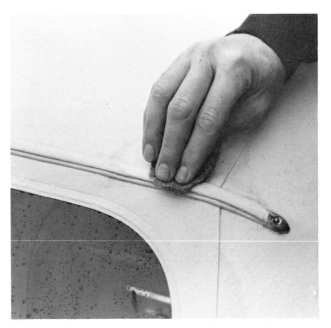

Mild application of an SOS pad quickly cleans the trim on this Corvette convertible top. Skiple prefers to use SOS pads over bleach or powder cleansers, in the belief that bleaching agents in the cleanser may damage paint. SOS pads are relatively soft and will not harm convertible material.

If the convertible top you are going to clean is in need of harsh cleansers, you might consider protecting paint from soap stains by covering in plastic. One roll of plastic was cut in half and afforded plenty of coverage for this Corvette. The front of the car was covered with one half and the rear with the other half. Plastic was placed under the top and secured when the top latches were locked and the windows rolled up.

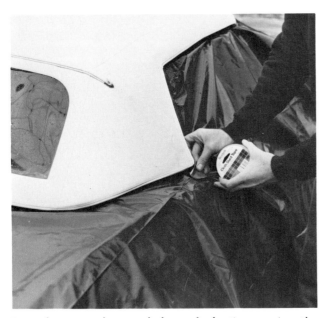

Seam between the two halves of plastic covering the Corvette body during ragtop cleaning is secured with duct tape.

The plastic protects the Corvette body and paint while the ragtop is scrubbed with a plastic brush and soap. This protection is not needed all the time, only for those occasions when tops are so dirty they require the use of heavy-duty detergents, like powdered cleansers.

Comet powdered cleanser is worked into a slurry by the plastic-bristled brush on this Corvette ragtop. Extra cleaning strength was needed to remove imbedded dirt. Minute abrasives in the cleanser, along with the brush, clean deep into the material. Save this type of vigorous cleaning for tops in extra dirty condition, such as those with mildew and stain problems.

Frequent rinsing with clear water is imperative during heavy-duty ragtop cleaning. Water applied through a nozzle works much better than out of an open-ended hose. When using a powdered cleanser, you may have to use the brush to help loosen cleanser residue. Thorough rinsing removes dirt and soap suds and lets you see the progress being made. Use the brush carefully around rear plastic windows, as the bristles can leave scratches.

Before using a powdered cleanser or SOS pad, try a liquid cleanser like Soft Scrub. They have good cleaning ability without the abrasives common in powders. Designed to clean plastic bathroom fixtures without scratching, liquid cleansers may clean just as well as powders without the abrasive damage.

Don't scrub convertible tops during extreme hot or cold weather. Cold temperatures cause the material to be brittle, and scrubbing may result in cracks. Hot temperatures allow the material to soften and cleaning may stretch it.

Dressings

McKee has owned his Jag roadster for almost seventeen years. The ragtop is black and looks new; this is because he has taken care of the car. He parks it in the garage whenever possible and washes it once a week. He has always used Armor All as a top dressing and has never had a problem with it. The key, he says, is to apply a thin coat, rub it in with a soft brush and buff off the excess. Dressing also helps the top to remain pliable, an important con-

cern when you put the top down and store it in its compartment.

Never store a damp top because it will mildew. Never store a dirty top either. Dirt will scratch the plastic window and will grind against fabric causing wear. Creases will suffer the most. If the car is to remain in the garage for an extended period of time, leave the top up and latches open.

This is especially significant for Corvettes. The back part of these tops lies on top of the rear deck. The rubber molding along the bottom edge will leave a mark on the paint. Let the top rest on the latch, away from the deck.

Plastic window care

Dusty plastic windows can be cleaned with lots of water and a very soft cloth filled with soap suds. Since scratching is so prevalent, you may have to polish the window periodically. McKee uses

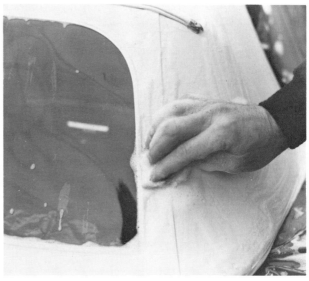

An SOS pad is used to clean around the edge of a rear plastic window on a Corvette ragtop. Use extreme caution around plastic windows because they scratch easily.

The vinyl top on a Porsche 911 Targa looks like new after cleaning and a light application of dressing. Light coats of dressing, applied frequently, will help a vinyl top look good and will protect it against weather and ultraviolet rays from the sun.

Meguiar's Plastic Cleaner #17 with good results. This can be followed by Meguiar's Plastic Polish #10. Eagle 1 Plastic Polish is good too.

Plastic cleaner and polish fill scratches and leave a protective film over the window. The film helps to reduce water spotting and dust accumulation. These products are also good for plexiglass, window tint film and motorcycle helmet shields. Severe scratches will require additional applications, maybe the two-step process with cleaner and polish.

Top replacement

Sometimes, a vinyl or convertible top is in such bad shape, no amount of elbow grease or special cleaner will bring it back. Save yourself work, and have a new top installed. Nothing looks better than a crisp, new white top on a candy apple roadster. The same holds true for vinyl. With a new top, you can start fresh with consistent upkeep and keep your top looking new for a long time.

If you love your car, but hate the vinyl top, have it removed. This is quite a project and the metal top must be repainted. In most cases, you will have to have a body shop fill in the holes left by moldings. Trim will have to be replaced too, since vinyl top trim and standard trim are different.

T-tops, sunroofs and moonroofs

Painted T-tops should be removed sometime during the detail to clean around the inner edges of the roof and the outer edges of the top. Polish and wax painted edges and treat rubber moldings with a light coat of dressing.

Sunroofs should also be opened to allow access to the same areas for cleaning, dressing and waxing. The painted tops of both roofs must be polished and waxed like every other painted part of the car.

Clear moonroofs are washed with the rest of the vehicle using a mitt and car wash soap. Use a paintbrush and toothbrush along trim. Tempered glass roofs are polished like other glass using glass polish. Plastic roofs should be polished with a quality cleaner or polish like Meguiar's or Eagle 1.

Light scratches on the plastic rear windows of convertibles can be polished out with Meguiar's Professional Plastic Cleaner. McKee has used this product for years on the plastic window of his Jaguar roadster to clean and to remove scratches. As you can tell by the picture, the window is in excellent condition.

Chapter 10

Tires and wheels

Tires and wheels have come a long way in recent years. Car people treat wheels and tires as part of the automobile's overall cosmetic appearance, rather than as a mere necessity. Frequently, the right combination of wheels and tires makes a car stand out better than best, especially when they are meticulously maintained.

Along with the new breed of wheels comes the dilemma of cleaning. You can use an all-purpose wheel cleaner with some results, but what is it actually doing to the surface of the wheel? Is it all right to use chrome cleaner on mag wheels? Will whitewall cleaner blemish certain wheels? If so, how do you get the whitewalls white? Plan a day to clean wheels and tires, including the back sides and the spare.

Do the wheels and tires on your car look nice from a distance, but just so-so close up? Next time you admire an exhibit at a car show, take note of the wheels and tires. You will see that they are cleaned and polished inside, as well as outside. Most newer wheels are slotted, allowing back sides to show through. Why spend an hour cleaning the front, when dirt is still visible from the back?

Choose a suitable work place and have cleaners, brushes and garden hose handy. Use a sturdy jack to raise the car and place jack stands under it. Then remove a wheel and tire. Clean one wheel and tire at a time. Before replacing, clean and paint the fenderwell and visible underbody.

Tires
Cleaners and cleaning

At the auto parts store, you will find an array of tire cleaning products all claiming to be the best and easiest to apply. These products are designed as step-savers, some claiming to clean tires with minimal rubbing and scrubbing. One such product is Eagle 1 Tire Cleaner. The label states its unique formula will instantly penetrate and dissolve grease, oil and road grime, while not using harsh petrochemicals, bleaches or abrasives. Whitewall cleaners, like Westley's, can also be used for blackwalls. Watch out for those cleaners containing bleach, as they may stain unprotected aluminum and alloy wheels.

Many car people have found the safest way to clean tires is with soap, water and brush. The plastic-bristled brush works well with Simple Green. Squire Tomasie, a Porsche mechanic and former motorcycle and auto race driver, likes Simple Green because it doesn't hurt metal. Before using Simple Green, he had problems with cleaners corroding aluminum engine parts. The same should hold true for wheels.

Stock wheels and tires have changed a lot in the last few years. This BMW wheel complements the rest of the car; wheels and tires have become an integral part of the cosmetic makeup for automobiles.

An entire day can be spent cleaning, polishing and dressing wheels and tires. These are two wheels off of Wentworth's 1970 Buick GS 455. The wheel and tire on the right looked like the one on the left before detailing. Soap and scrub brushes were used on the tire and SOS pads and chrome polish on the wheel. The center cap was purchased new from a GM dealership and new chrome lug nuts were bought at an auto supply store.

Even though the outside of this Porsche wheel looks clean, dirt and brake dust show through the slots and make it appear less crisp. Once a month, you may consider pulling the wheels to clean their back sides. In the interim, use a small cloth and your fingers to clean as much of the visible dust as possible.

Car wash soap, a small one-inch paintbrush and assorted toothbrushes are all you should need to clean spoked wheels in good to moderate condition. Wentworth concedes that chemical wheel cleaners do a great job, but worries about long-term effects on chrome nipples and spokes from acids and neutralizers used on a consistent basis. He saves chemical cleaners for the extra tough jobs on neglected wheels.

Using dish soap on tires often yields good results. Extra dirty and stained rubber has come clean with powdered cleanser and brush. Once again, you must consider if bleach in the cleanser will damage your aluminum or alloy wheel.

Wentworth prefers to use a bucket of dish soap and water, a spray bottle of Simple Green, a plastic brush and a toothbrush for complete tire cleaning. Rinse the tire, dip the brush in the bucket and start scrubbing. Spray Simple Green on stains and stubborn spots, then scrub. Rinse, and do it again. Continue until the tire is clean. Use a toothbrush along the rim and in tiny cracks next to lettering and tread. If need be, use a liquid cleanser like Soft Scrub for more cleaning punch. Apply the same cleaning technique to the inside of the tire.

Cleaning whitewalls

Use whitewall cleaners as you may, always following instructions on the label. Note cautions on the label such as "Clean one tire at a time and don't allow cleaner to dry on chrome, polished alumi-

The edge of an SOS pad is used to clean the thin whitewall on a Goodyear Wingfoot tire mounted on a Jaguar V-12 roadster. Whitewall cleaners and brushes do a good job cleaning whitewalls but many detailers prefer the low cost and maneuverability of SOS pads for cleaning whitewalls and raised white letters.

Washing tires with soap, water and a scrub brush works well and is safe for rubber and surrounding materials. Work up a good lather first with car wash soap and then rinse. Heavily soiled and stained tires can be sprayed with an all-purpose cleaner like Simple Green and scrubbed again. Repeat the process until the tire meets your satisfaction.

McKee has lightly applied Armor All to this Goodyear Wingfoot for over a decade with excellent results. He takes good care of his car, including washing, drying and dressing tires on a frequent basis.

num or painted wheels." Chemicals in some cleaners are strong and may blemish certain wheel surfaces.

Instead of whitewall cleaners, you can use car wash or dish soap and a whitewall brush. This small wire brush features short bristles cropped closely together. Used with soap, it scrubs whitewalls and raised white letters to their brightest.

Wentworth and Skiple prefer SOS pads. The combination of soap and soft steel wool makes short

work of whitewall cleaning. The side of the pad fits into thin whitewalls and into tight grooves where the outer white ring butts against the black.

For tough scuff marks, try the SOS pad and Simple Green. Rinse with plenty of water after each application. Keep at it until you are satisfied with the results. Damaged whitewalls can be touched up with quick-drying, flat white paint.

Dressings

A fellow once told me that tire dressing caused the tires on his car to split and crack after repeated weekly applications. He believed the exterior dressing contained a solvent that opened the pores in the rubber allowing silicones better penetration. He blamed the solvent for drying out the rubber, thus causing cracks and splits. To date, he is the only person I have heard mention this complaint.

The tires on McKee's car are the same ones that have been on it since new. He has used Armor All exclusively on a consistent basis, and this care has kept the Goodyear Wingfoots looking new.

Others have complained that once they use dressing, they have to use it all the time. If not, tires and vinyl look faded and dried out. Could it be that dressing makes those items look so good that anything else looks second rate?

I would much rather apply tire dressing than use tire black. Don't get me wrong. Tire black has its purpose and does a good job of making bad tires

To avoid overspray on wheels, spray the dressing cloth first and then wipe it on the tire. Use a fold in the cloth to reach under the lip on the outer edge of the rim.

Soak the back sides of tires with dressing during the once or twice a year cleaning. It is not a bad idea to let the dressing soak in for an hour before removing excess, since it will likely be some time before dressing is applied again.

170

look better. But, an intensive cleaning and proper application of dressing makes tires look more crisp, clean and original.

Tire dressing can be sprayed or wiped on. Spraying will result in some overspray, but will reach deep into crevices on sidewall tread and lettering. A good compromise is controlled spraying of the outer edge, buffing with the dressing towel and working the dressing into the tire with a soft brush.

For a heavy-duty one-time treatment, soak the tire with lots of dressing and let it sit for five to six hours. Then wash with mild soap and dry. The tire will look brand new without the glossy look of being freshly dressed.

A soft bristled brush is used to work dressing into the grooves on the side of this Goodyear Wingfoot. This method works much better than relying on an extra heavy dressing application to reach deep grooves. This brush also works well to work dressing into vinyl tops, ragtops and floor mats with unique designs.

Use the edge of a clean SOS pad to remove excess dressing from whitewalls and raised white letters. This is important, especially when using dressings that leave a blue film on whitewalls.

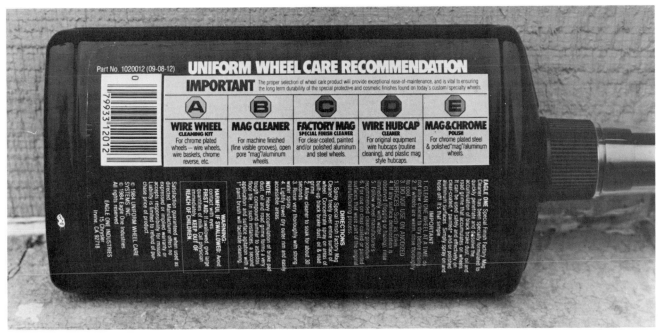

This is the Eagle I Uniform Wheel Care Recommendation chart found on the back sides of Eagle 1 wheel cleaning products. Working in conjunction with wheel manufacturers, Eagle 1 matches its wheel cleaning products with specific wheels to assure proper application. These charts are also displayed in many auto parts stores.

Use the edge of the brush to spread dressing along the border between tire and wheel and into grooves and tread patterns. Follow with a clean towel, buffing off the excess. Go over whitewalls and raised white letters with a clean, dry SOS pad. This will remove the blue tint from whitewalls, leaving the tire standing tall.

Dressing tires on motorcycles is a little different. You must take care to keep dressing out of the tread. The slippery dressing may cause the tire's sidewall to lose traction in a curve, resulting in an accident.

Wheels
Chemical cleaners

Eagle 1 leads the field in chemical wheel cleaners. Barney Li, owner of Eagle 1, has a special interest in wheels. Realizing that an all-purpose wheel cleaner must be weak to be safe for all wheels, he started a program to match certain cleaners with specific wheels.

The Uniform Wheel Care System uses a symbol system of color-coded letters to match wheels and cleaners. For example, the letter A in a yellow octagon denotes the Wire Wheel Cleaning Kit designed for chrome-plated wheels, including wire wheels, wire baskets and chrome reverse. The letter B in a green octagon stands for Mag Cleaner. The remaining three products—C, D and E—include Factory Mag, Wire Hubcap and Mag & Chrome Polish. Below each symbol is a list of wheels that the product will clean.

New wheels, made by a participating manufacturer, have one of these symbols attached to them on a piece of removable tape. It's a good idea to place this tape on the cover of your car owners manual or on another significant paper that remains in the glovebox. This will serve as a handy reference in the future, when you need to buy a wheel cleaner. Auto parts stores carrying Eagle 1 products also display a chart that lists in more detail the correct combination of cleaner and wheels.

Most chemical wheel cleaners contain hydrofluoric and phosphoric acid. This is the main chemical ingredient that dissolves brake dust, oil and road tar. Before applying any wheel cleaner, be sure the wheels have cooled down after driving. You can help them cool with water spray. This is especially important if you have driven to a self-serve car wash to do the cleaning.

Instructions advise the user to apply the cleaner and let stand for a specific amount of time, generally thirty seconds to two minutes. This is critical. Rinsing too soon won't allow the cleaner enough working time, and leaving it on too long may result in wheel damage. For extra tough grime and brake dust build-up, agitate the cleaner on the wheel with a paintbrush, according to instructions.

Rinsing is just as critical as the amount of time you let the cleaner sit on the wheel. Most instructions will suggest using high-pressure spray as opposed to a thumb over the end of a garden hose.

Cleaning around the bolts on this Lamborghini wheel is difficult: use a paintbrush and plenty of suds. The correct chemical wheel cleaner can clean just as well, and much faster. The best recommendation to keep areas like this from accumulating build-up is frequent cleaning and maintenance.

Scrubbing the chemical wheel cleaner with a paintbrush helps to remove stubborn stains and dirt build-up. Use caution working around these chemicals and consider wearing rubber gloves for this process. Also, be sure to vigorously rinse the paintbrush in clear water after using it on the wheel and before you use it on anything else.

Thorough rinsing is mandatory. You cannot rinse too much. Besides getting acid off the wheel, you should be concerned about removing residue from valve stem threads, lug nuts, center caps, spoke nipples and the like.

Cleaners for wire wheels

Like the Eagle 1 Wire Wheel Cleaning Kit, most wire wheel cleaners are two-step processes. The first step is a cleaner, the second a neutralizer. Rinse the wheel first with plain water. Next, spray the first-step cleaner liberally on rim and spokes, avoiding plastic center caps. Allow it to set approximately thirty seconds, and then rinse with water.

Step two, the neutralizer, is applied in the same manner as step one. The neutralizing agents in step two contain water softeners and specific agents that help to prevent streaks, stains and water spots. Rinse with plenty of water, and towel dry.

This type of product, used according to instructions, will make short work of cleaning wire wheels. Light rust, road grime, tar, oil and brake dust are easily and quickly removed.

Once again, however, one has to wonder about the long-term effects after repeated weekly applications. Wentworth will use such a cleaner once, then maintain wheels on a weekly basis using mild soap and water.

Basic cleaning for wire wheels

Chemical wheel cleaners will do an excellent job when used correctly. Applied improperly, they can cause streaks and stains, and remove polished finishes.

A small, one-inch paintbrush works well to remove dust and dirt from spokes and surrounding wheel features. After washing the wheel with the mitt, use this brush on the rim, around nipples, over the spokes and along the hub. Rinse with water, soap the wheel with the mitt and use a toothbrush for finishing work.

Cleaning spoked wheels is labor-intensive, to say the least. Armed with a toothbrush, clean each and every spoke and those spaces on the rim between them. The preferred toothbrush has a bend just behind the bristles. It allows better access to tight spots. A paintbrush also works well to clean around nipples and at those points where spokes are positioned close together.

Dish soaps designed to resist water spotting are good. You can also use multipurpose cleaners like Simple Green. Work up a good lather with the mitt and follow with the paintbrush. Rinse frequently,

The unique design of Reach brand toothbrushes is a noted asset when cleaning spoked wheels. The bend in the handle provides better access to areas under spokes and nipples. Note that the rings and bracelet on the hand of this detailer pose potential scratch hazards while cleaning, as well as during removal and installation of the wheel on the car.

A paintbrush and a toothbrush should remove most of the film and dirt on this chrome spoked wheel. Chrome polish can be applied by sticking your finger into a cloth, applying polish to the tip and maneuvering around the nipples. Extra tight spots can be polished with cotton swabs.

removing soap before it has a chance to dry and also to give you a better look at what you are doing. Clean both sides of the wheel.

Threaded parts of the spoke next to the nipples are common spots for rust. If the toothbrush and soap won't remove rust, try a little chrome polish on the end of a cotton swab. Remove the polish with a towel and toothbrush. If rust persists, apply polish with a toothbrush.

Since the back sides of these wheels generally receive so little attention, many are found in very dirty shape. Use an SOS pad to remove heavy accumulations of road grime, dirt and brake dust. The SOS pad works well on the spokes, too. Pitted and rusted rims will need polishing with Happich Simichrome or other chrome polish.

Wax the wheel for added protection, a good idea for the inside rim. Apply wax carefully, avoiding build-up at spoke bases. Remove build-up quickly with the cut-off paintbrush. Squirt a little WD-40 into all spoke ends to reduce future rust problems.

The center cores of knock-off wheels are lubricated. After a thorough cleaning, be sure to replace lubricant with the proper grease. You can also clean knock-off threads with a toothbrush and a towel. Once a year is not too often to check spokes for tightness. If you know how, tighten them yourself. If not, use the Yellow Pages to find a reputable wheel shop that can true spokes.

Cleaners for mags

True mag cleaners contain no acid. Instead, they contain solvents that penetrate the surface to remove accumulations of road grime and brake dust. Since acid is not used, a neutralizer is not needed, making mag cleaners a one-step process.

Apply according to directions. Rinse the wheel first with water. Spray the cleaner liberally on the wheel, and let stand for one to two minutes. Rinse thoroughly with a strong water spray.

Be sure to read mag cleaner labels before purchasing. Some cleaners are made for machine-finished and open-pore cast aluminum wheels, while others are for clear-coated, polished and painted factory mags.

If you are not sure what type of wheel is on your car, stop by a wheel shop and find out. Using the

The back sides of Wentworth's GS 455 tires. Both were identical until the one on the right was detailed. Lots of scrubbing with brushes, cleansers and SOS pads was needed to get the wheel on the right looking this good. Car enthusiasts like to clean the back sides of wheels once or twice a year—and sometimes more—depending on the style of wheel and the car it is on.

wrong cleaner may damage wheels, requiring repolishing or other repairs.

Cleaning other wheels

Painted, polished, clear-coated, cast aluminum and steel wheels are cleaned with mild soap and water. After scrubbing the tire, rinse the wash bucket and mix a fresh solution. Car wash soap or mild liquid dish soap is fine. Use an old wash mitt for extra dirty wheels, a newer one for those in good shape.

Wash the wheel first with the mitt. Push it into tight spots along slots and fins. Use the paintbrush liberally. You will be surprised at how well it cleans inside finned and gridwork patterns. Use a toothbrush around screws and inside slots. Don't be afraid to use your fingers. They can fit into places nothing else will, and you won't have to worry about scratching.

The back sides of some wheels may have to be scrubbed with a plastic brush to remove heavy accumulations of road grime and brake dust. This harsh cleaning is not good for the wheel as it can cause slight scratches from grit being moved around by the brush. Use this method only as needed to remove the really tough stuff. Detailed cleaning should be done afterward using a soft paintbrush or toothbrush or both.

BMW wheels can be a bear to clean. The gridwork pattern includes a lot of pockets difficult to reach. Persist with the paintbrush, using plenty of suds from the bucket. You may try using a special

toothbrush made for people with orthodontic braces. It is a soft brush with bristles shaped and located like cotton on a cotton swab. Don't force this brush into pockets, as it does have a metal rod supporting the bristles which could scratch.

Sometimes, the best cleaning tools are already attached to your hand. Here, the detailer uses his finger to clean dirt lodged along the edge of a recess featured on a stock BMW wheel. A paintbrush or toothbrush would have accomplished the same job, but in this case, a finger was quicker and easier.

Using the wrong polish on this alloy wheel could blemish the shine and the surface. If you are in doubt as to which polish to use on your wheels, go to a wheel store for advice. This wheel has never been polished; instead, it has been meticulously maintained with mild soap and frequent cleaning. If a stain were to occur, Happich Simichrome could be applied with good results.

Special wheels, like this race car's front wheel, can be damaged when improper cleaning products are applied. An SOS pad could severely scratch the surface and the wrong chemical cleaner could permanently stain it. To be on the safe side, use mild soap and water, a paintbrush and mitt, and lots of elbow grease.

Chrome-plated steel wheels as well as polished mag or aluminum wheels can be polished with Eagle 1 Mag & Chrome Cleaner. Painted wheels should be waxed. For badly abused and neglected chrome wheels, try Meguiar's Heavy Duty Chrome Polish or Happich Simichrome. Extra-heavy stains may require three to five applications of mild polish to completely clean and shine.

Cleaning wheel covers and hubcaps

Eagle 1 Wire Hubcap Cleaner is designed for original equipment wire and plastic mag hubcaps. You can use this or a comparable product, or clean by hand with soap, water, paint and toothbrushes. Some do-it-yourself detailers put wheel covers in the dishwasher with good cleaning results.

You shouldn't have to pull wheel covers every time you wash the car. Twice a year is sufficient, depending on the style of wheel cover and driving conditions to which it is subjected. Clean them inside and out. Clean the wheels, too.

Chrome covers are polished like any other chrome part. Paint touch-up is done with an artist's brush and appropriate paint. Damaged center cap decals can be replaced; check with the auto parts store or dealership carrying the same make of car.

This style of stock Corvette hubcap is susceptible to damage during removal. Refrain from using any tools to remove it. Instead, use your hands and apply the minimum amount of force needed. Treat it gently to avoid bends and wrinkles.

Pulling wheel covers and hubcaps

Most wheel covers and hubcaps are strong enough to withstand numerous removals. Even so, you must use care pulling them. Stock beauty rims and hubcaps on Corvettes bend easily. Do not use tools to pry them loose. Use your fingers, and pull a little at a time, constantly moving around the rim. I advise you to not pull this type of beauty rim and hubcap unless absolutely necessary.

Painted rims can suffer chipped paint during removal of wheel covers. Use a wide-bladed tool to pry loose an edge. Then, place a thin piece of cardboard or towel between the tool and the rim edge. This will help reduce metal-to-metal wear and prevent paint chips.

Just as much care should be given to putting the covers back on the wheel as taking them off. Be sure the valve stem lines up with the hole in the cover. Misaligned, the sharp edge of the cover may cut the valve stem causing a slow leak. Use your hands to get the cover in place, and secure it with a rubber mallet.

Painting wheels

Stock-painted wheels can be repainted. The best way is to remove the tire and strip old paint to bare metal. Sand and prime as necessary, then paint. The auto body paint and supply store can mix the proper paint, matching the original or creating a custom color. Enamel paint is most common because of its durability and because, unlike lacquer, it does not have to be buffed. Have the paint and an artist's paintbrush handy when remounting the tire. This will enable you to touch up any chips that occur during the process.

Wheels may also be painted with the tire attached, either on or off the car. The end result may not be as nice as a wheel that has been stripped, sanded and painted, but with care, a wheel's appearance can be greatly improved.

Prevent paint overspray on the tire with masking tape, grease or paint block. Masking tape will not stick to a tire that has been freshly dressed—a good point to remember. You can carefully mask next to the rim with quarter-inch masking tape and cover that with a wider strip three-quarters to one inch wide. Cover the rest of the tire with newspaper, taping it to the strip of tape already on the tire. The first masking strip you place next to the rim is the most critical. Take your time, and try to place tape behind the rim edge as much as possible.

A film of grease can be placed along the tire next to the rim. Paint will not stick to grease. This is a messy chore and you must not get any grease on the rim, as paint will not stick to that grease either.

A paint block can be made out of a piece of thin cardboard. The bottom of a shoe box is perfect. As you paint around the wheel, keep an edge of the paint block tucked closely between the tire and rim edge. Be sure the paint block is in position before you start painting. The block will have to be held in one hand while you paint with the other. Overspray should be minimized. If any paint gets on the tire, remove it with lacquer thinner and a rag.

Many foreign compact cars are equipped with silver wheels and plastic lug nut covers and center hubs. For good results paint these wheels with bright silver paint. The plastic covers clean easily with soap and water.

Chips on painted wheels can be repaired much like chips on body paint. Dab paint on the chip. Let it dry, and do it again. Allow the paint to build up higher than the surrounding surface. After a week of drying, mask off the chip and sand smooth with #600 wet-and-dry sandpaper. Remove masking tape, and polish to a fine finish.

Caring for lug nuts

Before replacing wheels, take a minute to service the lugs. Grease is removed with a rag and WD-40 on a toothbrush.

Chrome and painted lug nuts may scratch while being tightened by the lug wrench. To prevent scratches, place a piece of plastic over the lug nut before applying the wrench. One side of a heavy-duty freezer bag, such as a Ziploc bag, works well.

A heavy-duty plastic freezer bag was opened up and laid over the lug nuts before the lug wrench was applied. The plastic protects chrome and painted lug nuts from scratches during removal and installation. Start with a fresh section of plastic for each lug nut.

Chapter 11

Finishing touches

After cleaning, polishing, waxing and dressing, carefully check your car to see that everything is perfect. For maximum visibility, inspect the car in sunlight.

The loose edge on this driver's side floor mat poses a potential driving hazard. In a relaxed position, with the cruise control running the car, a foot could catch in the opening and prevent the operator's quick access to the brake pedal. An upholstery shop can restitch the seam in a matter of minutes.

You have to wonder, after spending days washing, cleaning, polishing and waxing an automobile, what else is there to do? Remember what Dan Mycon said earlier in the book about detailing? He sees it as a two-part process: cleaning, and getting things right. The cleaning is done; now let's get things right.

Parts replacement

How do the floor mats look? Do they match? Do they fit your car correctly? Are they the right color scheme? Why lessen the impact of a professionally detailed interior with a set of cheap, ugly floor mats? Go out and purchase a set that fits the car and blends with the overall appearance of the interior.

The same holds true for worn pedal rubbers and steering wheel covers. These parts are inexpensive, last a long time and provide the interior with a feeling of completion.

Under the hood, look at the battery and the plastic containers for windshield washer fluid and radiator overfill. A battery that looks old and worn probably is. Why clean plastic bottles if they are cracked and serve no useful purpose? You can purchase inexpensive batteries for under forty dollars, and those plastic bottles can be bought from an auto wrecker for around five dollars each.

If both heater hoses are black and one bursts, don't replace it with a red one. For that matter, if one broke, the other is about ready to; replace them both. Ditto for radiator and vacuum hoses.

The same approach holds for ignition wires. If one goes bad, replace the entire set. If you really want to make a car person laugh, replace a faulty black spark plug wire with a yellow one. Most engines are equipped with guides for plug wires. It is usually a bracket attached to a valve cover bolt. The bracket supports a plastic piece that holds each wire in place, keeping the wires from dangling over the edge of the valve covers. Make use of such brackets to keep wires neat and aligned.

Factory engine stickers add originality. Replace worn and torn stickers with new ones. Check with auto parts stores or a local dealership for availability. Radiator caps, fan belts, valve cover gaskets and battery cables all fit into this category. These parts are inexpensive and seldom have to be replaced. Spend an extra fifty or sixty dollars (more if you need a battery), and make the engine compartment really stand tall.

In the trunk, jacking equipment should be clean and usable. The diagram showing how to stow the

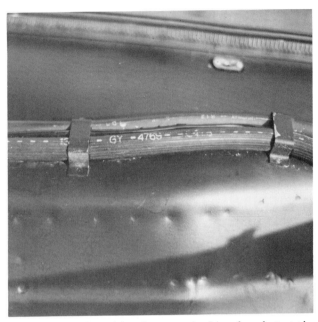

Minor paint chips like those on the hose bracket at the right of the picture can be touched up with a small artist's paintbrush. During a full detail, the hoses should be removed from the brackets, cleaned and dressed. At that time, the brackets and the area under the hoses can be repainted with semi-gloss or gloss black.

Dirt under the radiator overflow hose should have been cleaned before the radiator was painted. Use a damp towel to clean spots like this and look under all other hoses for similar oversights.

New decals for many older cars are available through auto dealerships and auto parts stores. A new GS 455 emblem for this Buick air cleaner can be purchased through a Buick agency's parts department.

equipment should be legible. If not, replace it. How is the trunk mat? Stock mats can be purchased at reasonable prices.

On the exterior, look at the wheel hubs. Wentworth's 1970 Buick GS 455 convertible originally came equipped with factory wheels exhibiting nice decals on the center hubs. Unfortunately, when he acquired the car, most of these decals were broken. To his surprise, the local Buick dealership was able to get stock replacements and now the wheels look perfect. He was also able to purchase the GS emblems for the front quarter panels. All stock emblems and decals belong on the car. You should make a sincere effort to find them starting at the auto parts store, dealership and auto supply store as well as in auto part catalogs.

For those decals, emblems and trim that suffer from paint peeling or fading, touch-up can be done at home. A visit to the auto body supply and paint store should provide you with the correct color and type of paint. Use an artist's brush for application.

Final inspection

Under artificial lighting, a detailed automobile may look perfect. In sunlight, the perception is much different. The sun will readily reveal smeared windows, swirls, lint, wax residue and much more.

Park the car in a dry, sunny spot. Have at the ready your cleaning gear, including the dressing-soaked towel, the cut-off paintbrush and a clean towel.

Interior

Open all the doors, and sit in the driver's seat. Check the dash for spots missed by dressing. There should be no need to spray additional dressing; wiping with the dressing cloth will bring up some excess from the surrounding vinyl.

Are the gauges clean? Check for smeared dressing marks, lint and dust. Vents can be touched up with cotton swabs. Spray swabs with a dab of household furniture polish, like Pledge. This makes the swab more dust absorbent. Afterward, adjust vents so that they point in the same direction.

Check the headliner and rearview mirror, front and back. Look in the corners of the windshield for dirt and around the mirror base for smears. The steering wheel should be squeaky clean, including grooves near the horn button and along the steering column.

Next, check carpet for lint and stains. A dry spot remover will work fine. Worn patches on carpet can be covered with rubber inserts at the upholstery shop. Secure loose carpet using double-backed tape.

Put tension on the seats to spread pleats, looking for lint and grit. Do the same thing to the bead

New center hub decals make this freshly detailed wheel and tire set look new. New chrome acorn lug nuts were purchased to complete the entire package on Wentworth's Buick GS 455. Check with auto parts stores and dealerships to locate similar items for different makes and models.

Wax build-up in the lettering on the lens of this sidelight does not stick out like a sore thumb. However, combined with a number of other subtle oversights, an entire automobile can appear less than appealing. Use a toothbrush or a cut-off paintbrush to remove this type of wax build-up. A clean soft towel will be needed to buff off resultant powdery wax residue.

and the area between the cushion and the backrest. Check the back seat area with the same intensity.

Finally, look at the door panels. All scuffs and marks should be gone. If not, clean and dress again. Check door handles and pouches, if so-equipped. Doorjambs must be free of dirt and grease. Squirt a little WD-40 on hinges and door latches for lubrication. Wipe off the excess. Are the door moldings OK?

Exterior

Open the hood and trunk lid. Look for and remove wax residue on the edges of these parts, including the area next to the windshield and rear window. The lip drain and molding for the trunk lid must also be clean and dust-free.

Inspect decals, emblems and trim. Squat down and check paint on exposed frame parts and fenderwells. Rubber bumper guards and vinyl trim should be dressed and lint-free. Carefully look into the corners of grille components and remove any rem-

nants of dust and dirt. License plates clean? Plate frames OK?

Look at all the glass. Sunlight will plainly show imperfections. Bull's-eye damage to windshields can be repaired, as opposed to requiring full glass replacement. Kits are available at auto parts stores for under ten dollars. They work quite well. If you

Wax dust and residue along the molding bead of this Lamborghini doorjamb should be quickly cleaned with the cut-off paintbrush. When inspecting a car, open the doors, trunk lid and hood to look for and remove wax and dust along their edges.

Bring color back to faded interior vinyl with dye designed for vinyl application. Most car enthusiasts recommend you not change the color of any vinyl. They would prefer to have all new upholstery installed in order to effect a color change. Dyes of various colors are available at auto body paint and supply stores.

Wax residue in the corner edge of this deck lid was not noticeable with the lid closed. A cut-off paintbrush will remove the residue easily.

Dressing application on tires should be uniform. Novice detailers spray dressing over the entire tire and leave it. You must buff off all excess dressing and work the poly-penetrant into the rubber. Worthington has maintained the tires on his 944 by wiping them with a cloth sprayed with dressing. Light and consistent coverage makes rubber look new and cared for, not just spiffed.

Lightly damaged flexible bumpers can be repaired using kits like this one from Bondo. Major damage will require a new bumper. Auto body paint and supply stores are loaded with various kits designed to repair minor damage to vinyl, trim and other items.

Bull's-eyes, such as this one in the windshield of a Porsche 911 Targa, can be repaired professionally by a company called Novus. Repair kits are also sold at auto parts and auto body paint and supply stores for do-it-yourself repairs. It is best to repair bull's-eyes and stars as soon as possible before a crack starts to creep along the windshield, making any repairs impossible.

Chrome weights look much better on chrome wheels than standard lead weights. When getting wheels and tires balanced, spend the extra money to have appropriate weights applied, would rather, a company called Novus repairs such damage. In some cases, it is reported that auto insurance companies pay for the service.

Look at wheels and tires to determine if the dressing was applied evenly. Many times, that part of the tire which was on the ground at the time of initial dressing will not have been touched. Whitewalls should be checked for pattern uniformity. Mismatched and damaged whitewalls can be repaired by tire cosmetologists; check with the local car dealer or the Yellow Pages.

Chips on black lug nuts, black trim and chassis can be touched up with a black felt pen. By no means a permanent repair, this quick fix will cover a blemish for a short time, until you have the opportunity to properly sand, prime and paint.

Dings in chrome bumpers can be cosmetically touched up with a tiny dab of bright silver paint.

Spray a tiny puddle on a piece of cardboard, dip a toothpick into it and apply to the ding. From a couple of feet away, you won't know the difference.

The windshield wiper blades should be replaced if not working properly. If in good shape, buff with the dressing cloth. There is no need to spray additional dressing; the excess on the cloth will be sufficient.

How do things under the hood look? In sunlight, you'll quickly notice paint flaws, dirt and lint. Adjust plug wires so they line up according to the design of the engine. Other wires should also run true to pattern. Remove any overspray with a dab of lacquer thinner on a rag. Chrome can be touched up with chrome polish. Look at the underside of the hood for flaws.

Louvers are notorious places for wax build-up. Check them along the cowling at the base of the windshield. Use the cut-off paintbrush for cleaning.

A broad black felt-tipped pen is a secret carried in just about every show car owner's detailing kit. By no means a permanent repair, these pens can quickly touch up wear marks and slight scratches on black-painted wheels, lug nuts and trim. Here, the pen is used to cover up wrench marks on the lug nuts of a Porsche wheel.

A toothpick is used to remove wax along the outer edge of a windshield washer nozzle on a 300ZX. In this case, a soft, cut-off paintbrush would be much better suited, as it does not pose a potential scratch hazard. Toothpicks come in handy to remove debris along the base of windows and windshields, and to scrape built-up crud from slots on steering wheels and knobs.

Marsha Templeton prefers to leave this bra on her 1977 Porsche 911 Targa at all times. She believes the bra protects paint from rock chips and other road hazards. Other

car people disagree. They feel bras do more harm than good by trapping dirt and grit underneath, causing scratches while they vibrate in the wind during driving.

Under the bra of Templeton's 911 you can see the accumulation of dirt particles and grit. Moisture is also trapped under the bra, adding to the problems associated with constant bra usage.

Walk around the car as many times as it takes. Look at it from every angle and height. Inspect every square inch. When you have made two trips around without finding a flaw, smile. Isn't it a beautiful automobile?

Protecting your detailed automobile
Bras

Protecting a beautiful, detailed car is important. Car enthusiasts have mixed emotions about bras and car covers. Bras protect paint against chips from road hazards. At the same time, they trap rain water and minute pieces of grit. As the bra vibrates in the wind, grit is rubbed against underlying paint, causing scratches. If you deem it necessary, put on the bra while traveling a particularly rough road. Remove it when you're past the hazard.

Bras themselves are maintained in much the same way as interior vinyl. Clean with the mitt and car wash soap, using a soft brush as necessary to remove build-up and bug residue. Hang the bra on a clothesline or other suitable spot to allow it to dry.

Break loose and whisk away lint and grit from the inner surface with a soft brush. Afterward, apply a light coat of dressing and be sure to buff off the excess and allow to dry before storing or re-installing.

Car covers

Car covers do an excellent job of protecting paint and interiors. Most important in the summer, good car covers protect paint from the scorching rays of the sun. They also keep the sun's ultraviolet

Cotton car covers, like this one covering Worthington's 1985 Porsche 944, are preferred among car enthusiasts. Beverly Hills Motoring Accessories carries a wide assortment for various automobile makes and models.

Good quality car covers protect the car's interior as well as the exterior. Blocking the sun's ultraviolet rays helps interiors resist fading and cracking.

To uncover the car, first fold each side of the cover up and onto the roof, trunk and hood.

With the cover folded onto the roof, trunk and hood, roll the cover from the front of the car onto the center of the hood. Then, starting at the back bumper, roll the cover up to the hood until it is confined in a roll. When you go to cover the car, simply place it on the center of the hood and reverse the process.

rays from penetrating interiors, drying vinyl and leather upholstery and fading fabrics.

Plastic car covers are worse than no cover at all. Heat is trapped inside with no place to go. Your car needs a cover that breathes. Cotton car covers are favorites among car people. Beverly Hills Motoring Accessories sells an excellent assortment of them.

There are no real tricks to putting on a car cover, or taking it off. The key is to never let it touch the ground, where it may pick up grit or grime. You will need some help putting it on the first time. After that, taking the cover off and putting it on is a one-person operation, which you will learn to do.

Imagine that the cover is on your car. Loosen one side and fold it to the middle. Do the same with the other side; now the folded cover is lying lengthwise on the trunk, top and hood. Next you fold the cover into thirds. Fold the far front up to the middle of the hood. Then, starting at the rear, fold the cover all the way to the hood.

When you cover the car, simply place the folded cover on the hood. Unfold to the rear, then the front, followed by each side. Tuck it around bumpers and mirrors.

Avoid sliding the cover on the car. The slightest grit will cause scratching. If you think it is going to

rain, keep the cover off. Rain won't hurt the car; a wet, moldy car cover will.

If you must park your car in the sun on a regular basis and don't have a cover, try alternating the car's position. Park in different spots, allowing the driver's side to catch the majority of sunlight one day, the passenger side the next. If only one parking space is available, back the car in one day and pull straight in the next.

Rattles and squeaks

Finicky Art Wentworth let laid-back Jerry McKee drive his gorgeous 1974 red Corvette roadster during an extended trip down the California coast. While on a rather remote and mundane stretch of highway, Jerry suggested Art take a short nap. Trying to relax, Art's finely tuned ear honed in on a vibrating noise coming from somewhere in the car's immaculate cockpit. The new rattle disturbed him and he began an immediate search for it.

Art moved his head about, listening intently for the irritating noise. He touched the console, pushed on the door panel, felt under the dashboard and covered every square inch of the interior he could reach with his hands, ears and eyes.

After about fifteen minutes of watching Art out of the corner of his eye, Jerry finally asked him what in the heck he was doing. Art explained he was looking for a rattle. Jerry said, "I don't hear anything."

Art went on in detail, describing the unique vibrating sound. At long last, Jerry said, "Oh, that noise!" and took his hand off of the steering wheel to show Art his ring. "The stone is loose in its setting and I guess it was rattling from the vibration in the steering wheel." Art just sighed.

I include this brief scene to demonstrate two things. The longer you listen to a rattle or a squeak, the more your ear gets used to it, finally tuning it out. Over time, the loose part will wear prematurely or break. On the other hand, as a true car enthusiast, seeking out new rattles and squeaks and repairing the cause will prolong the life and use of effected parts.

After a complete detail, go over the car, inside and out, and tighten screws, nuts and bolts. Tighten trim, grille pieces, license plate frames, lug nuts, hood bolts, valve covers, seat brackets, dash screws and so on. Use clean tools of the appropriate size and check every fastener you can see. As a preventative measure, you can do this once a month during the super cleaning, or concentrate on just one section of the car with each washing, using a system that ensures complete coverage once a month. During oil changes and lube jobs, concentrate on the screws, nuts and bolts under the hood.

If you discover a rattle or squeak while driving, take note of it and plan to track it down later. Don't start looking for it while hanging onto the steering wheel doing 55 mph down the freeway. Let someone else drive the car while you hunt for the noise, pushing and pulling as much as you please.

Chapter 12

Is concours any different?

A Concours d'Elegance is an event in which owners of restored and highly maintained automobiles compete to see which entry is the cleanest and most original. The amount of time these competitors spend detailing their cars is staggering. George and Kathy Ridderbusch have won almost eighty concours awards and have spent countless hours cleaning and detailing their 1979 Porsche 928 to perfection. When asked how many hours of work have gone into the car, George Ridderbusch replied, "I have spent a lifetime cleaning and preparing this car. It's a labor of love, a devotion and love of the car. It's like, how many hours a day can you love your wife?"

To get an example of how perfect a concours winner must be, I asked Mike Wiley how a brand new car, fresh from the showroom floor, would score. With six years' experience as a concours judge, Wiley said that a new car straight from the showroom would score 150 out of a possible 300 points. He also said that most winning cars generally score 295 to 297 points overall. That means a brand new car, never driven, is only half as perfect as a concours winner!

To say concours enthusiasts are perfectionists is an understatement. After reading this chapter, you may understand why.

Concours events

Concours d'Elegance events are held periodically throughout the world. Across the United States, you can attend competitions in many cities, from Forest Grove, Oregon, to Rochester, Michigan, to Pebble Beach, California. Various car magazines print calendars that include auto shows and concours events.

George and Kathy Ridderbusch's concours-winning 1979 Porsche 928. Purchased new, it took them hundreds of hours to remove all the Cosmolene, line up clamps and screws, trim threads, polish, clean and perfect this car into a consistent concours-winning automobile.

Generally, about half of the concours events are held outdoors in park settings. Cars are parked early on and competitors spend hours attending to minute details. Here, five entries are staged waiting for judging while enthusiasts admire and photograph favorites.

Said to have begun in France in the late 1800s, a concours was an event for the social elite; the car and entire family were judged. In England, competition in the Rolls-Royce category became so fierce that beautiful models, hired to show the cars, wore specially designed dresses that matched the interiors of the cars. Some entrants even went so far as to have picnic tables set up nearby with linens and accessories made to blend with the vintage and color of individual cars. It got so ridiculous that the cars were being overshadowed.

In America, competition is just as keen. George Ridderbusch used to drive his car to events. Arriving a day early, he would spend fourteen to sixteen hours preparing the car for judging. This was in addition to the three weeks of six- to eight-hour days he spent getting the car ready beforehand, even though the car was exceptionally clean to begin with!

Because competition has become so exacting, George Ridderbusch is now forced to tow the car to events in an enclosed trailer. By the way, in the trailer the car sits on wheels and tires put on just for the trip. The set reserved for judging are carefully placed on a rack in the trailer and not put on until the car is parked in its final position. Because wheels and tires are worth five points, he cannot afford the slightest scuff or blemish.

Each event hosts its own categories, depending on the number of entries and the varying vintages and models. For instance, the 1987 Meadow Brook Hall Concours d'Elegance in Rochester, Michigan, listed these eleven classes.

Class A Antiques through 1915
Class B Vintage, 1916 through 1924
Class C American Classic, (open cars), 1925 through 1934
Class D American Classic, (closed cars), 1925 through 1942
Class E American Classic, (open cars), 1935 through 1948
Class F Postwar Convertible
Class G Postwar Luxury, (closed cars)
Class H European Classic Prewar, (including Rolls-Royce)
Class I Classic Sports Cars through 1959
Class J Contemporary Sports Cars, 1960 and newer
Class K Featured Cars

These are actual score sheets used to judge the Ridderbusches' 928. The 288.7 points out of a possible total of 300 are mighty impressive, considering a brand new car fresh off the showroom floor can only hope to bring in about 150 points.

The Ridderbusch 928 undergoes extensive detailing for three solid days prior to judging.

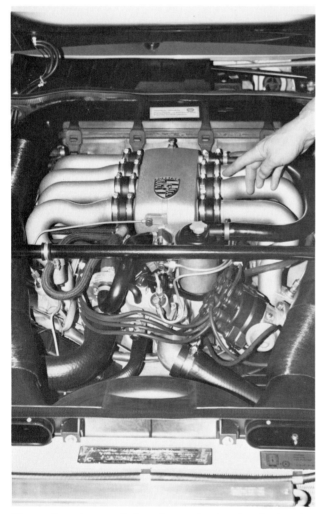

The perfect degree of gloss is required under the hood to earn maximum points. Note the total degree of consistency throughout this 928 engine compartment. Hose clamps are aligned, screw slots are all vertical, hoses look equally perfect and there's not a speck of dust anywhere.

Larger events include more categories. For example, the concours show held in Forest Grove, Oregon, listed thirty-five classes, some of which included Jaguar sports cars 1946 through 1973, one- and two-cylinder cars through 1916, and historic auto race entries.

After all the cars have been judged, each class winner is entered into the "Best of Show." This competition determines the best car of the entire competition. Since all the Best of Show entrants are winners of their classes, only the best car is given an award; there is no second or third place.

About half of the concours events are held outdoors in beautiful parklike settings. One of the most picturesque is the Vintage Car Show presented by the Chilliwack Rotary Club of Chilliwack, British Columbia, Canada. The cars are parked in designated spots on the grass throughout the Minter Gardens grounds. Surrounded by thousands of colorful flowers and acres of manicured lawns, the entries look spectacular.

Other concours events are held indoors. At one such show in Reno, Nevada, George Ridderbusch parked his 928 in the arena three days early. Immediately, the car was put up on jacks and the Ridderbusches went to work. Systematically, the couple went over every square inch of the car, making sure each item was perfect. An entire day was spent on the wheels and tires. It took two hours to bring up the perfect degree of gloss on a cast-plastic air cleaner element, which would be worth one-half point.

As a judge, Wiley points out that too much shine and gloss is not original and detracts from the true beauty of the car. At the same show, a vintage auto was delivered in a crate. It came in pieces fresh from the restoration shop. A crew of six worked feverishly to assemble the car within the prescribed time limits. This degree of perfection is understandable when you realize that George Ridderbusch has missed first place by only three-tenths of a point—caused by a misaligned screw.

Considered two of the top Porsche concours competitors in the country, the Ridderbusches are said to be the only people to have entered their car in three consecutive "Manhatten Circle" (Best of Show) events during the National Porsche Parade, a concours show exclusively for Porsche automobiles held at different locations across the country. The Ridderbusch car won the Best of Show at the 1987 Porsche Concours at Expo, the 1986 World's Fair held in Victoria, British Columbia, Canada.

George Ridderbusch estimates that out of 250 entries, only ten to fifteen will really compete. By this, he means that not everyone can spend the thousands of hours required to detail a winner. He notes that his 928 was purchased brand new and it took three to four years to bring it up to a consistent first- and second-place finisher.

Wiley and George Ridderbusch both agree that just entering and competing in a concours event is fun, and acknowledge that a car fresh from a good detail shop may place fifth or sixth in a field of seven. Most detail shops just can't afford the time it takes to detail a winner. It's when you get to the top two and three percent that it gets serious.

One can't help but wonder why people do it, especially when awards for winners consist of ribbons, plaques and trophies; there are no cash prizes in a concours event. George Ridderbusch says, "Concours is strictly a hobby and a passion—like a mountain, it's there to be climbed."

Preparation for judging

Depending on the concours, a team of three to six people will serve as judges. Wearing white coveralls or smocks, they have six minutes to evaluate each entry. Because of the limited time, showing the car is a critical element.

Contestants have been known to spend hours parking the car in just the right spot. They will determine the direction from which the judges will approach and position the car so that the best side is seen first. If one spot under the hood isn't perfect,

they will try to have the engine compartment positioned under a tree, hoping shade will hide the flaw. George Ridderbusch has even strategically placed his wife so that she blocked the judge's view of a tiny paint flaw near a quarter panel. "All's fair in love and war," he says.

During concours events held outdoors, competitors have manicured grass and pulled weeds to make the site more appealing. Some fanatic entrants gently push and pull their cars into position, not wanting to turn on the engine for fear of marring the engine compartment. Fanatical competitors restore cars and never place a drop of fluid anywhere in the car—no oil, gas, brake or transmission fluid—so they never have to worry about the slightest leak or telltale spot on the floor.

About the judges

Concouring today is more competitive than ever before. Along with ultimate cleanliness, judges look for originality. Owners spend thousands of dollars restoring classic automobiles to better than new and original condition. Money is spent on locating, restoring and properly installing original parts. Judges must be thoroughly familiar with the type and model of car they evaluate to be assured of fairness and accuracy.

Learning about the originality of a car is not easy. Judges research magazines, books, owners manuals and especially shop manuals. They learn

Judges, in white coats, go over the 928 with a fine tooth comb. Each of five to six judges is responsible for one part of the car—for example, interior, engine compartment and so on. Note the judge lying down next to the front tire inspecting the underbody. He is looking for dust, dirt, grit and grease on top of the transmission and anywhere else he can find it, and may even check to see if cotter pins are bent correctly around locking nuts.

From another angle, you can see judges inspecting the rear underbody, front underbody, trunk, interior, exterior paint on the driver's door—and one judge on the passenger side leaning over to check the engine compartment. The judges have six minutes to observe the car before tallying a score. Not much judging time considering the hundreds and thousands of hours concours competitors spend preparing their automobiles.

through years of experience, generally starting as a competitor in a particular class of automobile. Over the years, they develop a special knowledge for certain categories, such as German cars, English cars or old cars.

Because competition is so keen, judges quickly scan the obvious and hunt for peculiarities and dirt in the most hidden spots. Wiley has checked cotter pins on ball joint retainer nuts to see if they are bent the right way. To break a tie between two perfect cars, he opened the distributor caps to see which was cleanest. George Ridderbusch lost first place after a tie because of dust on the coil spring inside the windshield wiper of his car. One judge likes to stick a cotton swab into the spark plug wrench of Porsche tool kits to find dirt, and another checks engine oil for color.

Six minutes doesn't seem like a long enough period to judge a car, especially after the owner has spent thousands of hours preparing it. Therefore, each judge is only responsible for one part of the car. Depending on the event, one judge will be assigned to each of the following areas: exterior, engine compartment, chassis forward, chassis rearward, interior and storage compartment, bumpers and wheels. Each judge is given a score sheet for his or her particular area. The sheet lists a maximum point total for each of several categories for that area. Each category is judged on originality and preparation. For instance, the spare tire is worth two points: 0.4 for originality and 1.6 for preparation.

After judging, all the score sheets are tallied. It is not uncommon to find a winner with a final score of 296 or 297 out of a possible 300 point total. Better judges make brief comments at the bottom of their score sheets. This helps the owner to understand why the car was marked down in a certain area and to improve before the next competition.

Detailing for concours events

As mentioned earlier, a car detailed at a quality shop will generally score in the middle of the pack at a concours event. The exceptions are those cars prepared by select detailers with concours experience who charge more than $350.

If you detail your car according to the advice in this book, you can be assured of bringing it up to the baseline for a concours event. To get into the winner's circle, your car will have to be as close to perfect as you can get it.

You will have to research everything you can get your hands on that pertains to your car. Study shop manuals and parts books with emphasis on blowups of parts and assemblies to see how they are put together, how the cotter pins are bent and so on. Join a car club and become part of the support group for a fellow member active in concours events. Most of all, be prepared to spend lots of time cleaning, polishing, researching and detailing.

Detailing for a concours event is different from detailing for the street. For concouring, the car must be perfect for an eight- to ten-hour period. Long-

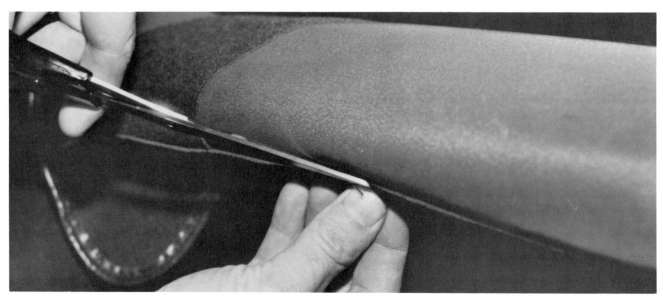

Part of the interior detail for concours preparation includes trimming stray threads from upholstery. After vacuuming, George Ridderbusch meticulously trims carpet nap with scissors to achieve a perfect surface.

lasting effects are not as important. For that reason, some of the detailing tips that follow may seem contrary to what has been already presented.

Tips for the interior

For the first-time detail on a potential concours car, the interior should be stripped. The degree to which it is dismantled depends on the age of the car. Older models may require removal of door panels and trim to allow for cleaning and dust removal.

George Ridderbusch can easily spend twenty-four hours cleaning the interior of the 928. After a thorough vacuuming, he uses scissors to trim carpet nap that doesn't conform to the proper level. He also inspects upholstery for loose stitching or threads, and trims accordingly.

Shampooing the carpet may be acceptable for a first-time detail, but concours people worry about shrinkage and slight color fading. Use the least amount of water possible, and consider a very light application of the properly colored carpet dye to bring back the original tint.

Concours detailers prefer to bring as little as possible into the interior during cleaning, including water and liquids. Some have found Tuff Stuff to be a good overall cleaner. They like the foam because it contains less liquid than other cleaners and it doesn't tend to fade colors. Many use dry cotton swabs to remove dust in grooves along the dash, although some spray the swab (outside of the car) with Pledge for added dust absorption.

Never use an all-purpose polypenetrant dressing on the interior. The silicones eventually adhere to almost everything and cause fisheyes on anything you try to repaint. Ridderbusch uses Lexol exclusively. Three days before judging, he will apply a light coat to leather and vinyl. His prescribed time span allows the conditioner to soak in and fade to a rich appearance without extra high gloss. The three-day period also allows vapors to dissipate which helps glass to stay clean for a longer time.

All interior metal parts on a concours winner must be free of paint chips. Brake and clutch rods, seat brackets and even the nuts and bolts securing the seat should be sanded and painted as needed. Metal dashboards should be polished with a mild glaze wax. George Ridderbusch prefers Meguiar's #7.

During cleaning and polishing, check to see that the heads of trim screws are in line, pointing in the same direction. Use a toothpick to remove dirt or wax inside the slots.

George Ridderbusch applies Lexol to the leather interior of his 928 three days before judging, without deviation. He has found through experience that it takes three days for the conditioner to fade to just the right degree of gloss for winning results.

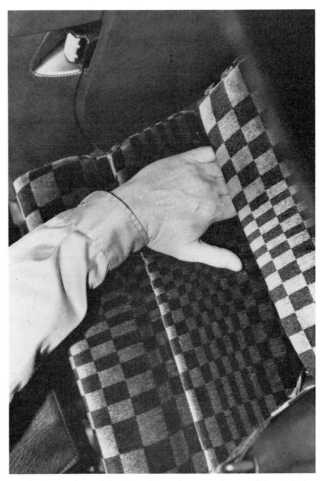

With the palm of his hand resting on the cushion of the rear seat, George Ridderbusch reaches into the space between the cushion and seatback to feel for proper staple spacing. He was marked down by a judge because one staple was out of position.

Kathy Ridderbusch prefers to use Glass Plus for window cleaning. She used water and newspaper for a time but has found that this glass cleaner works very well. She takes her time and cleans in small sections, never letting any of the cleaner dry on the glass. Before an event, she cleans each window three to four times and stresses the importance of using a clean cloth each time. At that, for concours judging, the insides of the windows only stay clean for thirty to forty-five minutes with the doors closed because of vapors emitted by interior vinyl.

Tips for the exterior

As a fellow member of the local Porsche club, Wiley (while not judging) participated in the club's support group helping George Ridderbusch prepare the 928 for a concours show. Wiley spent eighteen hours polishing the paint with Meguiar's #7. Totally by hand, he filled in or removed every swirl and hint of spider webbing, a small section at a time. To fill in and remove scratches, he would apply the glaze in any direction necessary. For final applications, he rubbed in a straight, back-and-forth motion. When finished, the paint was perfect.

Many concours people do not use carnauba protection wax on show cars. They feel this wax builds

The "Car of the year" sticker came stock with the car and has been maintained for originality. Only this and an "Unleaded fuel only" sticker are found on any piece of glass.

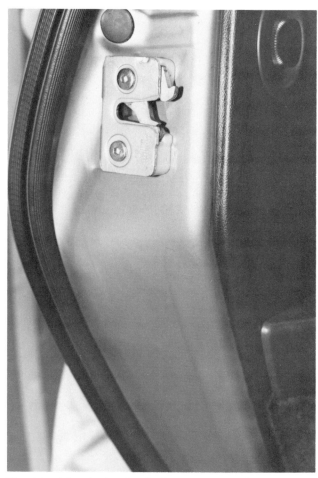

The 928 driver's doorjamb. No service stickers, no dirt, no grease and no paint chips. Note the rich appearance of the molding, achieved through light and consistent applications of dressing followed by concentrated buffing.

Many concours enthusiasts, like the Ridderbusch team, enjoy the sport and invite fellow car club members to events to help with detailing preparations. As part of the support group, friends help polish, dust and clean, as is being done here.

up and yellows over time. Instead, they wax with a glaze and keep the car out of the sun and the elements, usually in a separate, heated garage. The swirls and spider webbing remain invisible for about ten days. To prepare for the next event requires another treatment of the same intensity.

The degree of exterior paint gloss is another important factor noticed by judges. The high-gloss detailed look does not fare well. Orange peel (a rough paint surface that looks like the texture of orange rinds) is also a factor considered by judges. If a particular model came from the factory with a certain degree of orange peel, points are deducted if the car owner polished paint to perfection, flattening the original orange peel.

Chrome is polished as it is with any automobile. Some prefer to protect it with a coat of wax. For shows, Wiley applies a light coat of Windex. It brings up a brilliant shine without an oily film.

George Ridderbusch has had good results using Turtle Wax Clear Guard and Meguiar's #40 on exterior rubber. He applies it to every piece of rubber on

Gentle cleaning with mild soap, paintbrush and toothbrush keeps this 928 wheel and tire looking better than new. Note how the point of the Porsche crest in the center of the wheel points toward the valve stem. This seemingly trivial item has been the tie-breaking factor used to determine who took first place in a concours competition. The second-place finisher had the point of each tire's crest pointing down in uniformity. For originality, crests came from the factory with the points toward the valve stem.

All the Phillips-head screws are aligned in the same position on the taillight lens. This area is crisp because there is no wax build-up anywhere and the paint is polished uniformly.

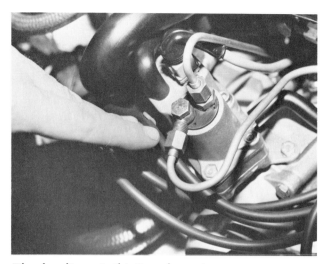

The cleanliness in this Porsche engine compartment even extends to the exposed threads on couplings. Constant upkeep with small brushes, clean towels, cotton swabs and lots of time are the key ingredients.

the exterior, including tires, bumper guards and wiper blades. A cotton swab is used to carefully wipe it on rubber trim next to paint.

Since long-lasting qualities are not the main concern for concours cars, Lexol has been used successfully as a dressing for vinyl tops. It makes the top look fresh without the glossy look silicone

dressings exhibit, and lasts through a four- to five-hour show.

The only time a concours car owner uses a chemical wheel cleaner is the first time used wheels are detailed. After that, they are consistently maintained with soap, water and plenty of elbow grease. George Ridderbusch had a problem with brake dust on the wheels of his 928. He used a wheel cleaner to get rid of dust build-up. Later, he bought a different brand of brake pad, which cured the dust problem.

Around the entire exterior of a concours winner you will notice strict attention to detail. Screw heads will point in the same direction, swirl marks will be nonexistent and you won't find a stray piece of dried wax anywhere. Glass will be perfectly clear, and tires will look better than new.

Tips for the engine compartment

In the engine compartment, judges have checked back sides of distributor cap clips for scratches and have probed into valleys on manifolds with cotton swabs looking for dirt and grease. Judges have also checked spark plug wires for correct curvature coming out of spark control boxes and proper light reflection bouncing off painted inner fenderwells.

George Ridderbusch and Wiley like the results they have had using Gunk engine cleaner. The product cuts grease and does not induce further damage. As with all cleaners and solvents, they use it sparingly.

Since all judges at all concours events are not Porsche experts, George Ridderbusch pulled the engine on his 928 in order to completely repaint the

The edge of this 928 radiator bracket came from the factory uncoated. Noting a minuscule amount of rust and discoloration on the edge, Ridderbusch sanded and painted it with a fine artist's paintbrush to match the face of the bracket.

The degree of concours perfection includes removing pieces of grit and debris from the radiator fins of the 928. Afterward, George Ridderbusch spent hours straightening each fin to near perfection.

compartment. Although this removed the poor finish applied at the factory, destroying that element of originality, he felt that the general appearance of a fresh compartment would add to the overall presentation of the car. When the motor was reinstalled, all clamps, screws and bolts were aligned. He even went so far as to repaint red marks on all the nuts, bolts and screws that were painted at the factory. These paint marks were originally made to denote that the part had been installed correctly and tightened to designated torque specifications.

Paying strict attention to detail, Ridderbusch noticed that the edge of the cadmium-plated bracket around the aluminum radiator was beginning to show rust. Since the bracket was cut after plating, raw steel was exposed on the outer edge. He solved the potential rust problem by sanding and painting. His eye for detail includes removing small rocks from the radiator face and straightening the fins afterward. This is the kind of detailing it takes to produce a winning concours automobile.

Tips for the underbody

The bottom of a car, front and rear combined, can be worth seventy points in a concours competition. Winners spend many hours on their backs cleaning and polishing undercarriages until you could eat off them. Gunk has been found to remove Cosmolene easily and with no ill results. For other hard-to-remove substances, Ridderbusch uses solvents and, at times, carefully planned applications of lacquer thinner.

Pledge furniture polish works very well to shine the fenderwells and underbody. Kathy Ridderbusch suggests you use the unscented type. It

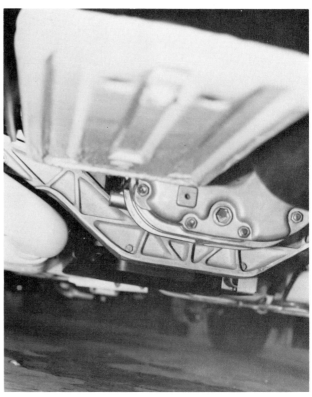

The underbody of this 928 is literally clean enough to eat off of—upside down. The marks on the nuts and bolts were made at the Porsche factory. They are placed on each nut and bolt to signify that it has been torqued to specification and needs no further attention. These red marks are common under the car and in the engine compartment. To maintain originality, Ridderbusch uses red fingernail polish to keep marks visible and to re-mark nuts and bolts that were loosened during repair work.

All of the factory decals and stickers are preserved under the hood of this concours 928. Harsh cleaners and high-pressure water are not used in this engine compartment.

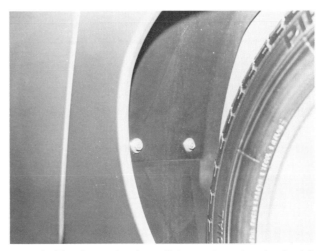

Detachable plastic fenderwell insert is maintained with Pledge furniture polish. Ridderbusch has two sets of fenderwell inserts. One set is installed for driving and during transportation to events, and the other is installed for judging only.

seems that lemon-scented Pledge attracts bees, who both disturb judges and leave unwanted droppings on the paint.

A winning concours underbody will be painted and undercoated the way the factory intended it to be. Determining the correct color and texture of undercoat may require extensive research in shop manuals and other resource data. To find out where to get the correct information, you will have to check with dealers, car clubs, friends and other concours enthusiasts.

Driving a concours car

Driving your concours car to a competitive event may require three days of cleaning once you arrive. Although most damage is done in the first twenty-five miles, George Ridderbusch drove his 928 to a Porsche Parade in Washington, D.C., a 3,000 mile journey.

To protect the large side mirrors, he placed self-stick shelf paper over them and then covered with a bra. He feels that the paper prevented scratches from the bra's vibrating in the wind and said that the paper didn't hurt the paint because the paint was in excellent condition. He also put shelf paper on the underbody with fair results.

He made a special plastic wind deflector for the front which reduced paint chip hazards for the bumper, license plate and hood. He used a different set of lug nuts and spare fenderwell panels for the trip. Upon arrival, he installed the good parts for judging.

Buying a car for a concours

Restoring an automobile to running condition can be fun. Restoring a classic car to concours perfection will be time-consuming, expensive and educational. Do some research before you buy a project car. Check periodicals and magazines to get a feel for the market and latest trends.

Find out if parts are available or if you will need to make them. Determine if you will have the time and money to see the job through. Join a car club that includes makes and models of the type you hope to buy. Ask fellow members about the availability of parts and research material. These fellow auto enthusiasts will be more help to you than anyone else. Talk to restoration experts, body shop workers and upholsterers to get an idea of the money you will have to spend.

A late model, used classic will also be expensive to rejuvenate into a concours winner. Plan to spend $2,000 to $3,000 the following year preparing the car. Plan on spending around $3,500 for a quality, high-tech paint job. It is expensive to have the

Clean 928 underbody parts next to the right rear wheel. Note the color consistency of the various parts and the uniform position of nuts and bolts.

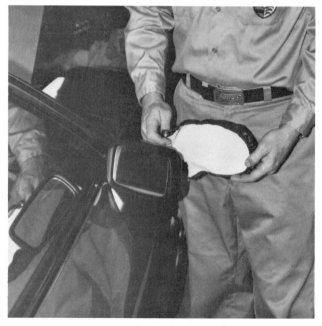

During trips, George Ridderbusch covers the painted portions of the large side mirrors with shelf paper before attaching the bra. He realizes that shelf paper will not hurt a part coated with good paint and feels the paper protects paint from the vibrations of the bra.

This is a custom wind and rock deflector Ridderbusch made for his 928 for protection during road trips. It even lends protection to the license plate.

These are all of the original accessories that came in the trunk of his 928 when George Ridderbusch bought the car new. Points are scored for having these parts, a real plus when you realize they cannot be bought without buying the car. They are not available as aftermarket items.

body stripped to bare metal, sanded, primed, color-coated and clear-coated.

It is very common for some true concours competitors to spend $30,000 to $40,000 bringing an older classic up to concours-winning standards. Money is spent on new parts, rebuilding old parts, body work, upholstery, wheels and tires. If you can afford to have a restoration shop do the work, plan on the final bill adding up to as much as three times the original estimate; this is due to hidden damage. Restorers can't determine all the damage until the car is dismantled. What may appear to be in perfect shape on the outside may be completely rusted through on the inside.

Final thoughts about concours

Please don't let this chapter discourage you from entering the concours arena. When George Ridderbusch entered his first Porsche Parade in Monterey, California, in 1973, he imagined himself a winner with his 1957 Porsche 356A, a car he restored himself over the previous nine years. He placed fourteenth out of seventeen entries.

Since that time, he has become an expert on Porsche automobiles. He did this through research and active involvement in the Porsche Club of America. He is also highly competitive.

If you have aspirations to become a competitive concours car owner, restorer and detailer, take the first step. Detail your car and enter an event. The worst that can happen is a last-place finish. Beyond that, you'll have fun, meet lots of auto enthusiasts, see beautifully restored classic automobiles and learn more about Concours d'Elegance, the ultimate test of all detailing challenges.

The spare tire cover is made from fiberboard and is susceptible to deterioration from moisture and heat. To preserve this piece of original equipment, Ridderbusch sealed it with clear lacquer paint.

200

Chapter 13

Upkeep and maintenance

For true car enthusiasts, there is nothing better than driving a clean car. Some are so fanatic that they have their cars professionally detailed twice a month. Others have been known to return home and retrieve a clean car because the one they were driving was spoiled by an inconsiderate bird.

Realizing that concours is a sport not really suited for cars that we drive on a daily basis, I believe most of us fall into a category somewhere between the twice-a-month detail enthusiast and the person who believes a good rain is sufficient to clean any car. No matter how much time and effort you put into detailing your car, it won't last forever. From a more realistic standpoint, consider undertaking a thorough detail twice a year with a weekly maintenance program to keep the car in stunning condition during the interim.

Weekly upkeep

Automobiles that are frequently driven need to be washed often. Once a week is not too much. During dry weather, dust collects on the body and finds its way into the interior, trunk and engine compartment. The longer it sits in and on the car, the more chance it has to penetrate pores of upholstery, vinyl, leather and paint. It is important to rid these surfaces of dust on a routine basis.

During wet weather, dirt is brought into the interior on your shoes and road grime is splashed on the body and into the engine compartment. This

Fanatical car enthusiasts like everything to be in perfect order, as in lining up screw heads so they all point in the same direction. The more they do to their cars, the more aware they become of imperfections and can always find something to clean or adjust. That's probably why their cars always look so good.

During the weekly wash, clean lower body areas to remove road film and to prevent grime from accumulating. This detailer is kneeling on the hose to keep his pants dry while cleaning the rear lower section of a 1985 BMW CSi.

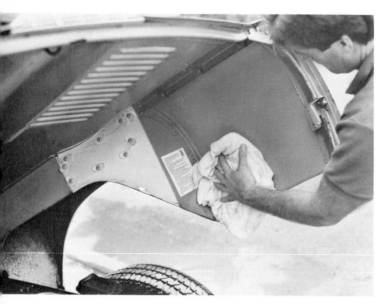

Fenderwells should be thoroughly rinsed with every wash. At least on a monthly basis, take time to wash fenderwells and scrub away accumulations of dirt and debris. The tilt-up hood of this Jaguar makes washing and drying the front fenderwells an easy task.

material not only is unsightly, but also can stain the interior, scratch paint and give rust a starting place in the fenderwells and underbody.

Weekly upkeep need not be as intensive as a full-blown detail. The basics have already been done. Protectorants on the interior should prevent permanent stains; wax will protect the exterior and undercoating will shield the underbody. A con-

scientious vacuuming, wash and rinse will remove potential hazards and bring the car back to brilliance.

Fenderwells and underbody

As described earlier, wash the underbody first so you'll have a dry surface to work on. You should only need to use the wash mitt and plenty of suds from the wash bucket. Since the underbody has already undergone extensive cleaning and repainting, dirt and road grime should easily wash off.

Concentrate on areas that tend to collect road grime and debris. These would be spots behind tires and along each side of the car. It is important to remove accumulations of leaves, pine needles and anything else that retains moisture. Should a stubborn patch present itself, use the plastic-bristled brush.

Since underbody paint is rather susceptible to chips and wear, consider covering visible frame areas with plastic coat. This material is hard and resists chips and wear better than most paints. You'll find these products at most auto body paint and supply stores.

Wheels and tires

Unless brake dust is a real problem, there should be no need for a chemical wheel cleaner. Car wash soap in the wash bucket with the mitt and

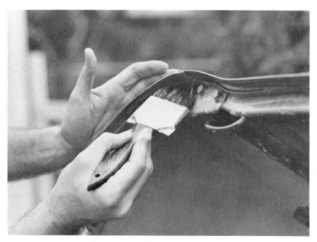

Maintaining a frequent cleaning schedule prevents dirt build-up and makes for easy cleaning. A paintbrush should provide adequate agitation strength to remove most dirt accumulations along seams, ridges and trim.

Fingers are used to clean between the fins on this BMW wheel. The painted wheel cleans easily during the weekly wash and fingers make for quick removal of the slight dirty film located between the fins.

paintbrush will clean wheels sufficiently. Use a toothbrush and your fingers in tight spots as needed.

Tires usually retain dressing for quite some time. The plastic-bristled brush will remove surface dirt and some scuffs. If you hit the curb extra hard in a parking maneuver, use an SOS pad to remove stubborn marks, especially on whitewalls.

Apply dressing only as needed. If the tire looks good after drying, don't dress it. On the other hand, if it looks flat, spray some dressing on a towel and wipe on. Use a soft-bristled brush to work it into pores and exposed side treads.

Body

After cleaning the underbody, fenderwells, wheels and tires, empty the wash bucket and bring up a fresh solution of car wash soap and water. Rinse the body to remove as much of the "big stuff" as possible. Wash one half of the top, windshield and rear window with a fresh mitt and plenty of suds. Use a paintbrush around drip rails, trim and windshield wipers. Rinse thoroughly.

Although the paintbrush may not remove bug residue on the first try, repeated applications will soon prevail and you can rest assured that the gentle cleaning will have caused no damage to paint. On the front of a 944, a paintbrush is used to remove road film from seams around light fixtures.

A paintbrush should be carried in the wash bucket and is used here to clean the wiper blade and trim around the rear window of a 944. Take advantage of the abundant suds left by the mitt by using the paintbrush right after it.

203

If you must work on the car in sunlight, wash the shady side first, using a paintbrush around mirrors, emblems, trim and sidelight lenses. Proceed to the rear and opposite side of the car. Around the grille and brightwork, use a toothbrush and paintbrush to remove dust and accumulated dirt in gridwork. Bug residue can be removed with repeated applications of the wash mitt and paintbrush.

Rinsing the entire body often is important, especially the side facing the sun. Keep the body wet until you are ready to dry. Unless you are using ultra pure water, water spots are bound to appear if water is permitted to air dry.

Interior

After the exterior has been washed and dried, take a few minutes to wipe down the interior. For the most part, a clean wash mitt rinsed in clear water is all you'll need.

Dressing vinyl interiors, rubber trim, bumper guards and tires serves a useful and cosmetic purpose. The material looks new, fresh and shiny, and it is rejuvenated with moisture. As with wax, too much is not too good. Dressing in lieu of cleaning is a common mistake. Although dressing will cover up some dirt, the lack of a clean surface detracts from true beauty. Take time to clean vinyl and rubber

first. Then, apply a light coat of dressing and buff off the excess.

Don't use harsh cleaners and chemicals on dusty surfaces. If the car is just dusty, use warm water and a towel for cleaning. Imbedded dirt, not dust, requires cleaners and soap. Use a dry towel to wipe off water droplets from gauges and knobs.

The carpet should be vacuumed. Once again, the crevice tool is your best choice. If pine needles are a problem, use an old hairbrush to break them loose before vacuuming. For the once-a-week spiff, a mini-vac or battery-powered vacuum cleaner will be sufficient. If a hardy amount of residue is gathered in the interior, use a stronger vacuum cleaner, or brush debris into a pile and remove with a mini-vac or battery-powered model.

As with tires, apply dressing only as needed. In most cases, a quick wipe with the dressing towel should be sufficient. For interior brightwork, try a light application of Windex instead of wax. It will provide a shine without the worry of wax build-up.

Engine compartment

On a weekly basis, the biggest concern under the hood is dust. Oil leaks should have been corrected during the primary detail. Along with wiping the inner fenderwells with a clean wash mitt, you should check the levels of engine oil, transmission fluid, radiator coolant, windshield washer fluid, brake fluid and power-steering fluid.

Used weekly, a cotton swab can easily remove dust from vents, slots and tight spaces around knobs. A quick pass over the vents each week on the dashboard of this BMW prevents dust from accumulating and becoming a real cleaning chore.

The upper grille area of this Nash Metropolitan can be quickly cleaned with a damp towel. Passing over this two-minute cleaning chore week after week will result in an hour cleaning task in the span of two months. After washing the body, open the doors, trunk and hood, and wipe down the jambs and edges.

Minor spots of oil or grease can be cleaned easily with a rag dabbed in solvent or Simple Green. Quiet squeaky belts by rubbing an ordinary bar of soap across them. Wax dull air cleaner housings and other painted surfaces. Hoses and belts should be touched up with the dressing towel, chrome shined with polish.

Waxing

Many auto buffs like to do something extra every time they wash the car. Many times, this consists of waxing a certain part of the car with each wash. Figuring the car is washed once a week, they wax the top, hood and trunk lid one week, one side the next, the opposite side the third week and chrome the fourth.

Waxing the doorjambs, underside of the trunk lid and metal dashboards can be saved for the super cleaning once a month. This will make any future

In your zeal to clean and shine, don't forget to return the windshield wiper blades to their proper position before opening the hood. Along those lines, plan your weekly washing jobs to encompass as much cleaning as possible in the time you have available. Do something extra each week in order to stay on top of things, rather than saving a lot of work for one specific weekend.

On a monthly basis (more often if necessary), use a damp towel to remove dust and dirt in the engine compartment. As grease or oil appears, dab a rag with solvent and clean it off. Apply a thin coat of wax to painted surfaces. Meguiar's Car Cleaner Wax is well suited for this chore since it does not produce a powdery dust when dry.

accumulations of dirt build-up easy to wipe away and keep parts looking good. While waxing in the trunk, check jacking equipment and tool kits for cleanliness, lubrication and mechanical operation.

Cautions

In freezing weather, car washing is impractical unless you have heated quarters. Washing a car in freezing temperatures will cause doors to freeze shut and may result in door molding tears or separation when doors are forced open. On cold days, above freezing, use warm water in the wash bucket; your hands will thank you.

If the car is dusty, not dirty, don't wash it. George Ridderbusch and Wentworth believe that it is not a good idea to wash a car and then park it, especially for any length of time. Water sits in inconspicuous places and gives rust a chance. They prefer to wash the car first and then go for a Sunday drive or rally. This way, water is blown off wheels, fenderwells, bumpers and trim. Upon returning, they will use damp fluffy towels to wipe away dust. Thick towels will trap minute particles of dust and grit deep in the nap, preventing scratches. Tiny swirls may occur but will be removed with the next waxing.

Auto storage

The best thing you can do for your special automobile is drive it. Regular exercise keeps inter-

Cigarette ashes and butts left in this Corvette ashtray during an extended storage absorbed and retained enough moisture to corrode the metal. Before storing a vehicle, empty, clean and dry all ashtrays. Do not apply any dressing, or shampoo any part of the interior either. The added moisture can attract mildew and can even cause upholstery stitching to rot.

nal parts lubricated and prevents settling moisture from corroding idle linkages and brake shoes. Consider storage "long" if it adds up to months.

Before starting a stored car, make a number of mechanical and safety checks. Check for proper fluid levels, tire pressure, headlights, brake lights, turn signals and windshield wipers. Since cylinder walls may be completely dry, you may consider squirting a bit of engine oil into spark plug holes and turning the engine over with plugs removed. Once you have started the engine, keep rpm low. Allow plenty of time for oil and water to circulate throughout the engine.

Extended storage may have resulted in dust and moisture settling on brakeshoes. Be alert to "grabby" brakes the first time they are applied, or worse yet, no brakes at all. While enjoying the drive, operate all the accessories. This helps to lubricate moving parts, gaskets and linkages, as well as exercise belts and cables.

Storing cars can be much more damaging than regular driving. Over an extended period of time, moisture can cause corrosion, mold and mildew. I would advise against the use of any dressings on the interior before storage. The moisture in the protectorant will likely attract more moisture and the problems associated with it. Consider placing a box of baking soda in the interior to reduce musty odors. You may also consider putting packets of moisture-absorbing agents, roach motels and mice killers inside as well. Be aware of anything that might retain moisture. Cigarette butts left in an ashtray will attract moisture and cause metal ashtrays to corrode and rust.

There are mixed feelings among car people about storage procedures for the engine and fuel system. Some prefer to store dry, others opt to keep fluid levels full. If you choose to keep levels full, consider filling the cooling system with antifreeze and distilled water. Put an additive in the fuel tank to reduce problems associated with water condensation. Since it may take years to put 3,000 miles on the engine, change the oil every six months. Disconnect the battery. You may even consider storing it outside the car to reduce any possible damage that may result from acid leaks or seepage.

Convertible tops should remain up. For those that rest directly on top of the rear deck, like Corvette roadster tops, keep the rear locking mechanisms open and the bottom of the top off the deck. This will keep the top's rubber molding from attaching itself to the paint.

Protecting the car from sun, moisture and dust can be enhanced by use of a car cover. Make sure the one you use will breathe. Plastic is a definite no-no as it will trap moisture and air inside the car. Cotton covers are favorites. Beverly Hills Motoring Accessories carries a good assortment of quality car covers.

Final overview

Throughout this book, I have contended that it is difficult to get car enthusiasts to agree on specific detailing methods. Each has a preference for various products and the means by which cleaning, polishing and waxing are accomplished. There is, however, one comment that I heard over and over again: Always use the mildest cleaning method first, even if it requires two to three applications. The enthusiasts I talked to viewed harsh chemicals and aggressive methods as potential hazards and preferred to spend whatever time necessary to achieve the same cleaning results using mild products and a soft touch.

Although car people may disagree on the style, performance and apparent beauty of different makes and models, they all recognize the enjoyment given us by the efforts of those who take their time to gently clean, polish and wax their cars to perfection.

The processes described in these pages are not necessarily intended to be the last word in car cleaning. They are, however, proven methods that work for some concours winners, race drivers, auto body people, detailers and many who simply appreciate fine automobiles. I hope the information in this book, along with your favorite, time-tested car care methods, will help you to achieve the ultimate detail.

A one-time full-blown detail, followed with a conscientious and frequent maintenance program, will keep your special car in top shape, looking crisp and a pleasure to drive and admire.

Index